# Contents

# Acknowledgements

I HAVE MANY PEOPLE to thank for their help, the loan or gift of books, discussion, and patient toleration of my obsessions: Peter Davidson, Winifred Temple and Simon Rees, as always, but also Sandra Raphael, Robin Smith, Martha Bayless, Nick Graham, Richard Sharpe, Sarah Barber and Alison Gill. The translation of part of 'Wulf and Eadwacer' is by Peter Davidson and Robin Smith. I am particularly grateful to E.D. Mackerness for generously sharing with me some notes on nineteenth-century women dramatists, and to Carol Morley for further research in this area.

The book is dedicated to Jean Gooder, Head of English at Newnham College, Cambridge, and to the group of Newnham English students who were my contemporaries, particularly Yopie Prins and Carol Morley. This is an expression of my personal debt to Newnham for giving me the freedom, within a supportive and largely female context, to develop a mind of my own in a room of my own, fifty years after the publication of Virginia Woolf's well-known essay.

*Sheffield, 1992*

# Introduction

THE RELATIONSHIP OF WOMEN to culture has historically been different from that of men. Schools and universities have been, until very recently, a male preserve, which has effectively excluded all but a handful of upper-class women from the resources of the official culture. Many educationalists as late as the nineteenth century believed that a woman needed to be literate enough to read her Bible, but should not aspire to the arrogance of authorship. Consequently, women's creativity has traditionally been expressed in anonymous, ephemeral forms: domestic arts such as cooking and embroidery; the creation and re-creation of ballads; and in private writing, particularly letters and diaries. Like all simplifications, this one can be challenged by a wide variety of exceptions.

Although the social and ideological constraints on women's authorship mean that there are far fewer English women writers than men, their contribution to the literary culture of England can be traced right back to the very beginnings of writing in England. The book is therefore organised chronologically, in order to show how women's writing changed over time in response to different historical situations. It reflects the increasing involvement of women in English literature over 1,300 years. Thus, the first of the five chapters covers some 900 years of English literature, the second approximately 100, the third, fourth and fifth, less than a century apiece. Each chapter contains a general discussion of the cultural history of the period, and moves on to a discussion of some of the most significant of its women writers, separated into novelists, dramatists and poets.

The first chapter thus deals with the span of nearly a thousand years from the very beginning of writing in England in the seventh century, to the seventeenth. Many aspects of human life changed greatly in this period, but one constant feature is that women were always second-class citizens in one way or another. Even such dynamic and capable women as the fifteenth-century Margery Paston or Chaucer's fictitious Wife of Bath were constrained by an extremely restrictive range of legal, social, cultural and economic conditions. In every century up to the twentieth, more men than women were taught how to write, which obviously acts as a crude filter excluding many women from even the remotest possibility of becoming authors. Furthermore, the consistently higher cultural valuation attached to the male rather than the female point of view in all centuries has led to the erasure of many literary works by women on the grounds that they were trivial, unimportant or uninteresting: for example, the entire output of one of the first English women poets known to us by name, the eleventh-century Muriel. There are other reasons, of course, why women's writing disappears into oblivion. One is suggested by the celebrated eighteenth-century bluestocking, Mrs Thrale, when she comments on Henry Fielding, known as one of the fathers of the English novel, and his attitude to his sister, Sarah, also a novelist:

> I have heard Doctor Collier say that Harry Fielding quite doated upon his Sister Sally till she had made herself through his – Dr Collier's – Assistance, a competent Scholar ...[she] became eminent in her Knowledge of the Greek Language, after which her Brother never more could perswade himself to endure her Company with Civility.[1]

Henry Fielding's sense of appropriate behaviour for a woman clearly overrode even family affection; and the anecdote suggests that his reactions to his sister's writing could never have been straightforwardly those of one author to another. Sarah Fielding depended on her brother financially, and also looked to him to present her writing to the public on her behalf, so she could not afford to shrug off his opinions. Another way in which a woman's point of view can be suppressed is suggested by the seventeenth-century diarist, Samuel Pepys, who has left us a vivid, idiosyncratic view of Stuart London. Mrs Pepys also wrote a diary, for a time. When her husband found and read it, he considered it:

> so picquant, and wrote in English and most of it true, of the retirednesse of her life and how unpleasant it was, that being writ in English and so in danger of being met with and read by others, I was vexed at it and desired her and then commanded her to teare it.[2]

The interest and value of Pepys's diary lies in its unusual frankness. In this passage, he acknowledges both the truthfulness of his wife's writing, and the effect it has on him, and orders the suppression of this uncomfortable document which has 'vexed' him. There could be no question of his right to do so: he was the head of the household.

The issues raised so far as constraints on women's writing are those which affect them for specifically gender-related reasons. However, all men did not have better access to self-expression than all women. Social class has operated as another kind of cultural filter from the seventh century to the nineteenth, so while men of the educated and propertied classes spoke with a privileged voice, lower-class men and women were equally disregarded, and upper-class women sometimes given a hearing. Before the eighteenth century, literacy, and thus writing, were far from being universal skills. In looking at women and English literature over a long span of time, therefore, we sometimes have to ask the crude question: which women, if any, were taught to write at all?[3] If they were, was anyone interested in their point of view? Writing materials were expensive, and the priorities of the learned classes tended to be in the areas of religious and practical treatises, or Latin literature. The later history of English literature, from the eighteenth century onwards, has constraints of its own, since it is intimately connected with the economics of printing and publishing, as well as with changes of taste and fashion. Some women have been lucky enough to find that their work in some way fitted the mood and tastes of their times; others have not. Women's writing did not have to be torn up like Mrs Pepys's diary for it to be completely lost within a few years of its composition.

It is obvious to anyone who looks at the whole body of writing known as 'English Literature', that is, the creative writing produced in this country between the seventh century and the present day, that the amount of writing by women has varied enormously over time. There are several linked points to bear in mind here. First, the amount of writing by women (relative to the amount of writing by men at any given period) is intimately connected with their historical and cultural position. Another issue, which does not affect what woman wrote before the twentieth century, but which is directly relevant to how much of it is known to us, is transmission: what happens to a text after it is written. The preservation, transmission and survival of all writing, whether women's or men's, is affected by cultural, and especially economic, conditions. If one is thinking about medieval women in particular, the problem of the survival and transmission of texts is particularly acute, since very few pre-modern or early modern compositions by either sex survive in their authors' own personal copies. The more often a composition was copied by subsequent generations, the more likely it was that it would survive – and women's writing has not always been taken seriously in the past, even by women. For example, several of the great Christian scholars of the fourth century, such as Saint Jerome, enjoyed friendships with highly educated and saintly Roman ladies. We know this, because the letters which Saint Jerome addressed to these women, and which refer to his friendships with them, and their researches into Hebrew and Greek theology, were lovingly kept by the recipients, made into collections, and preserved for posterity. Neither they, nor Saint Jerome himself, seem to have seen any point in preserving the women's half of the correspondence.[4] So we cannot assume that the voiceless women of medieval England, who are described by great poets such as Chaucer and Henryson, but who never seem to speak for themselves, were actually as silent as they seem. For instance, an Englishwoman named Muriel, who has already been mentioned, was apparently active some time in the eleventh century, and was described by male contemporaries as *inclyta versificatrix* ('the famous poetess'), but none of her writing is known to have been preserved.[5] The problem of the actual survival of texts particularly affects medieval studies, but the problem of transmission and availability has been relevant to the study of women's writing of all periods – as, indeed, it is to the study of all literature. There has been an enormous growth of interest in women's writing in the last two decades, and part of the reason for it is that publishing groups such as Virago and the Women's Press had the vision to see that there was a *market* for women's writing, and reprinted a large number of novels by women writers. It is now possible to find cheap paperback editions of all kinds of work by women, which used to be obscure and hard to find. The critic Joanna Russ mentions that as recently as 1971, the only novel by Charlotte Brontë (one of the very few women writers whose work has been widely studied in schools and universities since the nineteenth century) available in paperback in the whole of the United States was *Jane Eyre*.[6] It was simply not possible for Joanna Russ to tell her students that they might find it interesting to compare *Jane Eyre* with *Shirley* or *Villette*. As she goes on to observe, the inclusion of a very small number of books by women – such as *Jane Eyre* – in the canon of 'English Literature' normally taught to students tends to make such works appear isolated and contextless, if not downright freakish. Writers are easier to understand when we can see them influencing each other – Wordsworth and Coleridge, for example, or Keats, Shelley and Byron. But most students read Jane Austen without reading Frances Burney, Mary Brunton, or any of the other women writers she herself read, admired, parodied, and used as models,[7] and her achievement is thus deprived of the historical, social and literary context that a student of Coleridge or Shelley is normally offered.

Seeing women writers in isolation from one another naturally tends to make them appear somewhat anomalous. This is a problem for the reader. There is a further problem for women writers themselves, which results from the widely shared perception that a smallish subsection of the community, privileged by gender, class and race, is centrally significant.[8] Perhaps the earliest woman writer to focus on this problem is the fourteenth-century Frenchwoman, Christine de Pisan, who categorically denies in her *Book of the City of Ladies* that male writers' views of women are as accurate or as just as they claim. Many later Englishwomen were to express similar views, notably Aphra Behn and Virginia Woolf. What is too easily thought of as objective or disinterested writing in fact originates in a small subsection of society: male, white, highly educated, and metropolitan. In the classical world, the literary élite of Rome provided the cultural standard for the whole of the empire, which came to include all of Europe and most of the Middle East. In the late seventeenth century, London came to occupy a similar place in the development of writing in English, which was by this time the expressive medium of an aggressive and expanding imperialist culture. So strongly does an acceptable style of discourse emerge in this period that, effectively, all other writing, in any other style, was either marginalised or compelled to attempt conformity. Women's writing, regional or dialect writing, working-class writing and even the work of such poets as John Donne, were rejected by an increasingly self-confident and influential coterie of London-based professional literary men.

The belief in an objective tone, inherited from the literary standardisation of the late seventeenth century and common to most readers, creates obvious problems for writers whose viewpoint, whether for reasons of class, race or gender, is culturally off-centre. All writers, as they learn their craft, model themselves on their predecessors. They have to take up some kind of attitude to the literary tradition they inhabit. So, if that tradition is designed to express their own kind of perceptions, they can move confidently within it, expand it, quarrel with it, and take it for their own. Writers who do *not* fit – who are not white, not middle-class or not male – have a great deal more difficulty finding an appropriate stance and vocabulary for what they experience.[9] Women's writing has historically existed in an uncomfortable relationship to the tradition of English literature, as it is normally understood. I hope to argue in the course of this book that while this is the case, it is also true that there is an alternative tradition of women's writing which has been important to virtually all women writers: from the sixteenth century down to the end of the nineteenth, women's writing was shaped by what women were writing in the previous generation.

Such a book as this cannot aim at complete inclusiveness. My aim has been to discuss writers who were either outstandingly popular in their own time (and who therefore shed light on what was expected of, or permitted to, women writers at a particular historical moment), or who were unusually original. I have also attempted to bring out the links between one generation of women writers and the next. Works such as Janet Todd's *Dictionary of British Women Writers* name many women whom I have not included: I have included a 'Reference works' section in the Bibliography which is intended to help readers who wish to pursue this further. In the twentieth century, the sheer volume of writing by women forces one to select, and to hope that as many innovative writers as possible have been at least briefly considered; a process which gives one new sympathy for the king at the beginning of *Sleeping Beauty*. It is virtually impossible to see which of the many interesting writers now at an early stage in their careers will continue to seem interesting to subsequent generations.

NOTES

1 M.A. Doody, *Frances Burney: The Life in the Works,* Cambridge University Press, Cambridge, 1988, p.241.

2 Samuel Pepys, *The Diary of Samuel Pepys,* ed. R. Latham and W. Matthews, Bell & Hyman, London, 11 vols, 1970–83, IV, p.9.

3 The evidence for a differential literacy rate is hard to quantify until the seventeenth and eighteenth centuries. Lawrence Stone, *The Family, Sex and Marriage in England, 1500–1800,* Pelican Books, Harmondsworth, 1979, p.144, notes that in the eighteenth century, only one woman in three could so much as sign her own name in a marriage register, whereas most men could manage this minimal indication of literacy, and that there is every

reason to suppose that the difference was more extreme in earlier centuries: 'women at all levels of society were an educationally deprived group compared with men'.

4  A. Rousselle, *Porneia: On Desire and the Body in Antiquity,* trs. F. Pheasant, Blackwell, London, 1988, p.182.

5  J.F.P. Tatlock, 'Muriel: The Earliest English Poetess', *PMLA* 48, 1933, pp.317–21.

6  J. Russ, *How to Suppress Women's Writing,* Women's Press, London, 1984, p.63.

7  It is the great achievement of Ellen Moers, in her readable, witty and entertaining book *Literary Women: The Great Writers* (Women's Press, London, 1978), that she has brought out the connections and literary parentage of a whole range of important women writers.

8  This problem is by no means confined to women writers. Any kind of writing perceived as 'minority' or marginal can be effectively removed from serious consideration or academic investigation by a lack of reasonably priced teaching editions. Scottish literature is an obvious case in point.

9  The relationship between a writer and his or her predecessors is in many ways similar to the relationship between a child and his or her family, which is why metaphors about kinship so often come up in critical discussion. I am suggesting here that there is a subgroup of writers who are like the fortunate children of supportive parents, and several other groups whose relationships with their literary ancestors are strained, unhappy and difficult.

# Chapter 1

# From Anglo-Saxon times to the Elizabethan age

## The Anglo-Saxon age

### Ecclesiastical writing

The history of writing in England began at the end of the seventh century, two or three generations after the introduction of Christianity to the pagan Anglo-Saxons. The earliest English writers wrote in Latin, the language of educated persons in the Christian West. The missionaries who brought the Christian religion had been quick to open schools, and to begin bringing the Anglo-Saxon people into the great tradition of Western culture. At the end of the sixth century, Pope Gregory the Great, beginning to think about the conversion of the Anglo-Saxons, ordered that Anglo-Saxon slaves should be bought and educated (in Latin) as future missionaries. No priority was attached to the use of the converts' own language: for two centuries the native Anglo-Saxon culture, which seems to have concentrated on preserving epic tales of Germanic heroes, and customary law, existed mainly in the memories of the chief men (not, as far as we know, of the women) of each region and was not written down. Meanwhile, the imported Christian Latin culture thrived in the monasteries and cathedral schools, written, copied, and, potentially, preserved for posterity. It was not until the later ninth century that Old English prose and poetry were written down in any quantity, in a context in which professional religious writers had generally become more relaxed about writing in the vernacular, and a great deal less puritanical about Old English poetry, which they had earlier rejected as, at best, irrelevant to salvation, at worst, dangerously seductive. Alcuin of York, near the end of the eighth century, gave voice to Christian suspicion of pagan sagas when he posed the question, 'what has Ingeld [a pagan hero] to do with Christ?' The answer, obviously, was nothing. So it was clearly wrong for monks to enjoy, let alone copy, the epic of Ingeld.

Reading and writing were thus entirely associated with the Christian Church, the only institution which maintained schools in the early Middle Ages. It is therefore not surprising to find that all known English writers before the late tenth century, with the exception of the ninth-century King Alfred the Great, were in holy orders. Perhaps more astonishing is that right from the first generation some of them were female.

The earliest surviving English writer known to posterity by name is Aldhelm, bishop of Sherborne, who died in 709. His main works are a massive prose essay and a parallel long poem in hexameters, both in praise of virginity. Aldhelm's Latin prose style is tortuous and complex in the extreme, and both the poetic and prose versions make extensive and self-conscious reference to classical and Christian authors. His twin masterpiece was addressed to the abbess Hildelith and sisters of a nunnery at Barking, near London. Aldhelm's address to his female audience at the beginning and end of his treatise clearly implies that in seventh-century England, women, frail though they might be considered in other respects, were not thought of (or educated) as intellectually inferior. He refers not only to his female correspondents' study of the Bible, but to their 'rummaging through the old stories of the historians and the entries of the chroniclers' and 'sagaciously enquiring into the rules of the grammarians and the teaching of experts on spelling and the rules of metrics'. Thus, the nuns of Barking studied exegesis, history, grammar, orthography, and the rules for writing metrical Latin poetry: it is hard to see why they should have bothered with the last three subjects unless they were determined to *write* Latin (and Latin poetry at that) rather than merely being able to read it. Furthermore, it needs a Latinist of more than average competence to make sense of Aldhelm's enormously long sentences, and since he records that the nuns wrote letters to him, urging him to even greater literary efforts, the scholars of Barking were clearly able to cope.[1] It is typical of the difficulty in studying medieval women that the letters and probable poems of Abbess Hildelith and her fellow students have not been preserved.

A generation or so later, several women were involved with the Anglo-Saxon mission to the pagans of Germany. Some of their letters and poems have survived, moving statements of affection and minor everyday concerns from 1,200 years ago, an example being the collection of Saint Boniface.[2] The style of Latin written by these women does not differ from that of their male contemporaries, though their frank expression of emotions such as personal affection, loneliness and loss is noticeable against the cooler, less self-revelatory tone of their male correspondents. For example, the following letter is written by a nun, Berhtgyth, possibly of Hartlepool, to her brother Balthard, who is apparently in the mission-field in Germany:

'my soul wearies of my life' for love of you, my brother. For I am left alone and destitute of the help of relatives: 'my father and mother have abandoned me, but the Lord has taken me up'. Many are the seas between me and you, but we are linked by love, since true love is not broken off by the limits of place. But I say to you that sadness never departs from my soul, nor is my mind quiet in sleep, 'for love is stronger than death'. Now, therefore, I ask you, my darling brother, to come to me, or let me come to you, so that I can see you before I die, since love for you has never faded from my soul. I pray for you day and night as I do for myself, every hour and every moment, that you may always have health with Christ.[3]

The letter is then rounded off with a ten-line poem, which makes Berhtgyth one of the first named women poets in the history of English literature; the poem is an affectionate prayer for Balthard's welfare in this world and the next, in the style pioneered by Aldhelm.

We also have an account of St Willibald and his travels in the Holy Land, written by his niece, an Anglo-Saxon nun called Hugeburc, who introduces herself in her preface with a mixture of shyness and determination, excusing herself for her unfeminine temerity in writing by her personal closeness to the subject of her biography.[4] Her writing is lively and original in content: for instance, she reports with relish that the saint successfully managed to smuggle valuable balsam past the Customs and Excise officers of Tyre, which neatly illustrates the difference between her work and a conventional early medieval saint's life.[5]

Some of the anonymous writing, both English and Latin, which survives from Anglo-Saxon England, may also have been written by women. This information is beyond recovery, unless the subject-matter, or a direct authorial statement, signals a female author. As Aldhelm indirectly bears witness, no distinction was made initially between the education of monks and nuns. The gender-specific structure of the Latin language sometimes offers a clue: a writer, for example, may refer to himself as *peccator*, or to herself as *peccatrix* ('sinner'). This is not always helpful, unfortunately, since later copyists sometimes switched these gender-indicators round to suit their own circumstances. For example, a book of prayers copied in the nuns' convent at Winchester in the eighth century uses both masculine and feminine forms, sometimes in the same prayer. How could we tell which were originally written by nuns, unless we were lucky enough to have a context of information about authorship, which we do not possess? In the more complex context of personification and authorial identity offered by other forms of literature, such as lyric poetry, such clues are of even less help. Writers of one sex can express themselves through a character of the other, and this is equally possible in an early medieval context. If we cannot assume that the poem known as 'The Wife's Lament', with its first-person female speaker, is necessarily written by a woman, we should be equally reluctant to treat it as a matter of course that a poem such as 'The Seafarer', with its first-person male speaker, must necessarily be written by a man. The very limited information which we have about the contexts in which poetry was composed and performed (which associate it with groups of men relaxing in the hall) suggests that male authorship is always statistically more likely—but the possibility of women's authorship is always potentially there for any anonymous work, Latin or Old English, and almost always unprovable.

The first sign of a differentiation between the education of monks and nuns begins as early as the eighth century, as women began gradually to develop the techniques of the embroidery for which English nunneries were to become famous, and which is discussed below in the context of the later Middle Ages, when it was at its height.[6] This characteristically female art, initially merely an additional responsibility, signals what was to become a gradually widening gap between women's education and men's.

The learned women of Aldhelm's and Boniface's circles flourished in the seventh and eighth centuries, but their successors in centuries immediately following are less visible. The state of learning declined generally in England in the ninth and tenth centuries, probably because of the national crisis of the Viking invasions. A few named authors survive from the later tenth and the eleventh centuries (many of them now writing in Old English rather than in Latin, and at least two, King Alfred and the *ealdorman* Aethelweard (late tenth century), laymen), but none of them is female.

## Old English poetry

There is no evidence that even aristocratic laywomen were taught to write in the Anglo-Saxon period (though some of them could certainly read, for instance, King Alfred's mother). It is thus very far from certain whether we can reasonably look for a tradition of women's poetry outside the nunneries, where we would on the whole expect women to write in Latin. There are therefore difficulties in attributing any of the surviving Old English poems to women authors, since we either have to assume that nuns retained a somewhat inappropriate interest in romantic love, or that laywomen could write. And we have absolutely no way of telling whether the fairly strict technical rules of Old English poetry were taught to girls as well as boys, since we are wholly ignorant of how native Anglo-Saxon culture was passed from one generation to the next. The only surviving literature of pre-Conquest England which acknowledges a conceptual difference between masculine and feminine points of view is a little group of poems from the Exeter Book, an eleventh-century manuscript containing many Old English poems, including three which are known as 'The Wife's Lament', 'The Husband's Message' and 'Wulf and Eadwacer' (probably late ninth or tenth century).[7] All three emphasise the agony of passivity as the woman, speaking in the first person, waits for her husband and kin to resolve their difficulties, with no possibility of action on her own account. The poems recognise that the breaking of an alliance in the male sphere of action and retribution may leave the woman a helpless, grieving spectator of her own kinsmen, father and brothers, at war with her husband and sons. These women inhabit a sombre world of stoic endurance and divided loyalties. If these three poems are not by women, they are the work of poets with an extraordinary insight into the real difficulties and griefs of a woman's position. 'Wulf and Eadwacer' in particular, though the complex ambiguities of the poem as a whole will probably never be resolved, contains lines which communicate directly even with the modern reader:

I have wept for my Wulf;       in wide wandering thoughts,
It was rainy weather,       misery alone.
When the strong warrior       took me in his arms,
It was joy to me then,       but wretched also.
Wulf, my Wulf,       awaiting you,
Your rare return       has wasted me
Grief in my heart,       not want of food.

We also find in Old English that men usually portray women in a number of more or less stereotypical roles. The passivity of the woman's lot, represented from a first-person standpoint in the poems already mentioned, also finds sympathetic expression, though from a much more detached viewpoint, in the great Anglo-Saxon epic *Beowulf* (? eighth century). Terms of praise for aristocratic women include 'peace-pledge' (*frithusibb*)and 'peace-weaver' (*freothuwebbe*), honouring their political and diplomatic functions in smoothing over potential conflict in the male world, either the microcosm of the royal hall, or the greater world of alliance between tribes or kin-groups. *Beowulf* in particular recognises that this was not always an easy or pleasant role for a person to play.

More unexpectedly, there is also a strain of individual heroic activity by women celebrated in Old English, in a series of poems on great heroines of the Christian tradition. The most interesting of these works is *Judith*, a tenth-century Old English poem on the Old Testament heroine Judith of Bethulia.[8] Judith saved her people, on the point of surrender after a long siege, by paying a clandestine visit to the commander of the besieging army, Holofernes, charming him out of his suspicions, and cutting off his head as he lay in a drunken stupor. The incident is a familiar subject of medieval and Renaissance paintings, and most male artists who have tackled it have clearly done so with a certain anxiety, or masochistic relish. Not the Old English poet, whose readers (or more probably, listeners) were invited to identify completely with this *ides ellenrof* ('exceedingly brave/powerful lady') as she smote the head off the 'heathen hound' and carried it home in triumph. There is an absolute absence of stress on Judith's deceitfulness, and not a word of sympathy is spared for Holofernes, led to destruction by his own worst instincts.[9] In other words, this and other Old English poems about heroic women (such as the ninth-century *Juliana* and *Elene*) expect their audience's reactions and identification to be conditioned by the holiness, or otherwise, of the characters represented, and only secondarily, if at all, by gender. *Juliana*'s subject is the heroic death of the eponymous early Christian martyr, and that of *Elene*, the epic journey of Helena, mother of the first Christian emperor, Constantine, in the early fourth century to the Holy Land, to search for the True Cross. It is a classic 'quest' poem, in which the heroine struggles with, and triumphs over, all kinds of difficulties and enemies. To a very remarkable extent, for early medieval literature, these three poems treat their heroines as interesting and important *people*, not in essential ways any different from heroes of the other sex.

# The post-Conquest period

### Courtly love and Marie de France

We have no poetry or prose from the Anglo-Saxon world which reflects aspects of women's lives other than heroic endeavour or marital difficulty; no poems celebrating love, children, religious ecstasy or friendship. After the Norman Conquest of 1066, the picture changes considerably. Anglo-Saxon literature is centred on male experience; its action, metaphors and frames of reference are to do with battle, the social control of aggression, various forms of relationship between men, and the ethics of heroism. But from the twelfth century, Western European literature begins to express new moods, to appreciate elegance, and to give a new prominence to individual emotional states, above all, to love. Like the heroic literature which preceded it, courtly romance offers an entirely aristocratic perspective, but it focuses on the non-martial personages of court life, the ladies, serving-maids, squires and chaplains, rather than on the lords themselves, who continued to behave very much like their ancestors.

The literature of courtly love had its origins in France, and has always been particularly associated with the sophisticated court of Queen Eleanor of Aquitaine (1122–1204), who is sometimes credited with its invention. This literature was sometimes created, as well as enjoyed, by women, and was popular in all the courts of Europe. And one of the most popular authors of this new courtly writing was a woman known as Marie de France, active at the English court in the second half of the twelfth century. Nothing is known of her life except what may be deduced from her writing, which shows that she knew several languages and had a profoundly aristocratic outlook.

Marie is relevant to this account, even though she wrote in Norman French, because she is the first woman writer working in England who is known to have been widely read, and to have influenced other writers. She was the first woman of the Middle Ages to write successfully, at length, in the vernacular. Most non-Celts now forget that any languages but English have been used in Britain. But in the Middle Ages, matters were far more complicated. Apart from the native Celtic languages of the North and West—Scottish Gaelic, Welsh and Cornish—the court, and anyone with any pretensions to aristocratic culture, spoke French (or rather, Anglo-

Norman), and anyone with any pretensions to religious culture spoke Latin. This is why the fourteenth-century poet John Gower, who was almost as popular in his own time as Chaucer, wrote his three major works in three different languages, Latin, French and English.

The *lais* (narrative poems) of Marie de France are concise, confidently told and elegant stories, whose author comments freely on her characters' conduct.[10] Though they conform, naturally, to the expectations of their genre and the social class which supported it, they draw on the surrealist resources of the European folk tradition to produce strange and haunting images; in the *Lai of Yonec*, for instance, the lover transforms himself into a huge hawk, an image both of freedom and of predation. The *lais* function, like much subsequent fiction, as courtesy books, instructing young ladies and young gentlemen in the niceties of social ritual, aristocratic manners and, in particular, courtship. Marie's value-laden vocabulary makes it very clear what constitutes admirable conduct and what does not. But the *lais* also have a much wilder and more surrealistic element; individual stories turn on a husband who is a werewolf, a wife who brings her husband's mistress back from the dead, and a fairy mistress who takes her lover away to the other-world of Avalon. They use this folklore material to express a basic religious conviction, that God will reward the virtuous and punish the wicked. But the morality is personal, rather than social: the jealousy of the old husband, in *Yonec*, is presented as being completely wrong and ridiculous, because the wife does not love him. Yet socially (and legally) speaking, even an unlovable, ugly, nasty old man had a perfect right to prevent his wife from having a child by a handsome young lover. Marie was interested in her heroes and heroines, and not particularly concerned with their integration into society. If love breaks ordinary social bonds, she is always found on the side of the lovers. Adultery was therefore acceptable according to Marie's ethics, but she drew the line at murder: the wives in her *lais* who actually seek to make away with inconvenient husbands come to a bad end. Her heroines are resourceful, resolute and efficient, not stereotyped beauties. One arranges for her illegitimate baby to be spirited away and brought up by her married sister; another, whose father will only let her marry if her lover can carry her all the way up a mountain, promptly goes on a crash diet to lose as much weight as possible. Though these heroines have extremely limited freedom of action, and most are literally imprisoned, by husbands or fathers, they are certainly not lacking in self-respect, or even in initiative.

### The High Middle Ages and the decline of women's education
It is curious to find that the number of identifiable women writers actually decreases as we move forward through the Middle Ages. There were many powerful queens and many highly educated, articulate nuns in the predominantly masculine world of early Anglo-Saxon England, despite its

obvious literary bias towards male points of view, whether those of Germanic heroes or the Church Fathers. In the High Middle Ages, however, the education of nuns became more and more perfunctory. Eileen Power tells us that the teaching of Latin died out in most English convents in the fourteenth century, and in French ones in the fifteenth.[11] The energies of nuns were increasingly diverted into embroidery rather than reading and writing, which meant that the one outlet for intellectually ambitious women which had previously been available was almost completely blocked. Of course, much medieval writing was anonymous, and highly abstract or conventionalised in form. Thus, it is quite possible that some surviving prayers, for instance, were composed by women, but there is no way of knowing for sure. What is more, it hardly matters, since the manipulation of hackneyed rhetoric and cliché-ridden metaphor, however sincere as an expression of personal piety, tells us nothing about the literary capabilities of women other than their ability to turn out capable and workmanlike imitations of existing forms. The cultural context of Norman and Angevin England, however, suggests as a general principle that not very much of the surviving anonymous writing of medieval England was written by women. The nuns of the High Middle Ages were not as well educated as their Anglo-Saxon predecessors. Chaucer's Prioress, for instance, who spoke a little French 'after the school of Stratford-atte-Bowe', and no Latin, is a fair representation of real-life fourteenth-century nuns. The Church of the twelfth to fourteenth centuries combined an increasingly emotional and fervid attachment to the Virgin Mary with a profound, and in some cases hysterical, suspicion of her earthly daughters. It was also an increasingly wealthy institution, with an insatiable appetite for the rich, lustrous and exquisitely detailed embroidery for which English nuns were famous, and which was therefore called *opus anglicanum*.[12]

**Mystical writers**
The great writers of the English Middle Ages are all men, and so, indeed, are almost all the minor ones. Chaucer has given us a memorable set of portraits of fourteenth-century women, notably the Wife of Bath and the Prioress in the *Canterbury Tales*, but hardly any Wives or Prioresses have given us their own stories of English life at this time. The only two semi-autobiographical accounts of medieval women are of extremely unusual women, the lives of Christina of Markyate (*c*.1096/8–*c*.1155/66) and Margery Kempe (1373–1440). Both are accounts of women who struggled to escape from the lives ordained for them by their families into solitude, prayer and contemplation, 'ghost-written' by men, as narratives of spiritual heroism of a kind which is fairly common in Northern Europe in the Middle Ages.[13] Christina of Markyate was a girl of noble Anglo-Saxon birth, who was forced into marriage, but succeeded in getting her marriage annulled, thus gaining her longed-for independence.[14] Margery Kempe

belonged to a prosperous Norfolk family, and bore fourteen children between her marriage in about 1393 and her eventual success in persuading her husband to swear mutual vows of chastity in 1413. In the earlier stages of her life, she was a businesswoman, a brewer and miller, but she rejected this, together with her family life, in order to pursue her vision of Christ. Once released from wedlock, she travelled as far as the Holy Land and Rome. Her life was shaped by the literal enactment of Christian metaphors, such as dressing in virgin's white to symbolise her status as the bride of Christ.[15]

One of the very few English nuns (Christina, Margery and Julian of Norwich (see below) were anchorites) of the High Middle Ages to leave any kind of identifiable oeuvre was Katherine of Sutton (*d*.1376). She was the abbess of Barking Abbey from 1363 until her death. This is particularly intriguing in that Barking had been an outstandingly cultivated house under Hildelith and her immediate successors in the seventh century. One wonders if any part of its library could have survived the intervening seven centuries. Katherine of Sutton wrote liturgical dramas, elaborations of the Easter liturgy of a kind which had been in use in England since the tenth century: the idea was to dramatise the amazing events of the Resurrection, and bring them vividly alive in the minds of the worshippers. In her *Elevatio Hostiae* ('Raising of the Host'), the nuns in the congregation impersonate the Old Testament patriarchs who are confined in Hell until Jesus comes and takes them with him to Heaven. They are shut out of the chapel until the priest, representing Christ, comes and releases them, and they come in rejoicing, carrying palms in token of victory. Similarly, the *Visitatio Sepulchri* ('The Visit to the Tomb') has three nuns representing the three Marys who go to the tomb of Christ, find it empty, and interrogate the angels who give them the news of the Resurrection. The drama is comparable in style with contemporary liturgical dramas in France, but is original in its details.[16]

The most interesting English woman writer of the Middle Ages is the great mystic Julian of Norwich (*c*.1342–*c*.1416), author of the *Revelations of Divine Love*. Julian's writing is startlingly original in its pursuit of a vision of God which comprehends the noblest characteristics of both sexes: 'as truly as God is our Father, so truly is God our Mother.' She develops this theme into a meditation not on the Virgin Mary as the great mother-figure of the Christian tradition, but on Jesus as Mother:

> The mother can give her child to suck of her milk, but our precious Mother Jesus can feed us with himself, and does, most courteously and most tenderly, with the blessed sacrament which is the precious food of true life; and with all the sweet sacraments he sustains us most mercifully and graciously ... The mother can lay her child tenderly to her breast, but our tender Mother Jesus can lead us easily into his blessed breast through

his sweet open side, and show us there a part of the godhead and of the
joys of heaven, with inner certainty of endless bliss.[17]          (ch.60)

Christian theology does not in theory conceptualise the Trinity as male, but
the association of power and authority with maleness, as well as the
tradition of visual representation, have had the effect that mystical writers
almost always see God as male, in one way or another. Julian's vision is not
heretical, but it is extremely unusual.

## Secular writing

In all of medieval English narrative poetry, only *The Floure and the Leafe*
and *The Assembly of Ladies*[18] (both fifteenth century) have been attributed
with any confidence to a woman – both are narrated by a female voice, but
that is hardly decisive. *The Floure and the Leafe* and *The Assembly* are
allegorical dream-poems, one of the most familiar genres of medieval
narrative poetry. *The Floure and the Leafe* dramatises a contrast between
self-indulgent frivolity (servants of the flower), and chastity, constancy and
virtue (servants of the leaf), using for its allegorical structure a game, or
cult, of the flower and the leaf which was played in fifteenth-century court
circles. The narrator and her story are alike so elegant and courteous in
address that it is difficult to discern an individual voice beneath the
polished, formal structure. The poem is charitable, and exquisitely polite,
in a way which brings to mind the polite literature of three centuries later.
Bad taste of any kind is simply not admitted into the poem's texture; even
the servants of the flower, though the morality of the poem rejects them, are
never less than gracious in their behaviour. The narrator describes mysterious, elegant companies of ladies and gentlemen, riding for pleasure
dressed in green and white velvet. It is only gradually that her curiosity is
satisfied by discovering the inner significance of what she has seen. Thus the
reader, seeing the events through her eyes, is similarly presented with a
puzzle and its resolution. The poem is the product of a mind disciplined by
the customs and *mores* of a highly artificial society, and only makes sense if
it is read as such: we cannot look to such a work for any expression of
possible tensions between the individual and society.

*The Assembly of Ladies* is simpler and more conventional: the ladies
assemble to complain of the neglectfulness and unfaithfulness of men. This
was a familiar debate by the mid-fifteenth century, which had been given
considerable impetus by the writings of the fourteenth-century Christine de
Pisan, the first European woman known to have earned her living as a
professional writer (she had been left a widow at twenty-six, with three
children to support). Christine argued eloquently that women were no
worse than men, indeed possibly better, and her writings, themselves
responses to a misogynist tradition, provoked further response. *The
Assembly*, then, breaks no new ground in insisting that women are as often
mistreated by men as men are by women, and neither sex has a monopoly of

faithfulness or wickedness. The writer has none of the *Floure*-poet's talent for dialogue and action; the poem is very static, and the allegory lifeless. It deploys its allegory without the *Floure*-poet's finesse: the reader is simply told what all the allegorical women are doing, and why.

As the Middle Ages gradually moved towards the Renaissance, women's contribution to the development of lyric poetry is suggested by the group of French women poets active at the court of Queen Margaret of Scotland in the mid-fifteenth century, including the queen herself, and by several short lyrics in the 'Findern Anthology',[19] written in Derbyshire in the later fifteenth century, apparently by young women friends of the family who were assembling the anthology in question. The activities of these two clusters of women writers suggest quite strongly that by the fifteenth century many more women were probably writing than we now know about, and that the survival of their work has been very much a matter of chance.

These isolated examples apart, women's writing effectively disappears from the record in this period. Very few lay people knew how to read and write. Even though most nuns could probably read their own language, very few were taught to compose in Latin, the language of high culture. The declining number of women still learning Latin is highly significant, since it greatly reduced the chance that women's poetry would be written down. This was not only because the ecclesiastical establishment was increasingly suspicious of the subversive powers of the female intellect,[20] but because there was, in their view, a far more practical use for women's time, labour and creative abilities. The replacement of the nunnery scriptorium (writing-room) by an embroidery atelier meant that, on the whole, the only people who could enliven the spare half-page at the end of a theological treatise with a favourite poem were men. Thus, any poem or tract composed by a medieval Englishwoman had to appeal to male tastes in order to stand any chance of being preserved, not as the result of deliberate censorship, but for purely practical reasons. It is hardly surprising that if any medieval women expressed views which were radically discordant with male perceptions, their work has not reached us.

The totality of male domination over the literary tradition in medieval England can be demonstrated in many ways, one of which is to observe that of the surviving English carols (popular songs) written before 1550, there are no fewer than seventeen which deride women and marriage, but not one which casts a satirical eye on men from a woman's viewpoint. The most positive mood expressed towards a human woman (as distinct from the idealised projection of the Virgin) in these carols is the genial patronage of:

A woman ys a worthy thyng,
They do the washe and do the wrynge;
'Lullay, Lullay', she dothe the[e] syng,
And yet she hath but care and woo [woe].[21]

Others in the same collection of carols, edited by R.L. Greene, for example no. 407, express the frequently attested male conviction that women have recently become uppity to an unprecedented degree, and that in days gone by they used to behave themselves better.

The fifteenth century has also left us one or two slight, light-hearted lyrics in praise of men, written from a woman's point of view, and quite possibly by female authors. Their innocuous charm was presumably their passport to survival. Greene's no. 446, for instance, describes, with a fresh and zestful appreciation, a black-haired lad in a scarlet bonnet and satin doublet. The poem mentions no specific physical feature except his black hair, but details his fine, well-tailored garments, and tells us that he was extremely good at kissing. It expresses a mood, rather than creating a picture, and in this respect it is very different from most contemporary poems about beautiful women, which tend to list the purely external features of hair, skin, eyes, teeth and general figure. Another of Greene's poems, no. 451, explores a theme familiar in women's writing, from the Old English 'The Wife's Lament' onwards: steadfast affection for a lover who is not able, or willing, to remain with the speaker. The patient, but hardly resigned, passion of faithful women for absent men echoes down the centuries, achieving one of its most memorable expressions in Jane Austen's *Persuasion*:

> We certainly do not forget you so soon as you forget us. It is, perhaps, our fate rather than our merit. We cannot help ourselves. We live at home, quiet, confined, and our feelings prey on us.               (ch.23)

A further handful of medieval lyrics which may or may not all be by women are in the form of a first-person narration by a young girl, who fares forth joyously on a day's holiday, meets an attractive young man, one thing leads to another, they have a sexual encounter, and she becomes pregnant. To a reader who has waded through some part of the immense sea of medieval complaint-poetry by men railing against the hard-heartedness and obdurate virtue of their lady-loves, these lyrics are a salutary reminder of the connection between sexual intercourse and pregnancy. In a world without efficient contraception, any girl who allowed herself to be tempted by an importunate young man ran an enormous personal risk, something which the international convention of courtly love and complaint-poetry discreetly passes over. These lyrics may well have been intended as cautionary tales, indirectly advising young maidens to guard their virginity, but there is a refreshing absence of conventional Christian morality. They acknowledge, without condescension or outrage, the inevitable tendency of healthy adolescents to find one another sexually attractive. Their pragmatic recommendation of female chastity springs not from sexual anxiety, but from a clear perception of cause and effect.

Despite an almost complete lack of statistical information for the English

Middle Ages, there is some reason to think that literacy was on the rise in the fifteenth century. Various historical conditions were conspiring to alter the structure of society by creating an expanding, chiefly urban, literate middle class. The great mass of the population, of course, remained peasants, but there gradually came to be a sufficient number of people with a little spare money, a little education, and some leisure time to create a new buying public and alter the character of the book trade. We have some information about the consumers, rather than the producers, of fifteenth-century English literature from the Paston letters, the personal archive of a wealthy Norfolk family, written between 1420 and 1503. Beside their fascination for students of English social history, and the powerful impression left on the reader by Margery Paston, a dynamic, strong-willed matriarch, the letters additionally tell us a little about the family's reading habits. The Pastons belonged to the small section of society wealthy enough to buy manuscript books. They owned, between them, a large number of books, mainly practical, but they also bought fiction. Anne Paston owned a copy of John Lydgate's long poem *The Siege of Thebes,* and the men of the family owned many other literary works, including some Chaucer. The practical situation which lies behind these modestly extravagant purchases is the creation of commercial publishing-houses: teams of scribes producing straightforward manuscript copies of popular works as simply and cheaply as possible, even though paper, which was relatively inexpensive, was not made in England until the end of the fifteenth century. The development of a book market was further enhanced by Britain's first printing press, that of William Caxton, established in 1476. The creation of a book-buying public, which increasingly freed writers from direct dependence on a wealthy patron, and thus from the need to cater for an essentially aristocratic canon of tastes and values, cannot be understood without reference to these social and technological factors.

# The Elizabethan age

### Women and education

The educational context of sixteenth-century England is as relevant to the absence of any women's names from the canon of famous Elizabethan writers as is the closed nature of writing as a profession. The dissolution of the monasteries after the break with the Church of Rome in 1534 made the development of an effective secular educational structure a matter of urgent necessity. In order to facilitate the new entrepreneurial culture of merchant adventurers, and the development of an increasingly cultivated and flexible middle class, the endowment of schools became a popular form of charitable self-display. Many grammar schools and merchant company schools were first founded in this century, particularly in and around London. But while the monastic system had offered some, though increasingly perfunctory, educational opportunities to girls, the grammar schools offered none, since they were for boys only, as were the universities which functioned until the late nineteenth century on the theory that they were educating potential clergy for the Established Church. Girls' education almost always took place at home, and was therefore directly dependent on their parents' views of what was appropriate for them. Elementary and 'petty' schools taught some girls up to the age of seven – but from seven onwards, no formal education seems to have been available to them. It was only in the most unusual circumstances that a family would encourage, or allow, daughters to acquire a literary education, and very rare indeed for them to acquire even a superficial knowledge of the classics or of law. Since this was an era which required literature to exhibit a high degree of technical excellence, acquired knowledge, and polish in order to be successful, very few girls were in any position to compete as writers – though as the end of the previous section suggests, their passive influence on English literature as consumers of a marketable product became an increasingly significant factor in English book production from this century onwards.

**Royal authors: Elizabeth I and Mary, Queen of Scots**
The sixteenth century is rightly considered one of the most glorious periods in the history of English literature: the age of writers such as Shakespeare, Marlowe, Ben Jonson and many others; none of them women, as far as the general reader is concerned. Queen Elizabeth (1533–1603) herself read and spoke several languages. She produced an English translation of what is perhaps the greatest book written in the early Middle Ages, the sixth-century Boethius's *Consolation of Philosophy* (Boethius's humane and sophisticated wisdom also attracted translations from, among others, her ancestor King Alfred the Great and Chaucer, so the queen was in good company). Various original poems have been attributed to her, but it is always particularly hard to tell whether great and autocratic rulers actually did their own writing – Elizabeth's father Henry VIII also had cultural pretensions, and is credited with a range of compositions (most famously, the song 'Pastime with Good Company') which he almost certainly did not write. The lamentably poor quality of Elizabeth's translations argues against the acceptance of her authorship of the poems attributed to her.[22] Mary, Queen of Scots (1542–87) is sometimes said to have been a writer (almost certainly in French, since she was brought up at the French court). She certainly had a humanist education, and the discourse, calligraphy and presentation of her letters would support this, but it is easier to prove that she was an expert embroiderer, since many examples of her needlework actually survive, whereas little original writing survives which can be attributed to her with any confidence.[23]

Why Queen Elizabeth's writing is not better than it is is presumably a straightforward matter of talent: education does not in itself necessarily produce the ability to write well. Why the attribution of writings to Mary is such a tangled tale is a considerably more complex question: as a political figure who attracted vehement partisans, as well as enemies, and who was even put up as a candidate for canonisation, her writing might be expected to have survived, if only in the Vatican archives. The paucity of her writing preserved for us is an interesting example of the way in which the work of even the most prominent public figures of the sixteenth century can disappear.

Apart from Queen Elizabeth, women writers are hard to find. The life, opportunities and education of monarchs such as Elizabeth and Mary can tell us virtually nothing about the opportunities available to ordinary people, and certainly nothing about the opportunities available to women. The reasons why we do not have a list of Elizabethan women writers to set beside the many well-known male authors of this period have been dramatised by Virginia Woolf, in the memorable passage of *A Room of One's Own* in which she imagines what would have happened if Shakespeare had had an equally talented sister. First of all, she suggests, her family would have told her to stick to her housework, and no one would have taken her poetry seriously. Then, when she ran away and went to London, she would have been unable to make any impression on the all-male world of the playhouses (where even women's parts were played by men); unable to get work and sexually vulnerable she would have ended up pregnant, and killed herself. There is nothing unlikely or unnecessarily negative in this depressing scenario.[24] Much of the best poetry of the Elizabethan age was produced by upwardly mobile members of the new bourgeoisie, men who went to university, and abandoned their fathers' professions in favour of a life of letters. Women could not go to university, and could not (except as whores, such as Venetia Digby (1600–33)) attract the patronage of rich and powerful courtiers. So this rising tide of 'new men' simply could not, within the social structures of the time, include any women.

A recent collection of writing by sixteenth-century British women includes very little writing intended as literature, or intended to be published: there are prayers in prose and verse (many of them by women of the royal family), some letters and diaries. Almost all the prose and verse written for publication consists of polemical works of various kinds, religious or political.[25]

### The Sidney circle

From the Elizabethan age onward, any woman who wrote, and whose work was published, was likely to belong to the top rank of society, to a circle which valued learning for its own sake, and not as an aspect of competitive social advancement. Apart from the queen, the outstanding names are members of the Sidney family. Mary Sidney, Countess of Pembroke (1561–1621), sister of Sir Philip Sidney, was perhaps the best woman poet of the sixteenth century, and the centre of a circle of poets. Like Queen Elizabeth, Mary Sidney produced translations as well as original poems. Her English version of Petrarch's *Triumph of Death* was the best rendition before the twentieth century, and the only one to use Petrarch's own rhyme-scheme. In an era when the new Italian culture of the Renaissance had superseded that of France as the international arbiter of taste and excellence, the *Triumph* was valued above even Dante's *Divine Comedy*, so a good English translation was of considerable significance.

Mary Sidney's other main achievement, besides her involvement with the editing and publication of her brother's much better-known poems, is a metrical version of the Psalms; more than a translation in the strict sense, it is a kind of meditation and re-creation of what the Psalms meant to her. According to Waller, Mary Sidney's metrical Psalms are 'as important a part of the late Elizabethan literary revolution as the *Shepheardes Calender* and *Astrophil and Stella*.'[26] They were widely read in their own time.

Another Sidney poet of the next generation, Lady Mary Wroth (1586–1651/3), had greater difficulty in getting her work accepted. Mary Sidney was used as a stick to beat her with: 'repent you of so many ill spent years of so vaine a booke... you may follow the rare, and pious example of your vertuous and learned Aunt, who translated so many godly books and expecially the holly [sic] psalmes of David', said a reproving courtier, Lord Denny. This gives a clue to Mary Sidney's acceptability. Most of her writing could be seen either as devotional, or as promoting her dead brother's fame, which were both praiseworthy uses for her talents, since they did not thrust her own personality forward in an unseemly way. Mary Wroth, on the other hand, wrote love poetry, an erotic-political romance, *Urania* (1621), and a pastoral play (unpublished) called *Loues Victorie*. Her work is cynical and disillusioned, suggesting that women are happiest alone.[27]

**Lady Falkland**

Elizabeth Cary, Lady Falkland (1585–1639) was a contemporary of Mary Wroth's. Both women were therefore writing not in the sixteenth century, but in the beginning of the seventeenth, and therefore not so much in the Jacobean age as in that of Charles I and his cultivated Roman Catholic queen, Henrietta Maria. Henrietta Maria's court was execrated by the increasingly powerful Puritan movement, but the queen's interest in literature, drama and the arts offered hope and encouragement to literary Englishwomen. This was particularly significant to Lady Falkland, since a dominant theme in her life was her conversion to Catholicism, which estranged her from her husband and family. Her principal literary activity was the translation of the works of Jacques Davy, Cardinal Du Perron, dedicated to Henrietta Maria, and the writing of verse hagiography. But she was also, with Mary Wroth, one the first women playwrights in the history of English literature.

Her *History of King Edward II* was never finished, but her *Mariam, Faire Queene of Jewry* is complete, and may have been written between 1602 and 1604. Technically, the play is strictly classical. Only three speaking actors appear in each scene, following a rule of ancient Greek drama. Unities of space and time are observed: the play takes place entirely in Jerusalem (though this diverges from the historical narrative on which it is based), and occurs in the space of a single day. There are speeches by a Chorus, and these speeches are more varied in their verse structures than those of the principal speakers, which again are characteristics of Greek tragedy.

The subject is the tragedy of Herod and Mariam, more often called Mariamne, taken from *The Antiquities of the Jews* by the second-century historian and Jewish apologist, Josephus: there were French, English and Latin translations of this Greek work available in the late sixteenth century. The plot is eminently dramatic: Herod, a usurper, has married Mariam, a daughter of the displaced ruling family. He is passionately devoted to her, but considers it politically necessary to kill her brother and grandfather, among other close members of her family. He comes, inevitably, to doubt her loyalty, and in a paroxysm of jealousy, orders her execution. The play presents Mariam's dilemma rather than Herod's: at what point does a loyal wife withdraw loyalty from a husband who is a treacherous murderer? Has she a right to a conscience of her own? A principal issue in this play, therefore, is independent moral judgment. At the end of Act IV, the Chorus criticises Mariam for objecting to her husband's actions, but in terms which support her right to think for herself, and steer her own path between the different moral imperatives of family, marital and political loyalty:[28]

> The fairest action of our humane life,
> Is scorning to revenge an injurie:
> For who forgives without a further strife,
> His adversaries heart to him doth tie.
>  And tis a firmer conquest truely sed,
>  To winne the heart, than overthrow the head ...

> A noble heart doth teach a vertuous scorne,
> To scorne to owe a dutie over-long:
> To scorne to be for benefits forborne,
> To scorne to lie, to scorne to do a wrong.
>  To scorne to beare an injurie in minde,
>  To scorne a free-borne heart slave-like to binde.

In her own life, Lady Falkland's conversion to Catholicism caused political difficulties for her husband, estranged her from her family, and caused much personal unhappiness, since it was not compatible with her serious desire to do her duty as a loyal wife. Her presentation of Mariam as a woman who makes principled choices, even if they turn out to be wrong, is that of a woman who asserted her own right to moral seriousness, at enormous cost.

The entire dominant pattern of poetic discourse in the sixteenth century relied on male action, female passivity; women as subject, never as speaking voice. Though the Elizabethan theatre was remarkable for some of the most vivid and assertive female characters in the history of theatre, these studies of women's personalities were written by men, and played by boys. They demonstrated that the Elizabethan audience found women, as well as men, interesting; but not that they were prepared to let women speak for themselves. It was evidently difficult for Mary Wroth to write at all, let alone convey her meaning against a set of social conventions which insisted on her silence: 'as the echo answereth but one word for many, which are spoken to her; so a woman's answer should be in a word.' The women of this great age of creativity and expressive, individual speaking voices were all but imprisoned in silence.

NOTES
1 Aldhelm, *The Prose Works*, trs. M. Herren and M. Lapidge, Boydell and Brewer, Ipswich, 1979, pp.59 and 130.
2 See *The Letters of Saint Boniface*, trs. E. Emerton, Columbia, New York, 1940, for letters by Egburga (V), Eangyth (VI), Bugga (VII), Lioba (XXI) and Cena (LXXX). Boniface's affectionate and respectful replies are also translated here.
3 This is my own translation from *S. Bonifatii et Lulli Epistolae*, ed. M. Tangl, Weidmann, Berlin, 1916, pp.284–5.
4 Hugeburc's account of Saint Willibald in the Holy Land is in *The Anglo-Saxon Missionaries in Germany*, trs. C.H. Talbot, Sheed and Ward, London, 1954, pp.153–77. Hugeburc says of her work (p.153): 'it may seem very bold on my part to write this book when there are so many holy priests capable of doing better, but as a humble relative [of Willibald and his brother] I would like to record something of their deeds and travels for future ages.' Talbot's volume also includes the life of another female member of this circle, Lioba, written by a German monk.
5 *The Anglo-Saxon Missionaries in Germany*, p.170.
6 The Abbess Bugga, in about 720, sent Saint Boniface (as she writes in her letter (Emerton, pp.40–1, see note 2 above) 'fifty *solidi* [gold coins] and an altar cloth [i.e. an embroidered cloth], the best I can possibly do'. But Boniface wrote to the Abbess Eadburg in 735 asking her to make, not an embroidery, but a copy written in gold of the Epistles of Saint Peter (Emerton, p.65). Writing in gold ink was a very tricky and delicate business which only the most highly trained scribes could attempt. Boniface is therefore assuming that Eadburg is capable of the highest standards of craftsmanship in writing – and she could probably embroider, too!
7 *A Choice of Anglo-Saxon Verse*, ed. and trs. R. Hamer, Faber, London, 1970, pp.71–85.
8 See further J. Chance, *Woman as Hero in Old English Literature*, Syracuse University Press, Syracuse, NY, 1986, esp. pp.31–40.
9 *A Choice of Anglo-Saxon Verse*, pp.135–7.
10 *The Lais of Marie de France*, trs. G.S. Burgess and K. Busby, Penguin Classics, Harmondsworth, 1986.
11 E. Power, *Medieval Women*, ed. M.M. Postan, Cambridge University Press, Cambridge, 1975, pp.80–99.

12  R. Parker, *The Subversive Stitch: Embroidery and the Making of the Feminine*, Women's Press, London, 1984, p.25, points out that laywomen also embroidered professionally. King Cnut (or Canute)'s daughter Aethelswith set up an embroidery workshop near the monastery of Ely, and it is known that she worked there herself. See pp.40–3 for a description of *opus anglicanum* and its social context.

13  C.W. Bynum, *Holy Feast and Holy Fast: The Religious Significance of Food to Medieval Women*, University of California Press, Berkeley, CA, 1989, pp.150–88, discusses a number of comparable lives.

14  *The Life of Christina of Markyate: A Twelfth-century Recluse*, trs. C.H. Talbot, Clarendon Press, Oxford, 1959.

15  *The Book of Margery Kempe*, trs. W. Butler-Bowden, Oxford University Press, Oxford, 1954.

16  *The Ordinale and Customary of the Benedictine Nuns of Barking Abbey*, ed. J.B.L. Tolhurst, Henry Bradshaw Society, London, 2 vols, 1927–8. See also N. Cotton, *Women Playwrights in England, c.1363–1750*, Bucknell University Press, Lewisburg, NC, 1980.

17  Julian, *Showings*, trs. E. Colledge and J. Walsh, Paulist Press, New York, 1978, is a recent full translation of Julian's work.

18  Ed. D.A. Pearsall, Manchester University Press, Manchester, 1980.

19  Ed. R.H. Robbins, *Proceedings of the Modern Language Association*, 69, 1954, pp.610–42.

20  See, for instance, Bynum, *Holy Feast and Holy Fast*, pp.15–23, especially p.22: 'after the early fourteenth century, the forms and themes of women's religiosity aroused increased hostility...by the time of Catherine of Siena, Bridget of Sweden and Joan of Arc, the influence – even the survival – of pious women depended almost wholly on the success, in ecclesiastical and secular politics, of their male adherents.'

21  BL Harley 4294 (fifteenth century) in *The Early English Carols*, ed. R.L. Greene, Clarendon Press, Oxford, 2nd edn, 1977, no. 396, p.234.

22  A maximalist approach to the poetry attributed to Queen Elizabeth is presented in *The Paradise of Women: Writings by Englishwomen of the Renaissance*, ed. B. Travistsky, Greenwood Press, Westport, CO, and London, 1981, pp.19–20, 36–7, 93–4, and in *Poems of Queen Elizabeth I*, ed. L. Bradner, Brown University Press, Providence, R.I., 1964.

23  Translations of poems attributed to Mary, Queen of Scots are to be found in *The Paradise of Women*, pp.187–207. A more reliable account will be found in the new edition by Robin Bell.

24  Even in the eighteenth century, when women had considerably more freedom, when the talented and intelligent Elizabeth Inchbald ran away to London at the age of sixteen to become an actress, she had a variety of exhausting and unpleasant experiences before she was forced to admit defeat and go to her brother-in-law for help (S.R. Littlewood, *Elizabeth Inchbald and Her Circle*, Daniel O'Connor, London, 1921, pp.10–16).

25  *The Paradise of Women*.

26  G. Waller, *English Poetry of the Sixteenth Century*, Longman, London and New York, 1986, p.162.

27  *The Poems of Lady Mary Wroth*, ed. J.A. Roberts, Louisiana State University Press, Baton Rouge, LA, 1983. The first book of her *Urania* is in *An Anthology of Seventeenth-century Fiction*, ed. P. Salzman, Oxford University Press, Oxford, 1991, pp.3–208.

28  *The Paradise of Women*, pp.209–33, at p.232.

# Chapter 2

# The seventeenth century

## The historical context

**Women's social position**

From the seventeenth century onwards, we are in something more like the modern world. Seventeenth-century English is more comprehensible to a modern reader than medieval English, though of course, we must always bear in mind that central terms such as 'virtue', 'honour', 'liberty' have changed considerably in significance over the centuries, and thus present traps for the unwary modern reader. 'Virtue' and 'honour', with reference to women, were associated almost entirely with sexual chastity in the seventeenth century, and 'liberty' was a much less positive concept than it is for a twentieth-century reader. Thus, when we read works either by or about seventeenth-century women, we must try to remain alert to the differences between what the words convey to us, and what they can possibly have meant at the time.

While the position of women in early modern England was changing, there were no signs, however gradual, of an improvement in their status from the gloom of the Dark Ages to the enlightenment of the Renaissance. The extent to which we have surviving writing by women, or indeed writing of indeterminate authorship but sympathetically expressive of a female viewpoint, is bound up with the whole historical context of how women were perceived by men (and by each other) at any one time. To quote chapter 23 of *Persuasion* again, the heroine Anne Elliot declares: 'men have had every advantage of us in telling their own story. Education has been theirs in so much higher a degree; the pen has been in their hands.' That was obviously true when Jane Austen was writing in the early nineteenth century, and becomes even truer the further back we reach into the past – Chaucer's Wife of Bath is made to say much the same in her Prologue (lines 693–6). In the early modern period, the social position of intelligent and creative women was rather worse in many ways than it had been for a nun such as Hugeburc or Lioba in the eighth century, or for a courtier such as Marie de France in the twelfth. Women had great freedom, both to act and to express themselves, during the actual period of the Civil War and subsequent Cromwellian government (1649–60), but this was followed by a masculine clampdown at the Restoration. This is reflected in pro-Cavalier propaganda verse, printed after the Restoration. Thomas Jordan's poem 'The Rebellion' directly associates the self-expression of women and the working class with madness, anarchy and death:

> Come Clowns, come Boys, Come Hobeldehoys,
> Come Females of each degree,
> Stretch out your Throats, bring in your Votes,
> And make good the Anarchy;
> Then thus it shall be, says *Alse*,
> Nay, thus it shall be, says *Amie*,
> Nay, thus it shall go, says *Taffie*, I trow,
> Nay, thus it shall go, says *Jemmy*.
> Speak *Abraham*, speak *Hester*,
> Speak *Judith*, speak *Kester*,
> Speak tag and rag, short coat and long:
> Truth is the spell that made us rebell,
> And murder and plundering ding dong...[1]

This poem makes an absolute assumption that giving any public voice to the underclasses of seventeenth-century society brings ruin and destruction. The names (italics are in the original) are both male and female and identify the classes Jordan envisages: the male 'Jemmy' suggests a peasant, 'Taffie' a Welshman, and 'Abraham' a Puritan (or a Jew, but the Puritan fondness for Old Testament names is a more likely target here). The women's names are not so obviously differentiated, except that 'Judith' and 'Hester' again suggest Puritans.

The new authorial confidence of the Civil War generation is shown in the memoirs of the Royalist aristocrat, Ann, Lady Fanshawe (1625–80), as well as in those of the Puritan, Lucy Hutchinson (1620–?). There is a distinct change, reflected in non-literary sources,[2] and equally in the work of the so-called 'Cavalier' poets of the early seventeenth century and their 'Restoration' successors, between the culture of England under Charles I and England under Charles II. Much Cavalier poetry written by men for women is, essentially, marriage poetry. It celebrates long-term relationships, official or otherwise, and it is responsive to the concept of the female half of the partnership having a point of view of her own. It also assumes intelligence and education in its recipient.[3] By contrast, Restoration poets, particularly the Earl of Rochester, represent contact between the sexes as ruthless, predatory and impersonal; the women are damned if they do, and damned if they don't – succumb, that is, to the poet's advances – and what is more, doubly damned if they are foolish enough to believe that protestations of affection might lead to marriage. The

Restoration is the era in which English writers and publishers first begin to produce pornography,[4] another reflection of the new phallic ideology centred on the aggressively public sexuality of Charles II himself. Rochester sums up this aspect of his era with the trenchant lines:

Love a Woman! You're an Ass,
'Tis a most insipid Passion
To choose out for your Happiness
The silliest part of God's Creation.

Let the Porter and the Groom,
Things designed for dirty Slaves,
Drudge in fair Aurelia's Womb,
To get Supplies for Age and Graves.[5]

In this context of savage masculine contempt for women, it is hardly surprising to find that women writers are little in evidence.

**The literary market**
From the seventeenth century onwards, the expansion of the market for literature makes possible an increasingly clear distinction between people who write purely because they have something to say, and people who write, at least partly, for money. In our own time, almost all poetry and certain kinds of prose, complex in its structure, thought and style, are recognised as 'literature', printed in small editions, and read by relatively few people. Essentially, it is very seldom possible even in our highly literate society to make a living out of aesthetically complex writing, whether prose or poetry. On the other hand, many writers of spy fiction, horror fiction and romances, from Stephen King to Jackie Collins, continue to make enormously large sums of money. This is not to suggest, of course, that popular writing is necessarily bad. Charles Dickens and Shakespeare, for example, were truly popular in their own time. But the distinction between writing for the love of it – literally, as an amateur – and writing for money is relevant to many women writers. Writing for money tends to restrict the capacity of the professionals to express themselves through their writing, since it is very unusual for a writer to create, rather than respond to, a market. Characterisation, plot, diction and subject in commercial writing are expected, or made, to conform to the highly normative expectations of publishers and readers. In the case of women writers, the considerable powers of censorship which men had at various stages of the publication process further militated against the expression of unorthodox sentiments or the development of unconventional plots in which women implicitly or explicitly rejected the demands which were made of them.

Before the twentieth century, the only 'career' open to most women was marriage. A middle-class or upper-class woman from the seventeenth to the twentieth century who was left for some reason unsupported had enormous difficulty until very recently in earning a living, unless she happened to be the bourgeois widow of a tradesman or craftsman who could take over her husband's business. The choices for most women who could not be absorbed into a family as an extra pair of hands, were teaching children, as a governess or in a school,[6] or needlework of some kind, which was so poorly paid as to be virtually a slow route to starvation, and prostitution. No professions of any kind were open to women. It is therefore not surprising to find that an increasing public demand for fiction, as improved technology made printing gradually simpler and cheaper, led to more and more women trying their hand at writing for the market. The market for books continued to expand throughout the century, in step with the rise in the number of affluent middle-class people and of popular literacy. The increasing availability of light reading was significant to another set of women who were also a relatively recent by-product of social change: under-employed middle-class wives. The well-known diarist Samuel Pepys records on 13 November 1662:

> up – and begun our discontent again[7] and sorely angered with my wife, who endeed doth live very lonely. But I do perceive that it is want of work that doth make her and all other people think of ways of spending their time worse.[8]

Six years later the Pepys household had more money to spare, and he mentions buying her a four-volume romance, *L'Illustre Bassa* (by the French woman writer Madeleine de Scudéry), to amuse herself with (24 February 1668).[9] There were increasing numbers of bored, lonely wives of busy men, especially in London, and, as the century wore on, they created a steady and growing demand for new romances, which their less fortunate or less financially secure sisters could supply, and earn a living by so doing.

The women who did not write for a livelihood were mostly poets, and they often circulated their work in manuscript, rather than seeking publication. Male poets who wrote as amateurs often did the same, since they perceived themselves as speaking essentially to a small audience of like-minded persons, rather than addressing society as a whole; this applied to such well-known writers as Andrew Marvell and Henry King, neither of whom approved a collection of his poems in his lifetime. Katherine Philips (1631–64) is one of the best-known of the women poets under her *nom de plume*, Orinda. She was genuinely outraged by finding her work printed without her permission (pirate editions were very much a feature of the seventeenth-century literary scene), and wrote to a friend (Dorothy Osborne):

> I must never show my face among reasonable people again, for some most dishonest person has got some collection of my poems as I hear and

has delivered them to a printer...the most part of the world are apt enough to believe that I connived at this ugly accident. I have been on the rack ever since I heard it...[10]

The fact that the printer was made to apologise and withdraw the edition is testimony that this was not merely mock-modesty.

# Drama

### Women and the theatre

One of the innovations of the Restoration was the opening of the professional theatre to women, not just as actresses, but as box-keepers and orange-sellers – and playwrights. The first significant group of Englishwomen to earn their livings by writing is that of the women playwrights of the Restoration period. The theatre was closely tied to the court, which meant that the potential audience was tiny, and performance runs necessarily very short. Seats were expensive – from one to four shillings for a normal performance, which is to say, much, much more expensive, in real terms, than going to the Opera at Covent Garden today. But if the run stretched to a third night, the profits from that night all went to the playwright, which meant that a successful play could net its author a great deal of money by contemporary standards.[11] By the 1660s, there was an expanding writer's market for new plays, which was taken advantage of by a number of women, including Mary Pix (1666–1709), Mary de la Rivière Manley (?1672–1724) and, most notably, Aphra Behn (1640–89).[12] The first play written by a woman to appear on a public stage in Britain after the Restoration was Katherine Philips's translation of Corneille's *Pompée,* first performed in Dublin in 1663, and brought to London in the same year.[13]

Women writing for the theatre ran an enormous risk. According to the rhetoric of the Restoration, women should remain modestly silent. The aggressively masculine act of thrusting oneself on the attention of the public as an author was deeply resented by brother writers and critics alike. A woman called Elizabeth Cottington, some of whose letters survive, wrote to a male friend in 1669:

We are in expectation still of Mr Dryden's play. There is a bold woman hath offered one...some verses I have seen which are not ill; that is commendation enough: she will think so too, I believe, when it comes upon the stage. I tremble for the poor woman exposed among the critics.[14]

She was right to tremble. The critics were savage in their treatment of any woman rash enough to write for public performance; though women who confined their work to high-flown and impeccably moralising tragedy in the French manner (as Katherine Philips had done) were handled less roughly by the critical establishment. In spite of male disapproval, however, women were, and remained, involved with the theatre in all kinds of capacities, on and off stage. An indication of the roughness (not merely verbal) of the world which they faced, and their ability to cope with it, is suggested by an incident in 1705, when Mrs Hudson, the box-keeper at Drury Lane, stabbed an unruly member of the audience to death with his own sword.[15] Women were also important as members of the audience: protesting at plays which they considered insulting to women, and encouraging the kinds of plays they liked.[16] Several women are also known to have acted as theatre managers: the most successful was Lady Henrietta Maria Davenant, who managed the Duke's Company from 1668 to 1673. There is some reason to think that she favoured plays by women, or with strong female characters. She put on three plays by Aphra Behn, and also Etheredge's *The Man of Mode* (1676), which was extremely successful with women, and often requested by them in subsequent years. The Duke's Company also put on an unusually large number of plays with transvestite heroines, which offer an opportunity for examining the parameters which govern women's lives.[17]

## Aphra Behn

Aphra Behn, the most successful of Restoration women playwrights, suffered particularly severely from the critical assaults of male writers, and also put up the most spirited defence.[18] Friendless, alone, and recently released from debtors' prison when she began her career, she had little option but to persevere or starve. Part of the reason for the intensity of resentment she faced was that she was highly successful; though there were only two theatres in London, she had seventeen plays produced (out of a total of about twenty-two written) in seventeen years, and also wrote twelve novels (discussed below in the section on 'Prose fiction').[19] Her own comment on the unfair criticism she received was trenchant:

> Had the plays I have writ come forth under any man's name, and never known to have been mine; I appeal to all unbiased judges of sense, if they had not said that person had made as good comedies, as any one man that has writ in our age, but a devil on't the woman damns the poet...I am not content to write for the third day [i.e., for money] only. I value fame as much as if I had been born a hero.[20]

Two of Aphra Behn's plays have been revived in the West End in the last decade, *The Lucky Chance* (1687) and *The Rover* (1677), and have amply demonstrated her wit and her gifts for dialogue, plot and timing. Most of her plots turn, like those of her male contemporaries, on courtship and marriage: where Aphra Behn differs is to focus on the woman's side of the picture, the control exercised over her by her family, the problems of arranged marriages and marriages for money. She employs the old dramatic device of two contrasting pairs of lovers. *The Rover* was an extremely popular play, repeatedly revived, which remained in the repertory well into the eighteenth century, disappearing only when it was held to be too indecent for an increasingly refined public. It centres on an attractive rake, Willmore, and the equally high-spirited woman, Hellena, who ultimately captures his affections, offset against a more sentimental couple, Belvile and Florinda. The play is set in the exotic world of 'Naples, in Carnival time', allowing for ferocious restrictions on female behaviour, courtesans, the potential imprisonment of Hellena in a nunnery, and much play with masks and identities. The use of the alien setting of Catholic Europe allows Behn to manipulate the conventions of Protestant satire for her own purpose, which is to reflect the mores of contemporary English high society.

Her play *The Emperor of the Moon* (1687) lampoons another side of masculine activities by inventing 'the absent-minded scientist' as a comic character, and showing women much more capable of managing the world than over-intellectual men. The play has obvious contemporary relevance, in the context of the foundation of England's first scientific institute, the Royal Society, patronised by Charles II. She is acute in seeing that the new scientist is as removed from human concerns as any Renaissance magician: it is necessary for the resolution of the plot that the determined and witty heroines should take on the role of educators of their supposedly learned guardian, staging a fantastic masquerade to bring him to accept that even with the latest scientific equipment he cannot communicate with the inhabitants of other worlds. He is gently brought to a realisation of the importance of the world of human emotions. The women initiate all stratagems, and act with wit and determination to better their own condition.

# Prose fiction

### Lady Mary Wroth

The market for prose fiction began to establish itself before the Civil War. The first woman who is known to have published prose fiction in the hope of making money is Lady Mary Wroth. She suffered a severe financial crisis after the death of her husband in 1614 and her son in 1616: while, as a widow, she would have controlled her son's estate until he reached maturity, without him the estate reverted to the next male heir. She may have hoped that the political *roman à clef* aspect of her romance *Urania* (1621) would have made it financially successful, but it had the opposite effect, since Lord Edward Denny, furious at the scandalous light which her work shed on his own family, succeeded in getting the romance withdrawn from sale.[21] *Urania* begins with mysteries: a beautiful shepherdess, who has recently discovered that she is an adopted child and who does not know who her real parents are, and a knight, Perissus, whom she finds lamenting in a cave. The knight's story is immediately told, at some length, but Urania's identity remains an unsolved problem, though light is rapidly shed on it when

Urania meets with Parselius, who is looking for the long-lost sister of his friend Amphilianthus, king of Naples. The resemblance of the plot which is developing here to a play such as Shakespeare's *A Winter's Tale* (and ultimately to classical and Hellenistic romance) is obvious. The effect is, however, quite different to that of a play, because the structure is open-ended. Every person who appears in *Urania* sits down with the heroine and tells his or her story at considerable length: any one of these stories would make a play, but nested one within the other as they are, the narrative effect is much more like that of the more complicated parts of the *Arabian Nights*, when four or five stories are in play simultaneously. *Urania* is part of an international literary tradition; another woman who was conspicuously successful in this genre is the French writer Madeleine de Scudéry (1607–1701), the author of several enormous romances, including the ten-volume *Artamène, ou le Grand Cyrus* (1649–53) which is similar to *Urania* in construction, and also in its combination of exotic locations and characters of the utmost refinement. It was translated into English soon after it was written.

### Margaret Cavendish, Duchess of Newcastle
Another very early, though much briefer and highly anomalous, prose romance by a woman is *The Description of a New World Called the Blazing World* (1666) by Margaret Cavendish, Duchess of Newcastle (1623–73).[22] It is not the first piece of fantasy or science-fiction writing in English. Speculative writing began in England with Thomas More's *Utopia* (1516) and Francis Bacon's *The New Atlantis* (1620), or even with Roger Bacon, who predicted the invention of huge, machine-powered ships and land vehicles, and even aeroplanes, in his *Epistola de Secretis Operibus*, written around 1260. Such writing was given a new impetus at the Restoration with Charles II's interest in science, and his foundation of the Royal Society of London in 1662. Margaret Cavendish was not the only woman to be involved in this kind of speculation. Aphra Behn was also interested enough to translate from the French Bernard de Fontenelle's *The Theory of the System of Several New Inhabited Worlds,* though she treats natural philosophers satirically in *The Emperor of the Moon.* Susannah Centlivre (see below, pp.77–9) presents a charming young woman philosopher, Valeria, on stage in *The Basset Table* (1705): a comic figure in her earnestness, but with a certain integrity, and ridiculed only by those other characters who are themselves presented as foolish. She has, and keeps, the affection of Ensign Lovely, and she moves to a happy ending without making a speech rejecting her intellectual pretensions.

*The Blazing World* is a humorous exposition of Margaret Cavendish's fantasy world, and announced as such:

> though I cannot be Henry the Fifth or Charles the Second, yet I endeavour to be Margaret the First, and although I have neither power,

time nor occasion to conquer the world as Alexander and Caesar did, yet rather than not be mistress of one…I have made a world of my own, for which nobody, I hope, will blame me, since it is in everyone's power to do the like.[23]

Accordingly, the heroine of the story, transported from her own world when she inadvertently reaches its North Pole, finds herself made the empress of the Blazing World. The explanations of the heroine's various subjects allow Margaret Cavendish to give her views on physics, architecture, religion, and many other disciplines. The light-heartedness of this fantasy is suggested by the appearance of the Duchess of Newcastle's soul, summoned to be the Empress's secretary: 'Said the Empress: "You were recommended to me by an honest and ingenious spirit." "Surely", answered the Duchess, "the spirit is ignorant of my handwriting" ' – which, she is the first to admit, was almost unreadable. This is a cheerfully self-mocking fantasy, for which Margaret Cavendish makes no claims beyond her own pleasure in writing it, but this in itself is unusually assertive, since it implies that she feels entitled to take up the reader's time without apology or any pretence of doing good.

## Aphra Behn

Aphra Behn wrote a total of twelve 'novels', though this term may raise expectations which her prose fiction does not attempt to fulfil. She did not turn to prose until the very end of her life, when she was already ailing. In 1682, London's two theatrical companies merged into one, under the management of Betterton and Smith, halving the potential market for new plays. Betterton, moreover, preferred to revive old plays, and thus the professional playwright's life became a difficult one. Another problem for Aphra Behn was that she was a supporter of the Stuarts in a political climate which was turning against them. She was arrested in 1682 after the prologue and epilogue she had written to a play by Nathaniel Lee were held to defame the Duke of Monmouth, and this would have made managements cautious of giving her public space. These factors seem to provide the context for her change of direction. Only four of her fictional prose works were published in her lifetime.

Her earliest prose fiction is virtually journalism, the *roman à clef*, *Love Letters Between a Nobleman and His Sister* (1684), a more or less transparent fictionalisation of a contemporary scandal,[24] the elopement of Lord Grey with his sister-in-law Lady Henrietta Berkeley in 1682. Her writing kept pace with actual events, since the first of the four parts published takes events up to the end of June 1683, and appears in the Stationers' Register at the end of October in the same year. The characters are virtually all recognisable political figures, some so thinly disguised as Fergusano (Robert Ferguson), and thus the narrative offered the twin delights of erotic and political scandal.

Her most successful novel, *Oroonoko* (1688), is one of the first works in English literature to offer its readers an entirely sympathetic black hero. It was very widely read in its own time. Behn claims, apparently with some truth, that the story is, again, a fictionalisation of a true story she was involved with when she went with her family to Surinam.[25] Be that as it may, the plot combines classic features of romance, such as beautiful, virtuous but star-crossed lovers, a tyrannical parent, a heroine preserving her virtue in impossible circumstances, and a dauntless hero, with some completely unexpected features. The hero and heroine are both black, and have been taken to Surinam as slaves. Behn does not spare the feelings of her contemporaries in presenting the white slave-owners as corrupt and vicious tyrants over black slaves who are at least as good as they are. She presents a slave revolt, engineered in final desperation by her hero Oroonoko, completely sympathetically. *Oroonoko* is still well worth reading, in spite of its melodramatic plot.

After Aphra Behn, her successors, such as Elizabeth Haywood and Mary de la Rivière Manley, gradually turned from the diminishing opportunities offered by the theatre to the market for fiction which was beginning to open up: this will be discussed more fully in the next chapter.

# Poetry

**Problems of survival**

Before beginning the discussion of the women poets of the seventeenth century, it is necessary to consider the conditions which govern the survival of nearly all vernacular literature of this and the previous century. Although a considerable quantity of vernacular literature survives in printed form, it is not impossible for a whole edition to vanish without trace. Editions were by modern standards extremely small: there is even evidence that printed work of Shakespeare's may have disappeared.

With those works which existed for a long time only in manuscript, the case is even more complicated. Paper was still quite expensive, and the people who could afford to have manuscript books copied for their use were unlikely to put vernacular literature high on their list of priorities. Latin poetry and legal and theological notes are much more common in manuscript collections. This is to suggest that the disappearance of women's writing may arise from factors other than conscious suppression: very few women were taught to write in Latin, and so, written in the vernacular, their works had a reduced chance of survival, as had works by men in any other language than Latin (this was true of all Europe, not only of England). There are of course exceptions: it seems that the celebrated Sir Philip Sidney created such a personal reputation as a poet, diplomat and soldier that his literary works were sought after by contemporaries, but we should equally remember that so fine a poet as Andrew Marvell was barely published during his lifetime and that a collection of his poems did not appear until 1681. It was extra-literary, chiefly political and antiquarian, reasons which led to the first reasonably complete edition of his work being published as late as the 1770s.

This may also suggest that there is more women's poetry yet to be found: although most of the innumerable compilations and notebooks in the libraries of the world contain no poetry, those that do have recently yielded a good number of verses by women, and work in this area has scarcely begun. However, there is already a considerable quantity of poetry by seventeenth-century Englishwomen available, far more than from any earlier century.[26] Some new themes appear in women's writing: poems of resignation to the will of God after the death of much-loved babies and children, and poems addressed to husband and children by a woman who fears death in childbirth. We also find overtly feminist poetry for the first time in English, notably 'Philo-Phillipa's' poem 'To the Excellent Orinda', published with Katherine Philips's own poems in 1667. But for all this new activity and expressiveness, women's writing was still a tiny fraction of the total output of the century. Girls' education still gave needlework and household skills priority over writing, which many girls never had the chance to learn. And women who could and did write still faced inevitable prejudice. As the scholarship of the last decade has made increasingly clear, it was only in exceptional families that women were taught to write or encouraged to write (families which could be called, in the modern sense, 'intellectual'). Few women circulated their poems, and outside the specialised area of revolutionary religious writing, very few indeed sought publication. It is not surprising therefore that in the absence of precedent, women writers were treated, at best, as exceptional, freakish or unwomanly.[27] Margaret Cavendish, the Duchess of Newcastle observed:

> our sex is more apt to read than to write, and most commonly when any of our sex doth write they write some Devotion, or Romances, or Receipts of Medicines, for Cookery or Confectioners, or Complemental Letters, or a copy or two of verses.[28]

Thus the categories of religious, romantic, practical and private writing into which so much women's writing is pigeonholed in the twentieth century, were already established as early as the 1650s.

## Private and published poetry

Margaret Cavendish's own history as a writer is unique, in that she was not only interested in publishing her work, but determined to do so. A radical thinker and feminist, childless, and married to a wealthy nobleman of literary bent who adored her, she was outstandingly well placed to write as she pleased. Her almost total lack of any kind of education makes her actual work an exasperating disappointment, veering uncontrollably between flashes of natural acuity, epigrammatically expressed, and exasperating errors of all kinds. As already mentioned, she published quantities of ruminative, rambling prose and poetry on all kinds of subjects, the nature and position of women being one to which she frequently returned. She vacillated between accepting and rejecting the then accepted 'scientific' proofs of women's 'custom and use' which accounted for their lack of intellectual attainments. Perhaps her real significance in the history of women's writing in England is not to be found in her actual work, but in the mere fact of her unprecedented demand that the fashionable world accept her on her own terms, as an author, in spite of her sex: as she observed, with respect not to her writing, but to her style of dress, which also attracted opprobrious comment:

And if a Lady dress, or chance to wear,
A Gown to please herself, or curl her hair,
If not according as the Fashion runs,
Lord, how it sets a-work their Eyes and Tongues!
Straight she's fantastical, they all do cry,
Yet they will imitate her presently.[29]

It may have been her example, not as an innovator in dress, but as a woman author, particularly as the biographer of her husband (this work appeared in 1667), which nerved the Puritan Lucy Hutchinson and the Royalist Ann, Lady Fanshawe to defend their respective husbands' posthumous reputations – though in both cases, their work was merely handed down in the family, and not printed until the nineteenth century.

Katherine Philips (known as 'Orinda') is an example of a celebrated women poet who circulated her work privately, in manuscript.[30] She celebrated passionate female friendship, a new note in English literature. Her poem to her friend 'Lucasia' (Anne Owen) begins:

I did not live until this time
Crown'd my felicity,
When I could say without a crime,
I am not thine, but thee.

This carcass breath'd, and walkt, and slept,
So that the world believ'd
There was a soul the motions kept;
But they were all deceiv'd.

The poem continues in this vein, which is using to new ends the diction and assertiveness of male poetry of sexual love, including the masculinely authoritative stance of beginning the poem with 'I'. Unlike, for example, John Donne's poem which begins 'I wonder by my troth, what thou, and I/Did, till we lov'd?' (The Good Morrow', c.1600), which Katherine Philips's poem in many ways resembles, she does not pre-empt Lucasia's point of view by venturing to speak on her friend's behalf. It is possible that the echo of Donne is deliberate. Katherine Philips certainly reworked 'A Valediction: Forbidding Mourning', with its well-known image of lovers as a pair of compasses. But whereas Donne emphasised that the fixed foot, woman, stayed still, and the moving foot, man, travelled about, Katherine Philips's re-use of the image places stress on the equal inclining of one to the other.[31]

'Orinda' was not entirely the shy, retiring poetess that legend has made her. It is true that she was deeply distressed by the idea of venturing into print; it is also true that circulating manuscript poems to friends was still an ordinary method of communication between poets. The only public for which she cared was the one she could reach by this non-commercial means. She was a royalist, and a significant figure in royalist literary circles. Her politics differed from her husband's, and she stoutly defended her right to think as she pleased:

> My love and life I must confess are thine,
> But not my errors, they are only mine.[32]

Another seventeenth-century woman poet used the pen-name 'Ephelia'. Her identity is unknown, but her collection was printed in 1679, and she wrote some vigorously confident lyrics, including a poem which begins 'You wrong me, Strephon, when you say / I'm jealous or severe', which draws a subtle distinction between her lover's casual promiscuity, which she is prepared to overlook, and his serious attentions to another woman, which she perceives as an assault on her self-respect. She also wrote a highly entertaining poem beginning 'Why do I love?' which gives one of the most unflattering portraits of a loved one in the whole of English literature: plain, twice her age, less intelligent than she, rude, affected and vain. There is a breezy vein of invective and assertion of self-esteem running through the ritual prostrations of her allegedly fatal passion. Ephelia experimented considerably with the formal elements of poetry: rhyme, line-length and sound patterns. In her poems the figure 'Ephelia' is sometimes treated mockingly, or with irony; she is not the simple mouthpiece of a witlessly naïve authoress. The conventions of seventeenth-century verse are manipulated with wit and skill.

Aphra Behn, unlike Katherine Philips and 'Ephelia', published her poetry under her own name: as a professional writer, rather than a lady, she had everything to gain by taking public credit for her own work.[33] Occasional songs appear in her plays, the lyrics for musical interludes, for example, 'Love in fantastic triumph sat', and she published entertaining and mostly playful amatory verse addressed to various friends, much of it in the context of more or less public exchange of verses between well-known literary figures. Another side of her independent poetic work is public and political – and expresses her loyalty to the House of Stuart. These public poems are far more controversial than they pretend to be. 'A Congratulatory Poem to Her Most Sacred Majesty on the Universal Hopes of All Loyal Persons for a Prince of Wales' (1688) is a salient example. It begins:

> The Mighty BLESSING is *at last* arriv'd,
> Heav'n has, *at last* the Wond'rous WORK achiev'd.
> Long did th'ALMIGHTY pause, and long debate;
> For MONARCHS are not fashion'd at a Heat...
>
> If *Gods* we may with Humane Things compare,
> (For *Gods* and *Kings* ally'd most nearly are)
> This is the Second *Birth* the World e'er knew,
> So long expected, so much Wanted too.[34]

As a statement of fact, this is outrageous. The poem is in fact a blandly successful act of political effrontery, not a conventional loyal greeting. The succession of James II to his brother Charles II had met with considerable resistance, since he and his wife, Mary of Modena, were zealous Catholics, and the majority of the English people were by the late seventeenth century both firmly devoted to Protestantism, and alarmed by the Stuarts' extremely autocratic concept of monarchy. The birth of this child (the Old Pretender) in 1688 was in fact greeted by widespread public hostility, and precipitated the Glorious Revolution in the same year, which deposed James II and put the Protestant William and Mary on the throne of England. The extraordinary hyperbole of Behn's writing in this and her other loyalist poems is therefore not so much sycophancy as a dogged attempt to shift public opinion on to the side of the Stuarts. It is a reminder that Aphra Behn was an active political figure who had once been a spy in Antwerp on behalf of Charles II, as well as a successful playwright and very public woman of letters.

A clue to the treasures of women's writing which may have been lost, is the single surviving poem of Katherine, Lady Dyer (*fl.*1630/40). As far as we know, Lady Dyer never published a line of her poetry. Her own family, the D'Oyleys, were associated with the highly sophisticated and cultured circles of Lord Falkland (son of the Lady Falkland discussed at the end of the previous chapter). Since the Falkland papers were lost in a fire, we will never know if they included unpublished work by Lady Dyer. But one poem of hers survives, because she had it engraved on a monument she erected to her husband's memory in 1641. There may very well be other poems by women lurking in the nation's churchyards; it is one of the very few environments where women's writing, validated by its subject matter, could be excused. Her poem is one of the great love poems of the seventeenth century. The emotion is caught and held in the courtly phrases, exquisitely balanced between dignity and homeliness. The second half runs as follows:

My dearest dust could not thy hasty day
Afford thy drowzy patience leave to stay
One hower longer; so that we might either
   Sate up, or gone to bedd together?
But since thy finisht labour hath possest
   Thy weary limbs with early rest,
Enjoy it sweetly; and thy widdowe bride
Shall soone repose her by thy slumbring side;
Whose business, now is only to prepare
   My nightly dress, and call to prayre:
Mine eyes wax heavy and the day growes old,
   The dew falls thick, my bloud growes cold;
Draw, draw the closed curtaynes: and make roome;
My deare, my dearest dust; I come, I come.[35]

NOTES

1 M.A. Doody, *The Daring Muse: Augustan Poetry Reconsidered*, Cambridge University Press, Cambridge, 1985, p.34, from *Rump: Or an Exact Collection of the Choycest Poems and Songs Relating to the Late Times*, 'by the most Eminent Wits', Henry Brome and Henry Marsh, London, 1662.

2 See E. Hobby, *Virtue of Necessity: English Women's Writing 1649–88*, Virago, London, 1988, p.86: 'the king's [Charles II] behaviour... is the most visible evidence of a far-reaching male backlash against female liberty.'

3 A splendid example of this is the manuscript poetry collections produced by and for the women of the Aston family of Tixall in Staffordshire.

4 See R. Thompson, *Unfit for Modest Ears*, Macmillan, London, 1979.

5 *The Cavalier Poets*, ed. R. Skelton, Faber, London, 1970, p.211. There is a third verse, which I have cut for reasons of space, in which the poet exalts alcohol and male companionship as preferable alternatives to the love of women.

6 The charity-schools which were set up from the end of the seventeenth century onwards to teach literacy and other basic skills to orphans and the children of the poor also offered employment opportunities to women. The feminist Mary Astell (1661–1731) and the Anglo-Saxon scholar Elizabeth Elstob (1683–1756) both kept themselves at one time or another by teaching in such a school.

7 Mrs Pepys wanted a maid, essentially to keep her company, and Pepys felt that they could not afford to have one at that time.

8 *The Diary of Samuel Pepys*, III, p.257.

9 *The Diary of Samuel Pepys*, IX, p.89.

10 D. Spender, *Mothers of the Novel: 100 Good Women Writers before Jane Austen*, Pandora, London and New York, 1986, p.27.

11 Hobby, *Virtue of Necessity*, pp.102–3.

12 An account of these women playwrights, and a representative selection of their work, is in *The Female Wits: Women Playwrights of the Restoration*, ed. F. Morgan, Virago, London, 1981.

13 Katherine Philips suffered less than Aphra Behn from spiteful personal criticism, since her stage work consisted entirely of tragedies of relentlessly high moral tone, and she was more a translator and adaptor of French drama (as in the case of her *Pompey*) than an original dramatist. The difficulty with Aphra Behn, from the viewpoint of her critics, was her gift for comedy, the more particularly since she was frequently led to ridicule male pretensions.

14 Hobby, *Virtue of Necessity*, p.111.
15 J. Pearson, *The Prostituted Muse: Images of Women and Women Dramatists 1642–1737*, Harvester Wheatsheaf, Hemel Hempstead, 1988, p.26.
16 *The Prostituted Muse*, pp.36–40.
17 *The Prostituted Muse*, pp.31–3.
18 See A. Goreau, *Reconstructing Aphra: A Social Biography of Aphra Behn*, Dial Press, New York, 1980, for further information about Aphra Behn and her life.
19 Aphra Behn, *Five Plays*, ed. M. Duffy, Methuen, London, 1990.
20 Hobby, *Virtue of Necessity*, p.119.
21 *An Anthology of Seventeenth-century Fiction*, pp.3–208.
22 *An Anthology of Seventeenth-century Fiction*, pp.251–348.
23 *An Anthology of Seventeenth-century Fiction*, p.253.
24 *Love Letters Between a Nobleman and His Sister*, ed. M. Duffy, Virago, London, 1987.
25 *Oroonoko and Other Stories*, ed. M. Duffy, Methuen, London, 1986, pp.8–11.
26 See *Kissing the Rod: An Anthology of Seventeenth-century Women's Verse*, ed. G. Greer, S. Hastings, J. Medoff and M. Sansone, Virago, London, 1988.
27 See, for instance, Hobby, *Virtue of Necessity* for a more extended discussion.
28 K. Jones, *A Glorious Fame: The Life of Margaret Cavendish, Duchess of Newcastle*, Bloomsbury, London, 1988, p.83.
29 *A Glorious Fame*, p.75.
30 *The Collected Works of Katherine Philips, the Matchless Orinda. I: The Poems*, ed. P. Thomas, Stump Cross Books, Stump Cross, Essex, 1990.
31 Printed in Hobby, *Virtue of Necessity*, p.138.
32 'To Antenor', printed in *Virtue of Necessity*, pp.133–4.
33 *The Uncollected Verse of Aphra Behn*, ed. G. Greer, Stump Cross Books, Stump Cross, Essex, 1989.
34 *The Uncollected Verse of Aphra Behn*, pp.96–8.
35 'Epitaph on Sir William Dyer'. This, with other poems by seventeenth-century women poets, will be published in the new *Penguin Book of Cavalier Verse* (forthcoming), edited by Peter Davidson, to whom I am grateful for passing on this unpublished poem to me.

# Chapter 3

# From the Augustan age to the Romantic era

## The rise of the novel

### The literary and social background

The origins of the novel lie further back in time than some critics seem to think. As a genre, the novel evolved out of the interminable sixteenth-century prose fictions generally known as 'romances' (Cervantes's *Don Quixote* (1605–15) is the only representative of this genre still remembered), which in turn had evolved from the verse romances of the High Middle Ages. The earliest contributions of women to prose fiction in English go back to the seventeenth century, and have thus been discussed in the previous chapter. The eighteenth century, however, sees a very substantial quantitative rise in the amount of published fiction by women available to the reading public. Samuel Richardson (discussed below) did much to forward this process, both as a writer, and as a printer of women's writing. What Richardson so conspicuously achieved was to make the novel respectable, and to give subsequent women writers a suitable male model to whom they could point as a literary progenitor. He and, in the early nineteenth century, Sir Walter Scott (himself deeply indebted to the work of Maria Edgeworth) were the two male novelists who were of most use to their female contemporaries and successors.[1] Richardson extends the respectable novel into territory where women writers are at home; Scott not only highlights the importance of plot (an area of strength of eighteenth-century women writers) but also lends respectability to areas of poetic and historical investigation which are exciting but, beyond doubt, chaste. By making an idealised version of the past both respectable and fashionable, he opened up a new field of narrative possibilities, allowing heroines to escape from their drawing-rooms without prejudicing their chastity.

The nature and quality of women's contributions to the rise of the novel can be seen only in the context of their education, and the social constraints which shaped their actions, diction and choice of subject-matter. The later seventeenth century is the era in which girls' schools first appear in England: one of the first women writers whom we know to have gone away to school is Katherine Philips, who attended Mrs Salmon's school in

Hackney, London.[2] Hannah More's sisters ran a successful girls' school at Bristol, for which she wrote suitable plays such as *The Search after Happiness: A Pastoral Drama* (1774). Many other such schools sprang up in appropriate places such as Bath, where Sophia and Harriet Lee opened a school in 1781, Cheltenham and, of course, London. Such schools did not cater for the academically ambitious and some, such as a London school of the 1760s run by a cultivated alcoholic called Mrs Meribah Larrington, were disastrous.[3] They were intended for the daughters of gentlefolk (or would-be gentlefolk), and concentrated on the inculcation of pleasing manners and deportment, and 'accomplishments': fashionable varieties of craft-work, music, a smattering of general knowledge, and perhaps a foreign language – French or Italian. The inmates of such a school, and something of the texture of their lives, are described in *The Governess, or The Little Female Academy* (1749) by Sarah Fielding (1710–68; sister of Henry Fielding). Young women who aspired to more than this had to be lucky in their parents. They could only get any kind of academic education by sitting in on their brothers' lessons, or being allowed the run of their fathers' libraries – something which most fathers were extremely reluctant to permit, in case the girl read anything which might give her unsuitable ideas. Elizabeth Carter (1717–1806), who became famous for translating the works of the ancient Greek philosopher Epictetus, was the daughter of a clergyman who chose to give her exactly the same education as her brothers. Her name was bandied about by the increasing numbers of people who wanted to assert that women were as intellectually capable as men, since her various publications made this quite clear, but few parents chose to follow the Rev. Carter's example.

Education is crucially important. Having almost always been carefully excluded from the higher branches of learning, literary ladies have frequently been forced to make a virtue of amateurism. Although Aphra Behn, for instance, was an extremely competent professional playwright, her harsh comments about her classically educated male contemporaries and rivals are essentially defensive of her lack of such an education. She was, of course, perfectly right to assert that half a lifetime's acquaintance with Seneca and Aeschylus – especially as they were taught in the schools of the seventeenth century – gave absolutely no advantage when it came to actually learning how to write for the contemporary professional stage:

> we all well know that the immortal Shakespeare's plays (who was not guilty of much more of this [classical learning] than often falls to woman's share) have better pleased the world than Jonson's works.[4]

Fortunately for women writers, there is a long-standing tendency in English national culture to be somewhat suspicious of too offensive a display of learning (or pedantry), and a consequent toleration of, or positive affection for, writing which does not too visibly bear the tokens of strenuous mental effort and disciplined professionalism. Perhaps the first major figure to exploit this English idiosyncrasy was the early Renaissance poet John Skelton, who was not only university-educated, but moved in the most educated circles in the country. Yet his poetic style is notoriously engaging, conversational, and flowing to the point of being slipshod. In the later seventeenth century, partly as a result of the fashion for plain conversational prose which can be connected with the activities of the newly founded Royal Society, an informal way of writing became at least acceptable in a very few, strictly limited contexts.[5] The Latinate, university-trained prose which was to be the predominant ruling-class discourse of the next two centuries, of its nature tends to exclude and marginalise all groups (women, regional writers, working-class writers) who have no direct access to centralised higher education. Thus, the informal style was seized on by various aspirant writers outside the professional, metropolitan context, providing untrained women authors with at least an acceptable public means of expression. After Laurence Sterne had popularised an impressionistic, spontaneous and informal style of writing with his *Tristram Shandy* (1759–67), the virtues of a loosely constructed, conversational mode of writing as a camouflage, or a way of bypassing the literary establishment *per se*, were more and more widely appreciated.

## The influence of Samuel Richardson

There are certain qualities which may be found repeatedly in women's writing, and which may superficially appear to make writers as different in time, tradition and circumstances as Sappho (Greek, seventh/sixth century BC), Sei Shonagon (Japanese, eleventh century AD) and George Sand (French, 1804–76) sisters under the skin; for instance, a vivid, specific and sharply focused response to the world of the senses. But the social patterns governing the lives of women also recur – the need to charm, the educational disadvantages, the need to forestall criticism which springs from a culturally disadvantaged position. Perhaps it is not surprising that the principal model for the feminine style of the eighteenth-century ladies' novel was a man, Samuel Richardson, who was himself lacking in the formal classical education of the upper-class male. This suggests that the question of writing styles may essentially be a class issue rather than a gender issue, provided that we recognise that gentlewomen belong to a different class from their brothers and husbands.[6] Richardson seems to have developed his feminine speaking voice (that of an inexperienced working-class girl) in his first novel, *Pamela* (1740–1), as a screen for his inability to use the appropriate mode of discourse of the male literary establishment. The motivation behind his writing was essentially commercial: himself a professional printer, he began by writing a volume of model letters 'on such subjects as may be of use to country readers', became interested in one of his scenarios, and began to compose a novel. Its success more than justified him from a purely professional point of view. *Pamela* is still his most famous work. Its subject is the struggle between a virginal young servant girl and a master who makes determined attempts to seduce her. Her resistance to seduction is the central theme of the novel, and all the incidents of the plot are related to it. A principal reason why *Pamela* and *Clarissa Harlowe* (1747–8) were immediately fascinating to female readers, and remained profoundly influential in women's writing for generations, is that they deal nakedly with power and sexual politics, particularly as they affect women who are, for whatever reason, deprived of the protection of their families and required to test out their own frail defences against a predatory and hostile world.

With *Pamela*, Richardson invented the epistolary novel, a form which was seized upon by women writers in subsequent generations as an expressive and hugely popular medium. It had the enormous advantage of circumventing the need for 'fine writing' (as the concept was understood in the eighteenth century) by adopting the convention that the epistolary novel consisted of artless outpourings of candid feelings, exchanged between close friends or relatives. Thus the novelist, speaking as if from the heart, writing as if scribbling a letter to a dear one in the privacy of her (or even his) own chamber, was not constrained to write English as if it were Latin, or to adorn her prose with classical tags.[7] Letter-writing was an important social skill, and many volumes of letters from this period have been preserved: those of Lady Mary Wortley Montagu (1689–1762) are particularly lively and interesting, and were first published only a year after her death. The informality appropriate to good letters is indicated by Frances Burney's mentor, 'Daddy' Crisp, who advised her:

> Never think of being correct when you write to me ... if your letters were to be fine-labour'd compositions that smelt of the lamp, I had as lieve they travelled elsewhere. So no more of that, Fanny, an thou lov'st me. Dash away, whatever comes uppermost ...[8]

The illusion of speaking from the heart in the epistolary novel may be a considerably more complex matter than it first appears. Most of the women who wrote for publication in the eighteenth century frankly needed the money. Jane Austen, who began her writing career at the very end of the century, is one of the few who did not; though she certainly was not well-off, she never seems to have considered compromising with the expectations of the novel-reading public for the sake of larger profits. The satirical brilliance of her oeuvre must surely owe something to this simple fact. Moreover, nearly all eighteenth-century women writers had relationships with at least one male mentor, and were entangled in the silken thread of emotional, if not economic dependency (again, Jane Austen is the exception). They needed to please the public, and they also needed to please their fathers or patrons.

## Themes and concerns in eighteenth-century women's novels

Richardson's female followers did not risk, in print at least, the occasional heretical outbursts of anger against society's complacent acceptance of male dominance which he puts in the mouth of his beleaguered heroine, Pamela. It is as if the gifted, articulate and, for the most part, middle-aged women who wrote novels in the eighteenth century feared and avoided the potential self-exposure inherent in creating heroines in their own image. The apparent exception, Mme de Staël's *Corinne* (1807), is essentially a sibyl rather than a conscious artist – woman as conduit for a mysterious prophetic force, rather than a hard-working professional.[9] The writer-heroine had to wait for Elizabeth Barrett Browning's *Aurora Leigh* (1857).

Instead, the great subject of the eighteenth-century novel was courtship, and the heroine normally an inexperienced girl of no more than twenty. Jane Austen made her last heroine, Anne Elliot of *Persuasion*, a woman of twenty-seven, which in the eyes of herself and her contemporaries made her already old – 'her bloom had faded'. But Anne Elliot as she appears at the beginning of the novel has spent the previous eight-and-a-half years in a state of melancholic limbo, almost as if she had not advanced from girlhood to womanhood. Certainly, the passing of time is not described as having brought any possibilities for further development into her life. And when Captain Wentworth reappears in her life, she is *just* young enough to recapture her swiftly-departing youth by the hem of its dress. Even this twenty-seven-year-old is almost unprecedented in eighteenth-century fiction. Women in their later and middle years were quietly censored out, appearing as comic figures, malevolent influences, or *deae ex machinis* speeding the plot on its way. They were not placed at the centre of the narrative.[10] Sometimes older women are disposed of altogether: many novels, from *Evelina* to *Emma* and *Middlemarch*, have a motherless heroine with only a father or father-figure to guide her. Jane Austen's irony, of course, spared no one, but it fell with a particularly devastating effect on the complacency of comfortably settled middle-aged men. Other novelists, Frances Burney, Maria Edgeworth and Mrs Radcliffe, for example, were inclined to take this mentor-figure more at his own valuation. The perfect goodness and wisdom, the impeccable moralising of these paternal saints, the pure intensity of the devotion with which their daughters or protégées regard them – all of these attributed qualities in fiction are a somewhat backhanded testimonial to the role of more fallible and human mentors in the lives of the actual authors. In the case of Richard Lovell Edgeworth, however, generalisation must be avoided: he was outgoing, lively, and more sensitive than is commonly thought, and his effect on Maria Edgeworth was one of enthusiastic, if critical, encouragement. However, the gross flattery, which verges on apotheosis, of a particular male ideal of the mentor in several otherwise very critical and observant women writers of the eighteenth century does not simply represent a tiresome feminine addiction to stuffed shirts and shop-window dummies. The need for approval is a dangerous drug for female artists in any medium, and by indulging the fantasy, attractive to both sides, of the omnipotent protective male, these women could only too easily gain the approval of society at large, and especially of the mentors in their own lives. The cost, only too obviously, is the loss of clarity of vision, and the loss also of any ability to present such figures with all the complexity and fallibility of human nature.

The problem of filial affection and the search for paternal approval is formidably relevant to the oeuvre of many eighteenth- and nineteenth-century women. We must remember that women living in their fathers' houses were socially and legally in the position of children. Thus, a destructive emphasis on children (and women) as quaintly entertaining beings, beneath the serious attention of a rational man, tended to discourage such dependent women writers from striving for excellence, since the expectations of those whom they were conditioned to please were usually depressingly low. In our own time, no parent, however critical his or her taste, would attempt to assess their child's kindergarten Nativity play by the standards of the professional theatre. The warm pleasure which an adult can take in a five-year-old's inept achievement is an appropriate response, but praising the achievements of a fifteen-year-old or twenty-five-old daughter with the same uncritical warmth is condescending and unhelpful. Without real criticism – neither automatic praise nor automatic condemnation – the young author is thrown back on her own resources. Lack of real criticism may have been one of the most serious disadvantages under which these writers had to work. Hannah More (who was very much a supporter of the status quo) noted in 1799 that:

> there is one human consideration which would perhaps more effectually damp in an aspiring woman the ardours of literary vanity . . . she will have to encounter the mortifying circumstance of having her sex always taken into account, and her highest exertions will probably be received with the qualified approbation that it is really extraordinary for a woman. Men of learning, who are naturally apt to estimate works in proportion as they appear to be the result of art, study, and institution, are apt to consider even the happier performances of the other sex as the *spontaneous* [my italics] productions of a fruitful but shallow soil.[11]

A natural consequence of an identification of women's writing (by its practitioners, its critics, and even its admirers) with artlessness, shapelessness, naturalness and so forth, as against the male's natural tools of balance, form, intellectualism and precision, is that formless, 'stream of consciousness' writing is often characteristic of men's writing in the special case when the man is attempting female impersonation. Although Dickens and Sterne use this technique to express the consciousness of male characters, Samuel Richardson and James Joyce have both made particularly effective use of it to evoke female sensations and sensibility. This eighteenth-century atmosphere of condescending enjoyment of women's writing had many and obvious disadvantages, but, from a financial point of view at least, offered some advantages as well. Writing for the theatre was potentially lucrative, but risky. Successful seventeenth-century dramatists such as Behn and Manley were as desperate as they were courageous. They had complicated life-stories which had placed them outside the boundaries of male care and protection, and they were not the sort of women to oblige society by meekly lying down to starve. Yet, in order to put on a play, then as now, the playwright must involve him- or herself in a great deal of direct confrontation, arguing, nagging, bullying, wheedling, as appropriate. In a century which defined women's greatest virtue as a chaste and modest silence, most women playwrights were pilloried by their male competitors; their characters and abilities subject to continuous lively, savage and inventive abuse from which they have not yet recovered. Towards the end of Mrs Manley's life, however, the publishers began to realise that there was a growing market for fiction. And so, in the eighteenth century, women who wanted, or needed, to write gave their energies not to the stage, but to writing novels. Some reasons for this are obvious. A manuscript could be sent anonymously or pseudonymously[12] to a publisher. After whatever correspondence was required, the publisher would attend to the negotiations within the business world, and out would come the volumes, with 'by a Lady' or 'Currer Bell' on the title-page. A lady novelist could therefore, if she had talent and pleased the public taste, earn herself a modest income without once appearing in public, and risking the loss of her good name. A woman novelist could in this sense have her cake and eat it too. Judy Simons, writing of Frances Burney, reminds us of how difficult it was, even in a post-Richardson literary world, for a virtuous young woman to think of venturing into print:

> to remain respectable, respectable women needed to retain their privacy. The stigma of unchastity that clung to early women writers was not necessarily based on scandalous events in their lives or in their writing but was a corollary of self-exposure, at odds with the contemporary code of female reticence.[13]

Lady Mary Wortley Montagu published essays and poems from 1716 onwards, but not one of her publications bore her name during her lifetime. Her play *Simplicity*, written in 1735, was never printed, and not produced on a stage until 1988.[14] Thus she was able to express herself, and to achieve recognition, while the more or less transparent veil of anonymity enabled her to retain her position as an aristocrat and woman of fashion.

The novel, however, was a domestic art form, which could not only be written at home, but which could also confine itself imaginatively to a feminine sphere and still find a market. Some writers took the high moral ground by claiming to write only from necessity (not from vanity, or immodesty, or for fun): one Sarah Emma Spencer told her readers that her novel was 'written by the bedside of a sick husband, who has no other support than what my writings will produce'; another authoress and family breadwinner claimed 'I ... may safely say, that it was in the *observance*, not in the *breach* of duty, I became an author' (her italics).[15]

### Early women novelists

The two generations which separate Aphra Behn and the writers of Restoration romances from the much politer world of Richardson and his female heirs is certainly not barren of women writers, but very few of their works are easily accessible today.[16] Mary de la Rivière Manley continued to write mildly salacious (and lucrative) pulp fiction (as well as plays) until her death in 1724. A rather similar writer, Elizabeth Haywood, born in the 1690s and so a generation younger, began her career by writing plays and semi-pornographic novelettes in the style of Mrs Manley. But she lived to see a major transformation in public taste; and though her first response to *Pamela* was to write *Anti-Pamela: or, Feign'd Innocence Detected: Syrena's Adventures Published as a Caution to all Young Gentlemen* (1741), her sensitivity to the literary market caused her, after that, to join the side of the angels, and to finish her career writing Richardsonian epistolary novels with delicately virtuous heroines.[17] It was Elizabeth Haywood who first introduced into English fiction the familiar opposition of an aristocratic villain harassing a virtuous girl of lower social rank, even before Samuel Richardson's Mr B.: a fictional formula which was to have a long life before it,[18] underlying as it does the plot of *Jane Eyre* and the whole tradition of female Gothic writing.

Charlotte Lennox (1720–1804) was profoundly admired as a writer by Dr Johnson, Samuel Richardson and Henry Fielding, all of whom went out of their way to support her efforts;[19] and Sarah Fielding was similarly admired by many contemporary critics, including Richardson and Johnson,[20] who thought her work better than her brother's. The increasing success of these women writers is different in kind from that of their seventeenth-century predecessors. Although the higher reaches of literature remained a jealously guarded male preserve, a niche appears to have been developing which could accommodate the woman writer. All a capable woman had to do to be modestly successful was to assent to the place allotted to her. Previously private forms of writing – the letter, the diary, the conduct-book, which were seen as legitimately part of women's province – now became public, and were incorporated into the novel. Other women writers gained fame as *belles lettristes*, notably Lady Mary Wortley Montagu, who published essays and verses during her lifetime, but became known after her death for her informal letters. Women writers were accepted on the basis of their femininity; not as equal competitors in the same field.

The earlier writers, Behn, Manley and Haywood, who really had competed with men on the common ground of the commercial stage, became unusable as models for eighteenth-century women because of their 'unchaste' lives, which were a greater focus of interest than their fiction itself. By contrast, the great claim of the women writers of the eighteenth century to public attention was not their gift for plot, dialogue and characterisation, but their chaste delicacy, propriety and feeling. A revulsion, in both sexes, from the manners and modes of the Restoration towards new ideals of modest simplicity and naturalness freed women's pens as they had never been free before. Now, a woman could write (as long as she wrote 'chastely') without sacrificing her reputation. And now that an elaborate parade of learning had been devalued, women's educational disadvantages were no longer such a handicap.[21]

The shift of literary interest from the robustly aggressive world of Restoration fiction, with its emphasis on action, to a more inward-looking, sentimental focus and intention, is one of the great revolutions of taste in the history of English literature. In the eleventh and twelfth centuries, polite taste turned decisively away from epic, as represented by *Beowulf*, or even *Judith*, and towards romance, which focused on psychological drama rather than physical action. Similarly, the discovery of sensibility, with the increased significance attached to the interior life of the individual, would almost seem a renaissance of the tradition of courtly love – though of course, like all other 'renaissances', the cult of sensibility differed in fundamental ways from its precursor.[22]

Charlotte Lennox's *The Female Quixote* (1752) highlights some of the differences between earlier fiction and the new English novel. Her title and plot allude to Miguel de Cervantes's great romance, *Don Quixote*, whose hero interprets the ordinary and mundane details of his life within a romantic convention of knighthood. Charlotte Lennox's book expresses a characteristically English concern with didactic and morally improving fiction, and is one of the first examples of the rather incestuous sub-genre of novels about novel-readers, of which the most famous example is Jane Austen's *Northanger Abbey*. Both the comedy and the moral are found in the gap between literary conventions and real life. Charlotte Lennox's heroine Arabella has been brought up in virtual isolation, avidly devouring the French heroic romances of the seventeenth century, with their impossibly noble characters and wild sequence of improbable incidents. The result is a ludicrously false and inverted sense of values, in which she runs away from the supposed designs of her father's gardener, believing him to be a prince in disguise, and unhesitatingly accepts the assistance of a total stranger who appears, in fact, to be about to take the proffered opportunity to abduct and seduce her. Arabella's constant errors of judgment spring from a naïve and heartfelt desire to be a good person, and do the right thing; and thus her mistakes arouse pity and sympathy both in the reader and in her foil, Mr Glanville, a decent young man who can see her good qualities as well as her embarrassing absorption in fantasy. *The Female Quixote* sounds the new novelistic note of realism – the imperfections of human nature with its mundane difficulties and capacity for making mistakes – contrasting it with the impossibly ideal nobilities of *Clelia, Pharamond* and other romances which are constantly alluded to in the text. However, *The Female Quixote* owes one salient feature to the romance, which is its almost total indifference to structure. Arabella falls in and out of adventures, invariably making the same type of mistake, just as haplessly as the heroines of the romances. This shapelessness relates partly to the exigencies of writing: for commercial reasons, Charlotte Lennox had to produce at least two volumes, and so began to spin out and pad her material as she progressed. The idea of a third volume was vetoed by Samuel Richardson himself, and thus after a second volume, much of which is superfluous, the story of Arabella is summarily concluded by an interview between the heroine and a Johnsonian Doctor (Bk IX, ch.11) which causes her to see the light in a single short chapter, after which, as a reformed character, she marries Mr Glanville and lives happily ever after. Charlotte Lennox could not affort to revise the novel completely, as she really needed to do, because of her financial situation which required her to publish it as quickly as possible, and in practice, once published, she found that its considerable virtues in comic plotting and crisp dialogue made it reasonably successful.

Another very early woman novelist was Sarah Fielding. She was financially dependent on her novelist brother Henry, with whom she lived in London, so the income from writing was materially important to her. Her long novel *The Adventures of David Simple* (1744) is a picaresque tale of an innocent young man in search of true friendship and happiness. This loose structure enables Sarah Fielding to let a variety of characters tell their life stories to the enquiring David, and to exhibit various kinds of moral failing for the edification of the reader. The effect of the novel is of a psychological study of human types, and the relationship of character to opportunity and environment, which analyses human emotion rather than dramatising it as later novels do.

Frances Sheridan (1724–66), mother of the playwright Richard Brinsley Sheridan, was another writer of the period who owed much to the example of Samuel Richardson. She was herself an influence on the work of her son, who appropriated incidents from her best novel, *Memoirs of Miss Sidney Bidulph* (1761), for his well-known play, *The School for Scandal*. The *Memoirs* are dedicated to Richardson, and the plot bears resemblances to that of *Clarissa Harlowe*, in that the heroine Sidney acts with sense, good feeling and filial piety, only to fall into misfortune after misfortune. Her troubles derive in the main from her mother who has instilled in her such delicate principles of daughterly affection: the picture which is transmitted by Sidney's loyal and loving prose (for the novel is, like *Clarissa*, epistolary in structure) is one of a hasty-tempered, arrogant, narrow-minded monster of selfishness. In Volume III, doubt creeps faintly across Sidney's mind when her mother is dying – which, due to the complexities of English inheritance law, will leave her penniless:

> 'Tis strange, my Cecilia, that this best of parents, who had always so tenderly loved me, expresses now not the slightest uneasiness at the forlorn condition in which she must soon leave me. Her thoughts are employed on higher objects.                    (letter dated 15 September)

The higher object, of course, is herself, or rather, her own prospects in the next world. Sidney's capacity for blind loyalty is further shaken by the discovery that her mother had forbidden her marriage to a man who truly loved her on the basis of her impression of a letter she had not troubled to read through to the end (29 October). Sidney's story is one of virtue entirely unrewarded, and may carry within it the first faint intimations of the dangerous idea that sometimes girls might be better judges than their elders, a theme which Maria Edgeworth exploits in *Belinda*, and Jane Austen in *Mansfield Park*, but which bordered on social heresy in the middle of the eighteenth century.

Charlotte Smith (1749–1806) is another writer temperamentally inclined towards telling uncomfortable truths. Her novel *The Old Manor House* (1793) combines a romantic plot based on the love of Orlando, a dependent younger son, for Monimia, a penniless orphan, with a left-wing perspective which attacks war in general, and particularly the British position in the American War of Independence (to which she despatches her hero):

> when he considered a number of men thus packed together in a little vessel, perishing by disease; such of them as survived going to another hemisphere to avenge on a branch of their own nation a quarrel, the justice of which they knew little, and were never suffered to enquire; he felt disposed to wonder at the folly of mankind, and to enquire again *what all this was for?*                    (Bk III, ch. 11, her italics)

Another radical concern is with the injustices of the English law of inheritance, demonstrated by the way in which a wealthy old lady effectually blights the life of her family of second cousins: the oldest boy goes spectacularly to the bad since he believes wealth will one day descend on him, and the second son spends month after month hanging about the manor house, Rayland Hall, reading rather than preparing himself for a career. The novel is also unusual in representing the life of servants as complex, and involved with the same issues of precedence and status among themselves as the lives of the gentry; for example, towards the end of Bk II, ch. 12:

> Mrs Lennard, who thought herself fortunate in having all the suspicions

fall on Betty, kept as a profound secret those she entertained herself relative to Monimia, whom she resolved narrowly to watch till Orlando was gone. And Pattenson, glad that the young minion was to go, as he termed it, for a soldier, reconciled himself by that reflection to the failure of his original plan which had been totally to ruin him with Mrs Rayland... Such were, at this juncture, the politics of Rayland Hall.

**Polemical novelists: Mary Wollstonecraft and Hannah More**
Women writers of all kinds, responsive to the large and increasing public demands for novels, began to express themselves in this form. Enthusiasts for all varieties of social reform, attracted by the opportunity for mass communication which the novel now offered, seized their pens and began creating fictionalised accounts of the ills of society, with a variety of success. They include some overtly feminist writers, notably Lady Mary Hamilton (1739–1816), whose *Munster Village* (1778) offers a pleasing picture of a small feminist Utopia; and Mary Hays (1760–1843), a radical and friend of William Godwin, who like him expressed her principles in fiction as well as in polemical prose, most notably in her *Memoirs of Emma Courtney* (1796), which shocked contemporaries with its depiction of a woman pursuing a reluctant man, and in particular, with her offer to live with him outside marriage.

Mary Wollstonecraft (1759–97) is the outstanding woman writer in this radical group, though her principal claim to fame is not, of course, as a novelist. Her *A Vindication of the Rights of Woman* (1792) is the work on which her reputation rests, though her *Letters Written during a Short Residence in Sweden, Norway and Denmark* (1796), with its combination of scene-painting and the expression of a warm sensibility, won her many friends in her lifetime, and offset the frigid impression produced by her capacity for hard-hitting argument. Her capacity as a novelist was not calculated to enhance her reputation in any direction whatsoever. Her first attempt, *Mary, a Fiction* (1788) and *The Wrongs of Woman* (1798) which was left half-finished at her untimely death, both suffer from her inability to express character either by action or by diction. All speaking voices sound exactly the same, and they all sound like Mary Wollstonecraft: even, with the grossest implausibility, that of a working-class prostitute turned prison wardress who tells her pathetic tale in the middle of *The Wrongs of Woman*. The abrupt end of *Mary*, which creates the impression that the author was so depressed by her own fiction that she could not bear to go on with it, leaves the heroine trapped in a loveless marriage and looking forward eagerly to death, prefiguring later heroines like Catherine Earnshaw in Emily Brontë's *Wuthering Heights*, and Rachel Vinrace in Virginia Woolf's *The Voyage Out* whose circumstances are so far at odds with their temperaments that death is the only possible solution.

Propaganda of another kind was offered to readers by the indefatigably worthy Hannah More (1745–1833), herself the first to recognise that her talent as playwright, poet and writer of fiction was second-rate at best. Her earnest endeavour to turn the nation towards conservative politics, piety and Sabbath observance made her a strikingly influential figure; her brainchild, the *Cheap Repository Tracts* (1795–8), improving literature for the working classes, sold in their hundreds of thousands. Nor did she neglect the reform of the upper classes: *Thoughts on the Importance of the Manners of the Great to General Society* (1788) and *Estimate of the Religion of the Fashionable World* (1790) were, perhaps surprisingly, best-sellers. She even reached so high as to attempt the reform of the Royal Family itself with her *Hints Towards Forming the Character of a Young Princess* (1805). The unfortunate Princess Charlotte's comment is worth preserving:

> The Bishop of Salisbury is here, and reads with me an hour or two every day from Mrs Hannah More's *Hints* ... This, I believe, is what makes me find the hours so long. *I am not quite good* enough for that yet.[23]

Nor can we know if Charlotte was improved by the experience: she was dead in childbirth before her twentieth birthday.

Hannah More resembled the radicals of her day in her methods, and sometimes in more than that: the bluestocking Mary Berry was highly amused to observe that Hannah More's *Strictures on the Modern System of Female Education* (1799) and Mary Wollstonecraft's *Thoughts on the Education of Daughters* (1787) agreed on all salient points, though written from completely opposed ideological positions, and of course, unbeknownst to Hannah More. Like Mary Wollstonecraft, Hannah More eventually expressed her position on the woman question in a novel, *Coelebs in Search of a Wife* (1808), which ran to twelve editions in the first year of publication, though it is hard to see why. It appealed to the growing public interest in reformist, Evangelical Christianity, and also offered a sort of guide to good conduct for young ladies as the relatively robust social *mores* of the Regency gave way to increasingly refined standards of personal conduct. The heroine is the epitome of all nineteenth-century feminine virtues – selfless, pious, and faultless in her propriety – and the plot is no more and no less dramatised propaganda than Mary Wollstonecraft's.

### Frances Burney

The first English woman novelist to achieve wide popularity and critical acclaim which has lasted beyond her own century was Frances (Fanny) Burney (1752–1840). (She used the pet name 'Fanny' only in her family circle, and was not referred to by it in a literary context till the twentieth century.) One of the most salient features of her character was her dependence on her father's approval,[24] so it is hardly surprising to find that her fiction is marked by anxious conservatism and a determined upholding of patriarchal attitudes. *Evelina* (1778), *Cecilia* (1782) and *Camilla* (1796) were extremely popular, and yet so respectable in tone and sentiment as to give rise to the somewhat backhanded compliment of appointing her Second Keeper of the Robes to Queen Charlotte, which proved in the event not so much an honour as five years of mindlessly tedious servitude, which only ended because she became too ill to continue. Distinguished writers were often given nominal employment as a form of patronage at this period, but women could not be given a position such as an office in the Board of Trade, even nominally. Her court position was so far from being a sinecure that she was continually on call from six in the morning to twelve at night, summoned by a bell, like a housemaid. The court post paid her £200 a year, which as Moers points out, was 'probably the highest salary a woman had ever received for respectable work, or would receive for generations to come'. *Camilla* made her £2,000 – and a governess, half a century later, might get £20 a year, which casts a practical light on why the market was, by the mid-nineteenth century, flooded with 'silly novels by lady novelists', as George Eliot called them.[25]

Frances Burney's work is in various ways indebted to that of other women writers, predecessors and contemporaries. She was a close friend of Mrs Thrale, and through her knew most of the other cultivated women in London society, such as Hannah More. The plot of *Cecilia*, in which the heroine is left at the mercy of a trio of wholly unsuitable guardians of radically different character, is probably a serious reworking of the plot which Susannah Centlivre uses in *A Bold Stroke for a Wife* (1718), in which the heroine's dashing suitor must gain the consent of each of her four wholly different guardians. Frances Burney was a enthusiastic playgoer, and this play was performed nearly 150 times between 1750 and 1800, as well as appearing in seventeen printed editions. Elizabeth Griffith's *The Times* (1779), with its depictions of the reckless squandering of money by fashionable people, is another possible source-text.

Frances Burney's great subject in all three of these novels is the misfortunes and misunderstandings which befall a very young woman on her way to a safe and respectable marriage. Burney had a gift for creating genuinely charming heroines who make little mistakes out of adolescent awkwardness, inexperience or imprudent generosity, and then find they get into one scrape after another trying to cover up for themselves. The world she depicts is nightmarish, in that the heroines' trivial blunders could genuinely wreck their future happiness, since the world in which they awkwardly manoeuvre is one which sets great store by appearances. The most agonising moments are those in which the girl is seen by the man she admires in some mortifying situation which is open to misinterpretation. For example, Evelina accidently becomes separated from her companions on a trip to the London pleasure-gardens of Marylebone (letter LII), and finds that she is mistaken for a prostitute. It is thus, inevitably, that the man she would least wish to see runs across her. Similar predicaments are common to all Burney heroines. In *Camilla*, the heroine is apparently unchaperoned, at a play, when her lover (who is, for complex reasons which do him little credit, disinclined to give her the benefit of the doubt) comes in and sees her:

> Camilla now began to regret that she had not accompanied Mrs Arlbery. She had thought only of the play and its entertainment, till the sight of Mandlebert told her that her situation was improper; and the idea only occurred to her by considering that it would occur to him.[26]

Frances Burney here, and indeed frequently throughout her work, is anatomising the double standard. She does not present herself as seeking to undermine the laws of society; in fact, she clamorously upholds them. Yet the mere exposition of the minute confines within which an inexperienced girl had to conduct herself, and the essentially censorious, predatory and ungenerous nature of male judgments upon her, have an implicitly ironic effect. Her novels are, in part, sketches of How Not To Do It. Without criticising the society she knew, she offered her readers considerable insight into how it worked. Any young woman preparing herself for the launch from her schoolroom into the marriage market, conscious that even small errors could be fatal and that she was, to put it crudely, a rapidly depreciating commodity, could learn a great deal from Evelina's or Camilla's mistakes. This is an aspect of the novel, not as moral instruction, but as preparation for life, which was of great concern to novelists, educationalists and readers alike in the eighteenth century.[27] The usefulness of this guidance is suggested in Jane Austen's last unfinished novel, *Sanditon* (ch. 6). The heroine sees a drawer full of jewellery at the subscription library (it was common in the eighteenth century for libraries to sell knick-knacks and trinkets) and finds them attractive. Then she picks up a copy of *Camilla*, and recalls the difficulties Camilla brings upon herself in just such a situation: 'she had not Camilla's youth, and had no intention of having her distress, – so she turned from the drawer of rings and brooches, repressed further solicitation and paid for what she bought.'

The double standard of behaviour for young men and young women is brought into almost ludicrous prominence in *Camilla*, even though this novel, written out of a dire need for money after Burney's marriage (at the age of forty-one) to a penniless French refugee, avoids all contentious subjects and even the faintest suspicion of politics or controversy.[28] At the beginning of her adventures, Camilla, leaving her family for a long visit to Tunbridge, is given £20 for new clothes and incidental expenses. Her brother manages to extract this money from her, leaving the girl to entangle herself in a morass of petty debts. One thing leads to another, and the final grand total of her debts is £118.9s.[29] The payment of this enormous sum[30] distresses her almost to the point of insanity. By contrast, her brother Lionel is seen to extract money by threats from his uncle in Lisbon, wring £700 from his uncle Hugh, the friend and benefactor of Camilla's whole family, and force Camilla to accept on his behalf a loan of £200 from her admirer Sir Sedley Clarendel. He then does his best to marry her off to that gentleman so that he can milk him further.[31] Lionel's further debts, revealed towards the close of the novel, amount to more than £500 (his father has an annual income of £600). The money has gone on gambling, adultery (with the necessary paying-off of blackmailing servants), and miscellaneous self-indulgence. Neither of the young gentlemen appears more than momentarily contrite about the near-ruin in which they have involved their families. The contrast between the respectability of the various girls of the family, loyally aiding one another with the minute sums of money at their own command, and the vast extravagance of their utterly selfish (if not necessarily vicious) brothers, is marked, though never specifically remarked upon by Frances Burney.[32] Many later novelists, notably Anne Brontë in *The Tenant of Wildfell Hall*, were to follow Burney in anatomising the evils of a social system which encouraged the sons of good families to be as selfish as their sisters were selfless.

Frances Burney's last novel, *The Wanderer, or Female Difficulties* (1814), is an extremely sombre tale, which puzzled contemporaries. The novel opens with a group of refugees flying from France during the Reign of Terror. A nameless young woman is reluctantly granted a place on the boat. This woman, Juliet, is forced to try and act as an independent person: it is almost impossible for her to do so. The first question which anyone wants know is who she is, and she cannot tell them. In fact, she does not know, in patriarchal terms, since (though she is still a virgin) she was forced into marriage in France with a man whose name she does not know. She inhabits a sort of limbo, no longer entitled to use her father's name, but without her husband's. Sisterhood is a principal theme of the novel (Elinor, her foil, is her most consistent and effective supporter). Another is the extreme difficulty which eighteenth-century women faced if they needed to work.

### Elizabeth Inchbald

Elizabeth Inchbald (1753–1821), a contemporary of Frances Burney's, led a very different life: she was a professional actress, and a reasonably successful playwright – it is her English version of Kotzebue's *Lover's Vows* (1798) that Jane Austen's characters attempt to act in *Mansfield Park*.[33] She also published two novels. Her claim to fame rests on the first of these, *A Simple Story* (1791), which was very widely read, and not only in her own time, since there were at least five editions between 1840 and 1890. *A Simple Story* is structurally faulty: the first half of the book is the story of Miss Milner and her guardian, Dorriforth, in the year in which Miss Milner is eighteen; then, after a gap of seventeen years, the second is devoted to

Miss Milner's daughter, Matilda, at about the same age. Dorriforth is a handsome, youngish man in the first part, a Roman Catholic priest; Miss Milner, his eighteen-year-old ward, is very beautiful, kind-hearted and generous, but wilful and vain. The tension in the story lies in the fact that the pair are in some sense in love; but the semi-parental relationship and Dorriforth's commitment to celibacy prevents this from ever moving on to a conscious level. In consequence, Miss Milner not only tests the bonds of Dorriforth's authority over her in an ordinarily adolescent way, she quite clearly also tries to provoke him as a man, by flirting with a dissipated peer, Lord Frederick. Her intentions towards both men, as far as she herself understands them, are entirely innocent, as Mrs Inchbald repeatedly says. The dénouement comes when Dorriforth succeeds unexpectedly to a peerage, and is given a special dispensation to marry; thus the romantic Miss Milner's passion, which had been in the safe realms of fantasy, is unexpectedly gratified by marriage to a somewhat cold-blooded and narrow-minded individual temperamentally incapable of responding to her. We learn at the beginning of the second part that the marriage lasted four years before Dorriforth had to go abroad, and that his wife, left behind, committed adultery with Lord Frederick. Dorriforth (now Lord Elmwood) refuses even to see his daughter Matilda, who is brought up in virtual isolation. She has, however, a mentor, Dorriforth's old confessor, and a friend, Dorriforth's dead brother's bastard son, and a considerably better education than her late mother's. All ends happily for the second generation, with all parties reconciled, and a marriage between Matilda and her cousin. The interest of the story is dependent on the character-drawing, particularly on the interplay between basic temperament and the effect of environment.

**Two Anglo-Irish writers: Maria Edgeworth and Sydney Owenson**
The writing of Maria Edgeworth (1767–1849), a somewhat younger contemporary of Frances Burney's, has some significant points of resemblance with Burney's work. One is that Maria Edgeworth was obsessed with her father's good opinion to an extent which made Burney's reverence for the principle of paternal authority look almost moderate.[34] The dynamic, self-absorbed and talented Richard Lovell Edgeworth was the father of, in total, twenty-two children by several successive wives.[35] Maria was his oldest daughter, and his right hand in managing this huge family. Being physically tiny, and conscious that she was not beautiful,[36] she never sought a life of her own (though she received a serious proposal of marriage, she refused it), but was content to subdue herself to her father's interests. The family lived, from the time Maria Edgeworth was fifteen, on an estate in Ireland, and it was her experiences of Ireland which led her to produce an utterly original and highly entertaining novel, *Castle Rackrent* (1800), written and published without her father's knowledge, just as

*Evelina* was written and published without the knowledge of Dr Burney.
She excused its creation by the only means available, which was to claim
that the story spontaneously came to her, and she simply recorded it.[37] A
woman could excuse the arrogance of authorship to the world and to herself
either by claiming that she wrote only at the command of a male mentor (as
Maria Edgeworth was later to do), or that she was, in the biblical sense,
inspired, a mere conduit for narrative, like Balaam's ass. The first option
denied the woman writer the status of an original artist; the second denied
her the status of a craftsman.

*Castle Rackrent* – with which Maria Edgeworth was first inspired at the
age of eighteen – tells the story of several generations of dissolute, hard-
drinking Irish squireens, as seen through the eyes of their loyal steward,
Thady. It is written in the first person, in Thady's broad Irish brogue; it is
cynical, irreverent, and touches on many subjects that women's fiction of the
time generally avoided, from alcoholism to political corruption. Of course,
once it was published, Maria Edgeworth's doom, like Frances Burney's,
was sealed. Thereafter, she contentedly wrote novels exhibiting a strong
moral and political sense, of the kind her father approved, under his
continuous supervision. He told her, as she wrote in a letter to a friend, that
'to be a mere writer of pretty stories and novelettes would be unworthy of
his partner, pupil and daughter',[38] an irresistible form of flattering coercion
for a woman of her cast of mind.

*Belinda* (1801) is a completely different kind of novel, displaying the same
gift for characterisation, but nearly sinking under a freight of didacticism.
Maria Edgeworth was never to return to the indecorous, improper use of a
male voice first-person narrator, but *Belinda* and her later fiction are works
of considerable interest and attraction. Richardson had given the world a
drama of courtship in which inflexibly virtuous young women confronted
male characters equally incapable of moral or personal development.
Burney develops the Richardsonian novel by showing us the process of a
young girl growing up, and changing as she does so, but continues to play
her heroines off against men whose characters are already formed, like
Lord Orville. Jane Austen, Edgeworth's contemporary, tended to do the
same, and so her Mr Darcy and Mr Knightley are considerably older and
sounder in their judgments than her heroines Elizabeth Bennet and Emma
Woodhouse. By contrast, Maria Edgeworth was interested in young men's
painful approach to adulthood, self-knowledge and mental maturity, as well
as young women's. Her heroes, therefore, though not necessarily of an age
with her heroines, are still in the process of learning by their mistakes. She
is not always as 'proper' a writer, in a negative sense, as she is sometimes
thought to be. For example, Dr Johnson's essay on the art and function of
the novelist states that:

> virtue not angelical... but the highest and purest that humanity can
> reach, which, exercised in such trials as the various revolutions of things

shall bring upon it, may, by conquering some calamities, and enduring others, teach us what we may hope, and what we can perform. Vice, for vice is necessary to be shown, should always disgust; nor should the graces of gaiety, or the dignity of courage, be so united with it, as to reconcile it to the mind.[39]

Yet in *Belinda*, Edgeworth created a gay and worldly near-villain, Lady Delacour (the name is significant, in suggesting that she is completely immersed in the superficial public life 'of the court'), whose superficiality and contempt for her husband are set off against her genuine love for Belinda herself, and the courage with which she confronts her private fear that she is dying of cancer of the breast.[40] As a woman who makes herself look worse than she is, out of bravado, she could hardly be more antithetical to Johnson's ponderously phrased demand for contemptible villains and shining examples of virtue. Another symptom of Maria Edgeworth's quiet radicalism (which she shares with her contemporary, Jane Austen) is her treatment of the generation gap. Belinda's parents are never even mentioned, and in contrast to Frances Burney's Evelina, whose guardian is all-knowing, all-wise, and inexhaustibly sermonising on the proper duties and conduct of young virgins, Belinda has as guardian her aunt, Mrs Stanhope, whose advice is so blatantly cynical that even the most conservatively minded of contemporary readers were forced to side with Belinda in her resolute rejection of it. Mrs Stanhope turns the letter of advice, a great fictional set piece by this time, on its head: she describes, sombrely, the unsuccessful husband-hunter, who:

> finds herself at five or six-and-thirty a burden to her friends, destitute of the means of rendering herself independent (for girls I speak of never think of *learning* to play cards), *de trop* in society... (ch. 1)

The vision of old maids resigning themselves, not to the intolerable tedium of governessing, but to the far more adventurous career of a professional card-sharp, is delicious and completely unexpected. It is one of many touches which show that the author of *Castle Rackrent* was never completely suffocated by Mr Edgeworth's dutiful daughter.

*Ormond*, written in 1816, and the last of her novels to be supervised by her father (who died just after the first draft was completed) returns to some of the themes of *Castle Rackrent*, setting relatively genteel members of the Irish landowning classes against a much more unorthodox group of Irish peasants and representatives of the native Gaelic-speaking nobility. The narrative is, however, distanced from its sometimes rowdy and unrespectable cast of characters by being couched in the third person: Maria Edgeworth did not return to her early experiment with a first-person dialect narrator in *Castle Rackrent*. *Ormond* also evinces her continued strong interest in education and the forming of the personality; the likeable but somewhat boorish young Harry Ormond is gradually formed, by a combination of experience, instruction and reading, into the kind of person a good heroine deserves to marry. The specifically feminine sense of values attached to different strands in the English novelistic tradition is shown in Chapter 7; Harry, discovering the pleasures of reading, comes within an inch of moral ruin by admiring Henry Fielding's *Tom Jones*, and ingenuously modelling his developing personality on its cynical and self-absorbed hero. Fortunately, he goes on to read Samuel Richardson's *Sir Charles Grandison*, and comes to realise that it is possible for a man to be virtuous without making himself look like a fool in the eyes of his fellows, or ceasing to be attractive to women:

> all the generous feelings which were so congenial to his own nature, and which he had seen combined in Tom Jones, as if necessarily, with the habits of an adventurer, a spendthrift and a rake, he now saw united with high moral and religious principles, in the character of a man of virtue as well as a man of honour; a man of cultivated understanding and accomplished manners.

Maria Edgeworth's novels were widely read, and highly regarded, not only by the public, but by fellow writers like Sir Walter Scott, who publicly acknowledged his debt to her, as indeed did the Russian writer Turgenev. Ruskin claimed that he had read *Patronage* (1814) and her tales 'oftener than any other books in the world, except the Bible', and Jane Austen sent her a copy of *Emma* on its first publication.[41]

Furthermore, she made £2,100 from her novel *Patronage* alone, so her earnings in total must have done a great deal to keep the family financially prosperous. Two recollections of her rare, shy appearances in the literary world tell us a great deal about her. Joanna Baillie (1762–1851), a talented though now almost forgotten poet and dramatist, remarked that Maria Edgeworth, though shy, 'tells her little anecdote or story (when her father does not take it out of her mouth) very pleasantly'.[42] Byron, similarly observant, commented that, 'one would never have guessed that she could write *her name*; whereas her father talked, *not* as if he could write nothing else, but as if nothing else was worth writing.'[43]

Maria Edgeworth was directly indebted to earlier women novelists, notably Frances Burney – her *Belinda* assumes that the reader is acquainted with Burney's *Cecilia* – and Elizabeth Inchbald. She was deeply impressed by Mrs Inchbald's skill in character-drawing.[44] Another aspect of *A Simple Story* which was particularly relevant to her own concerns is its stress on education: the mother and daughter are presented as temperamentally similar, but the daughter's better education leaves her not only a happier woman, but much better able to deal with the crises of her life.

Another Anglo-Irish woman writer of the same period, Sydney Owenson, Lady Morgan (178?–1859), was much less distinguished, but shared Maria Edgeworth's deep concern for promoting understanding between England and Ireland. *The Wild Irish Girl* (1806) is a loyal, if clumsy, attempt to defend the Irish against the ignorant contempt of their English masters, using the same formula as Edgeworth's *Ennui* (1809) and other novels: an English-educated hero, visiting family estates in Ireland, is gradually weaned away from his unthinking prejudices. The novel sinks under the weight of its good intentions: the text is burdened with learned footnotes on the Gaelic language, early Irish law, and aspects of native Irish society, and the characters cannot be said to develop any life outside their exemplary and didactic functions. In the event, the novel won its author considerable social success and a highly advantageous marriage, without, however, doing much to improve Anglo-Irish relations.

### Two Scottish novelists: Mary Brunton and Susan Ferrier

Regionalism, as exemplified by the Irish novels of Maria Edgeworth, the pioneer, Sydney Owenson and the Scottish novels of Sir Walter Scott, became an important strand in the development of the English novel at the end of the eighteenth century and the beginning of the nineteenth. Two Scotswomen also followed the Anglo-Irish Maria Edgeworth in exploring the differences between southern England and other parts of the country, Mary Brunton (1778–1818) and Susan Ferrier (1782–1854). Both write from a specifically Scottish perspective.

Mary Brunton was read by Jane Austen, who found her work extremely comic: her *Self-control* (1810) was, in Jane Austen's estimation, 'an excellently-meant, elegantly-written work, without anything of nature or probability in it. I do not know whether Laura's passage down her American River [by canoe!] is not the most natural, possible, everyday thing she ever does'. Mary Brunton belonged to the school of didactic writing which sacrifices character and plot to message. Jane Austen, developing her uniquely subtle analysis of the relationship of the individual to society, inevitably found an element of the grotesque in this naïve fiction; all the same, she read and re-read *Self-control* and *Discipline* (1814), and shared many of Mary Brunton's moral values. Mary Brunton follows in Maria Edgeworth's footsteps in exploring the contrast between the manners and habits of upper-class Londoners, previously the central focus of almost all novel-writing, and the sometimes grotesque social and cultural codes of remote parts of the island. Several of Edgeworth's novels, notably *Ennui*, contrast a hero whose taste has been formed by polite London society with a provincial Irish life of which the value, as well as the comedy, is presented by the author. Similarly in *Discipline*, the spoiled beauty, Ellen Percy, suffers a series of reverses which take her, almost penniless, to earn her living as a teacher in Edinburgh, and thence, by means of a chance acquaintance with a poor Highland woman, Cecil Graham, to a Highland retreat in Castle Eredine, where she eventually lives happily ever after, since the man she loved all along, though she was too proud to admit it (like Emma's Mr Knightley, he was apt to object to her frivolous conduct), turns out, by a stretching of coincidence, to be the son of the house. Mary Brunton holds middle-class Edinburgh manners, with their meannesses and pretensions, up to ridicule, but she is as serious in her portrayal of the warm, socially cohesive world of the Gaelic-speaking Highlands as Sydney Owenson had been about Gaelic Ireland. Her purposes are dual: the moral education of her heroine (the plot of *The Female Quixote*, among other predecessors), and an apologia for Highland Scottish manners in the style of *The Wild Irish Girl*.

Susan Ferrier's tastes and talents were more satirical in tendency. Her best novel, *Marriage* (written 1810, published 1818), expresses its plot and its message through a set of very broadly drawn caricatures. It uses the by now familiar device of the regional novelist transplanting a fashionable London socialite to her chosen region, to a more markedly comic and grotesque effect than Mary Brunton sought to achieve. In *Marriage*, proud, selfish, elegant and bird-brained Lady Juliana marries for love, and is horrified to find herself and her penniless but romantic young hero trapped in a remote Highland castle with his old father and a crew of equally bird-brained vulgar Scottish spinsters – his aunts, Miss Jacky, Miss Nicky, Miss Grizzel, and his sisters, five awkward, lumpish girls. Susan Ferrier's talents show to best advantage when her ill-assorted characters are grouped together for dreadful meals or agonising visits, entirely missing the point of one another's remarks. The ultimate point of her novel, despite the unrestrained grotesqueness of her characterisation, is a serious one: how girls should be educated for marriage, and to what extent they should be left to make their own decisions. The heroine of the book, Mary, is Lady Juliana's neglected daughter, brought up by a kind and intelligent sister-in-law. Her education enables her to appreciate the virtues of the rational, wise and courteous man who eventually becomes her husband. This straightforwardly happy tale is contrasted with a wide variety of more or less failed marriages: her mother married for romantic love, but was quite unable to envisage life without the luxuries she takes for granted:

> 'Are you indeed so changed, my Julia, that you have forgot the time when you would prefer a desert with your Henry, to a throne with another?'
>
> 'No, certainly, not changed; but – I – I did not very well know what a desert was; or, at least, I had formed a rather different idea of it ... I had fancied it a beautiful place, full of roses and myrtles, and smooth green turf, and murmuring rivulets, and, though very retired, not absolutely out of the world ...' (ch. 3)

By contrast, her favoured daughter marries for magnificence, like Maria Bertram in Jane Austen's *Mansfield Park*, and, like her, repents her bargain within a year and elopes with the man she finds physically attractive. Many other forms of marital folly are displayed; and, like Jane Austen before her, Susan Ferrier comes down firmly on the side of the woman's right to choose, and the importance of education and sound Christian principles in enabling her to make the right choice for the right reasons. The two successful marriages in the novel are those of Mary herself, a true love-match like that of Emma and Mr Knightley, and of her foster-mother, whose sense of duty, religious convictions and philosophical habits of mind enable her to make a success of marriage to a man she esteems but does not love, having given up the man she did love at the command of his mother, to whom she owed a debt of gratitude. This story seems designed to enforce the point that a properly educated woman makes her own happiness, regardless of circumstances.

**Ann Radcliffe and the Gothic novel**

Mrs (Ann) Radcliffe (1764–1823) was a niece of Thomas Bentley, the partner of the great china manufacturer Josiah Wedgwood, and spent part of her childhood in his home. This is of some interest, since Bentley was in touch with most of the literary and scientific figures of his day, and this may have helped to form her intellectual interests.[45]

Ann Radcliffe's Gothic romances are naturally of a different order from the social comedies of Maria Edgeworth and Frances Burney. She had very little interest in characterisation, and her heroes and heroines, in particular, are almost entirely without individuality. 'Female Gothic' now holds such a low place in critical estimation that Radcliffe is now seen as irrelevant to the development of the novel. Yet for more than a generation, it was true to say that anyone who read fiction at all had read *The Mysteries of Udolpho* (1794). It has been reprinted at least once a generation since it was written; it is an absolutely seminal work for the Romantic movement, an acknowledged source for Byron, and was equally evidently drawn on by Coleridge and Keats, Scott, Thackeray and Dickens, as well as, of course, by Jane Austen and Mary Shelley.[46] It was read and enjoyed at all levels, from those who, like Jane Austen's ingenuous Catherine Morland, read it for the thrills, to the writers of the nascent Romantic movement who found direct inspiration in its blend of intellect and emotion and its resolute stance against soulless materialism. It also remained a source of inspiration 'long after male writers had succumbed to the prevailing antiheroic, quiescent temper of the bourgeois century', to women writers, including the French George Sand, and the Brontës. 'The Victorian woman writer's interest in Mrs Radcliffe ... is a minor but interesting sign that women's literature flourished on its own traditions.'[47]

One of the salient features of Ann Radcliffe's writing is her very strong sense of plot. In *The Mysteries of Udolpho*, a series of incidents play strongly on the reader's curiosity. Why is the picture in the gallery at

Udolpho so horrific that when Emily lifts the veil, she falls in a dead faint? What awful secret can her eminently respectable father have harboured? Why is there mysterious music in the park surrounding the château of Villeroi? Are the closed rooms in the château haunted? Can Emily possibly be mistaken in her parentage? The reader is adroitly kept in suspense on all these questions, and the eventual dénouement is elegantly comprehensive.

Another salient feature of Ann Radcliffe's writing is her interest in landscape. Her scene-painting in *The Mysteries of Udolpho* is the result of research rather than personal experience, but it is convincing in its effect, which is very much that of the romantic landscapes of painters such as Salvator Rosa:

> On every side appeared the majestic summits of the Pyrenées, some exhibiting tremendous crags of marble, whose appearance was changing every instant, as the varying lights fell upon their surface; others, still higher, displaying only snowy points, while their lower steeps were covered almost invariably with forests of pine, larch, and oak, that stretched down to the vale. This was one of the narrow vallies, that open from the Pyrenées into the country of Rousillon, and whose green pastures, and cultivated beauty, form a decided and wonderful contrast to the romantic grandeur that environs it. Through a vista of the mountains appeared the lowlands of Rousillon, tinted with the blue haze of distance, as they united with the waters of the Mediterranean...
>
> (ch. 5)

The sense of what constitutes a truly picturesque landscape evidenced in this description is that which the romantic Marianne displays in *Sense and Sensibility*: contrast, particularly between wild and cultivated landscape, and changing light effects, and, especially, mountains, are principal elements in the ideal vista.

The success of Ann Radcliffe's writings not only made her an influence on many of the serious writers of the nineteenth century, it also inspired more or less crude imitations. The sensationalist feminine picaresque novels which resulted, for example, the presumably pseudonymous Mary Anne Radcliffe's *Malfroné, or The One-handed Monk* (1799), exhibit the sensational features of her works without her gift for plot or sense of overall purpose. They are amusingly represented as a genre in a poem by Mary Alcock (*c.*1742–98), published in 1799, 'A Receipt for Writing a Novel':

> ...Rack well your hero's nerves and heart,
> And let your heroine take her part;
> Her fine blue eyes were made to weep,
> Nor should she ever taste of sleep;
> Ply her with terrors day or night,
> And keep her always in a fright...
>   Now, at your fable's close, devise

Some grand event to give surprise –
Suppose your hero knows no mother –
Suppose he proves the heroine's brother –
This at one stroke dissolves each tie,
Far as from east to west they fly;
At length, when every woe's expended,
And your last volume's nearly ended,
Clear the mistake, and introduce
Some tattling nurse to cut the noose;
The spell is broke – again they meet
Expiring at each other's feet;
Their friends lie breathless on the floor –
You drop your pen; you can no more –
And ere your reader can recover,
They're married – and your history's over.[48]

## Jane Austen

With Jane Austen (1775–1817), we come at last to a woman writer whose name is part of the common currency of English culture. She was steeped in the work of her predecessors, and goes out of her way, in *Northanger Abbey* (written 1797–1803), to defend them. When *Camilla* was published by subscription in 1796, the 300 subscribers included many names famous in their day – and also the names of Mrs Radcliffe, Miss Austen and Miss Edgeworth, the three young women who were to become the seminal woman novelists of the early nineteenth century. Jane Austen was not only a faithful reader of contemporary fiction herself, she assumed the same familiarity in her readers.[49] Much of the joke of *Northanger Abbey* turns on the reader's familiarity with Mrs Radcliffe's *The Mysteries of Udolpho* and its Gothic imitators. Using common knowledge in a different way, in the same novel she underlines the loutish stupidity of John Thorpe by having him first fail to realise that *Udolpho* is by Mrs Radcliffe, and then add to his crimes by abusing 'that other stupid book written by that woman they make such a fuss about; she who married the French emigrant' – the despised book being, of course, *Camilla* (ch.7).[50]

Jane Austen has caused a great deal of trouble for readers and critics who confuse charm with weakness. Her power as a writer is recognised, but resentfully. Her self-deprecating remarks about the nature of her art tend to be taken entirely seriously, and are constantly quoted. She spoke to a niece of '3 or 4 Families in a Country Village' as the very thing for a novelist to work on, and, to a brother, of her 'little bit (two Inches wide) of Ivory'.[51] Such words, and her lifelong spinsterhood, have combined to create a vision of her as petty, old-maidish, and very limited in her knowledge of life. But Jane Austen was part of a large, talented and complex family. Real life, as lived by her brothers, sisters and associates, was a great deal more melodramatic than she allowed it to be in her novels. An index of this may be found in her juvenilia, which are very different in range from her mature novels. Plot elements include adultery and madness, alcoholism, murder and robbery.

Jane Austen deliberately chose an area of concentration; it was not forced upon her, just as Virginia Woolf, who R.L. Chambers said 'did not know enough about business and about India' to write about such themes, had access to a great deal of information which she deliberately chose not to use since the focus of her interest was elsewhere.[52]

Jane Austen has sometimes been seen as a writer without an ideology; involved almost entirely with character. But Marilyn Butler has shown that Jane Austen, though she does not mention, or involve her characters in, the French Revolution or the Napoleonic Wars, fits into a distinctive partisan context. She may be described, says Butler, as 'a "Tory radical", which is accurate provided we recognize that over all in the novels her toryism carries more weight than her radicalism'.[53] Jane Austen was on the side of the Tory gentry, the squirearchy, rather than on the side of the great Whig aristocrats. She produces a memorable caricature of the aristocratic Whig in the extraordinarily unappealing Lady Catherine de Bourgh, Mr Darcy's aunt, in *Pride and Prejudice* (1813). She was also, as some of her contemporaries noticed, and modern readers usually do not, a deeply Christian writer. It may be true that no one in *Emma* (1816), for instance, is ever said to set foot in a church except in order to get married, but the great Christian theme of a gradual progress towards self-knowledge through a consciousness of one's own faults is central to all the novels. This is quite specifically a moral process, from revelation, through shame, to repentance.[54] Jane Austen and Maria Edgeworth were compared by the critic Richard Whately in 1821, and he came down firmly on the side of Austen, because Maria Edgeworth's novels struck him as essentially irreligious, in that:

> virtue [is] studiously inculcated with scarcely any reference to what [we] regard as the main spring of it; [and] vice [is] traced to every other source except the want of religious principle.

By comparison, Jane Austen is 'evidently a Christian writer; a merit which is much enhanced, both on the score of good taste, and of practical utility, by her religion not being at all obtrusive'. In other words, readers who would turn away with bored disgust from a 'dramatic sermon' in the style of the indefatigably moral Mrs Hannah More, would find Jane Austen's novels the sweeetest of sugar-coatings for the bitter pill of Christian moral judgment.[55]

All her novels have at their centre a young heroine, who by the last page of the novel is happily married to an entirely suitable man. The choice of the right husband is the great business of these heroines' lives, and the story does not seek to pursue them beyond the altar. Like Burney and

Edgeworth, Austen has the problem of anatomising the lives and extremely limited opportunities of young girls without appearing to launch a radical attack against the structure of society. She was not a feminist in any modern sense of the word: in fact, she had fewer radical and liberal sympathies than Maria Edgeworth. It is a twentieth-century assumption to think that merely to analyse the terms on which women live under patriarchy, as Austen does, is automatically to have one's consciousness raised. She does not suffer from any silly optimism about everything being for the best in the best of all possible worlds, but she is a defender of conservative values, opposed to social experimentation. What she particularly champions is a form of Christian conservatism which goes back ultimately to St Paul, but which has been relevant to the entire history of Christian Europe: the answer to the problems of society is individual moral regeneration. Mr Knightley of Donwell Abbey and Mr Darcy of Pemberley are not only good in themselves; their just, charitable and upright dealings with their dependants create little oases of happiness in a corrupt, self-seeking and venal world. Emma's and Elizabeth's futures as the partners of these men are such as to admit of their lives being of use to others than themselves.

Jane Austen is, however, often cynical about marriage. Plain, poor and intelligent Charlotte Lucas in *Pride and Prejudice* would make just as virtuous and efficient a mistress of Pemberley as her friend Elizabeth, only there are never enough Darcys to go round, and she is not blessed with a pretty face and sparkling wit. She therefore marries a self-important ninny, Mr Collins, for the sake of achieving the only career open to her, and efficiently arranges her life so that she will see as little of him as possible. In twentieth-century terms, rationalisation of this has more to do with employment than with sexual relationships. Some lucky and talented women, in our own world, are able to have interesting careers, make a lot of money, and become public figures; but most women have to settle for boring jobs which they do not find especially fulfilling or interesting. When marriage was the only real job available to women, as it was in Austen's time, it was unwise for a girl to keep on refusing offers from tedious men in the hopes of the true and perfect prince coming along some day. The whole business had much more to do with economics than with romantic love. Only Emma Woodhouse, who already has an establishment (she looks after her father's house, since he has long been a widower), a fortune and high social status, is in a position to look forward confidently to old-maidhood (*Emma*, ch. 10).

For all her Toryism and conservative stance, Jane Austen was far from being an unequivocal supporter of the patriarchy. The fathers in all the novels consistently fail their offspring, sometimes simply (as in *Sense and Sensibility* (1811)) by dying and leaving their female dependants without home or security. Other father figures range from the sarcastically indifferent Mr Bennet, through the querulously self-absorbed Mr

Woodhouse, to the intimidatingly pompous Sir Thomas Bertram, and the ungovernably arrogant General Tilney. Not one of the fathers who play a main part in the action of an Austen novel is notably better or wiser than the next generation, and most of them are worse, or more stupid. Other male authority figures do not always fare well at Austen's hands. In *Northanger Abbey* (1818), although Henry Tilney can talk rings round the young and ignorant Catherine Morland, her instinct that the General, Henry's father, means her no good is entirely correct, and Henry's arrogant overthrow of her perceptions in the name of rationality is ultimately wrong. Only Mr Knightley in *Emma* judges consistently better than the heroine. Knightley is the nearest thing Austen ever produced to an unqualified hero. Even though Emma, in the fullness of her self-approbation, manages to be gloriously and consistently wrong about everything and everybody, her relationship with Knightley is the most sexually charged that Austen ever described. The way they work together as a team is shown in the few sentences they exchange while everyone else at a dinner-party is fussing:

'Your father will not be easy; why do not you go?'
'I am ready, if the others are.'
'Shall I ring the bell?'
'Yes, do.'                                                           (ch. 15)

The action of the novel is, of course, on a plane of utter physical and verbal decorum. But their consciousness of each other's physical presence is made very clear; on Mr Knightley's side by his unexpectedly abrupt response to Emma's teasing comment that they are not really like brother and sister – 'Brother and sister! no, indeed!', he says, and there the chapter ends (ch. 38); and on Emma's side by the unexpected revelation, in conversation with the harmless Harriet, that she can remember exactly where Mr Knightley was standing in the room on an occasion weeks before (ch. 40). These minor but revealing incidents, only a few pages apart, serve to show how much, though below the level of conscious intention, the pair are drifting towards one another.

Jane Austen, in effect, while upholding traditional values, can be seen simultaneously as mounting a critique of the fundamental base of English social structure as it affects women in a variety of blatantly unjust ways. Irony and charm are the weapons which permit this sleight of hand, or sleight of mind. Her concept of Christianity, which in early nineteenth-century England was very far from being a radical religion, enabled her to defend the concept of the individual value of her intelligent and lovable heroines, and to recognise the atrocious traps in which they were caught by law and social custom, and yet to maintain the necessity of the status quo. Emma Woodhouse is the most dangerous of her heroines because she is very near to being the queen of her little world; she is financially independent, and also independent in spirit. It is necessary, therefore, that

Emma should always be wrong. Otherwise, she would run an enormous risk of falling into the satanic sin of pride. Satan, as Milton made clear, sinned irreparably by stepping out of his place in the hierarchy and seeking emotional and existential autonomy. For all the acuity of Jane Austen's social analysis, she was writing in the nineteenth century, and even if she was quite merciless in her mockery of self-important patriarchs, she was very far from advocating total independence.

The Christian position has always been that people (of either sex) should weigh up the demands made on them by those in authority, and refuse them if they go against conscience. Nothing, however, should permit the breaking of a vow, once made. Jane Austen's stance on this is clearest in *Mansfield Park* (1814), her most overtly moralistic novel. Timid Fanny Price obdurately withstands the combined assault of all the male authorities in her little world in refusing to marry a man whom she mistrusts. For all her filial dependency, she absolutely refuses to 'oblige her friends' by making an irrevocable promise to a person she cannot value. She is not a hypocrite, even though her virtues may appear negative, narrow and smug to a reader who does not share Jane Austen's values. Conversely, even though Maria Bertram's husband is a ninny, her sin in running off with her lover Henry is unpardonable. Mary Crawford, Henry's sister, judges this adultery pragmatically, as we are likely to do, as folly. To Fanny Price, it is sin, and there can be no doubt that this was Jane Austen's own view.

Yet there is doubleness in Jane Austen's Christian Tory morality. Feminist criticism has sought in Jane Austen the quality which is now sometimes seen as the touchstone of an authentic female voice, that is, anger. And under the irony, the charm, and the conventional morality, they have found it. Jane Austen's own life, as an unmarried woman whose emotional life was centred on a deeply-loved sister, and whose métier was not managing a husband and household, but learning and practising the craft of writing, was very far from the lives she sets out for her heroines. As a novelist, she can run with the hare and hunt with the hounds, by giving expression and life to viewpoints which she explicitly invites the reader to condemn. Furthermore, women whom she overtly disapproves of – managing, shrewish Aunt Norris in *Mansfield Park*, Lady Catherine de Bourgh in *Pride and Prejudice* – are essential in furthering the plot. Aunt Norris is the person who introduces Fanny Price to Mansfield Park, and Lady Catherine inadvertently unites Darcy and Elizabeth while attempting to part them.[56] Self-repression and submission to the due order of society is the lesson which Jane Austen's heroines have to learn. They must seek their happiness within the social structure, and not in opposition to it, which is pragmatic wisdom in any age. Jane Austen's own art, however, contradicts the limits she assigns to her characters.

# Drama

### The eighteenth-century theatrical scene

The extraordinary assault on the stage by Aphra Behn and her contemporaries is now well known. However, it is generally believed that subsequent generations retreated from dramatic writing instead of consolidating their victory, which is not entirely true. The theatre changed in many respects after the political demise of the Stuarts. Physically, theatres became larger, the separation between the audience and the stage was more clearly defined: spectators were no longer permitted to sit on the edges of the acting area. This tended to make theatrical performance more decorous, since the audience was less able to get involved, and it also tended to make drama less verbal and more visual. The dramatic tableau, freezing the action at a moment of high emotional intensity to leave a memorable picture printed on the audience's mind, was developed at this time. Acting techniques also began to stress emotional expressiveness rather than maintaining the momentum of the play as a whole. Both these developments devalued narrative coherence and refocused the attention of audience and playwrights alike on the creation of show-stopping episodes.

Theatres proliferated in the London of the 1700s. This changed abruptly in 1737, when the first British act of theatre censorship, the Licensing Act, was introduced, reducing the number of theatres to two and bringing all drama under the censorship of the Lord Chamberlain. This drastically reduced, as it was intended to, the opportunities for topical, satirical drama such as had got Aphra Behn into trouble when she endorsed, by writing a prologue and epilogue, an anonymous play attacking the Duke of Monmouth in 1682. The new playwrights of the early eighteenth century concentrated on sentimental drama, moral, emotionally stirring and visually spectacular, or on comedies based on the exploration of character. The decline in the number of London theatres was counteracted by the increasing importance of theatres outside London, notably in Bristol, Bath and Edinburgh.

### Character comedy: Susannah Centlivre

Susannah Centlivre (1670–1723) is a particularly important transitional figure in the change from Restoration drama to the new performance styles of the eighteenth century. A generation younger than Aphra Behn, she began her life by putting herself outside the bounds of conventionality in a similar way: she left home before she was fifteen, because she disliked her stepmother intensely, and became a 'strolling player', travelling from town to town, mostly in East Anglia. Her name was associated with a number of men from a very early age, so whatever the truth may have been, she had lost her 'honour'. However, after a hard-working and increasingly respectable career as a writer and an actress specialising in male roles, she married at thirty-seven Joseph Centlivre, who managed Queen Anne's kitchen, and successfully lived down her complicated past. Between 1700 and her death in 1723, she had nineteen plays staged, making her one of the most prolific playwrights in England at that time. Two of her plays, *The Busy Body* (1709) and *The Wonder: A Woman Keeps a Secret* (1714), were continuously popular from their first appearance right through the nineteenth century: not only are they well crafted, they provide wonderful opportunities for actors. David Garrick chose *The Wonder* for his final performance in 1776, and it was still being described as a 'favourite' acting play in 1884.[57]

*The Busy Body* is a particularly well-plotted and effective comedy. There are two young couples: the girls have problems with, respectively, a guardian and a father: Miranda's elderly guardian is in love with her, while Isabinda's father wants her to marry the son of a wealthy merchant. The subsequent complications, masks, disguises and so forth, are enormously complicated by a memorable comic figure, the well-intentioned Marplot, who is another ward of Sir Francis's, and a friend of both the young men. Marplot blunders through the action, trying to be helpful to his friends, and nearly spoiling everything. The character of Marplot moves the conventional comedy of intrigue on to another level, adding a new element of suspense, and a sketch of an easily recognisable, but un-hackneyed personality to the conventional gallery of lecherous and avaricious old men, young lovers and quick-witted chambermaids. The play was performed about 500 times before 1800.

*The Wonder* is also a tightly plotted comedy, with a Peninsular flavour, set in Lisbon.[58] All the main characters are sympathetically drawn. The principal hero and heroine are Don Felix and Donna Violante; the principal secret is that Don Felix's sister Isabella has fled her home in order to escape a forced marriage, and, after attracting the honourable affections of a Scottish colonel called Britton, has taken shelter with Violante. Felix is a classic portrait of a Mediterranean grandee, adoring, but jealous, touchy, and with a strong sense of family honour. In order to protect Isabella, Violante must hide her from her brother, lest he return her to their father as a matter of family honour, while hiding Felix himself from her father, who intends her to enter a nunnery, and allowing Colonel Britton reasonable access to the house so that his courtship of Isabella can proceed. Her actions, therefore, provide abundant opportunities for the jealous Felix to misunderstand her, and repeated temptations for her to justify herself to him by revealing her secrets. The plot is thus furthered by character as well as by incident, particularly by the dilemma Violante experiences between the need to protect her 'honour', meaning her reputation, and acting as a genuinely honourable person in respecting the secrets entrusted to her. There are moments of pathos and suspense in the comedy which make the eventual happy ending all the more welcome.

Mrs Centlivre's comedies are high-spirited and entirely unmalicious, very carefully constructed, and featuring frank, attractive characters, particularly strong-minded, independent and decisive young women. Her plays are also entirely unsalacious, either in subject or in language. The heroines are virginal, the heroes reasonably respectable in their behaviour, and the plots end in marriage: all these are features which allowed the considerable merits of her plays to be put before the public for the following two centuries. Mrs Centlivre's early history was not one of chaste respectability, and since she was unlucky enough to stand in opposition politically to Pope and Swift, she received her share of scurrilous abuse during her lifetime. Yet, in startling contrast to the later reception of the work of Aphra Behn and Mary de la Rivière Manley, editors and commentators of the early nineteenth century were prepared to gloss over her past and defended her as a woman of 'beauty, generosity and talent': this is understandable in Mrs Inchbald, a generous-minded woman who had once been a struggling actress herself, but it is more surprising to find such a stance taken in Cumberland's *British Theatre* (1829).[59] It is strongly suggestive of the sheer attractiveness of her work that whereas the names of other women playwrights became anathema to polite audiences, a sort of collective amnesia permitted Mrs Centlivre's plays to remain in the repertoire.

## Other women playwrights

The whole question of women's plays in the eighteenth and nineteenth centuries is somewhat confused by the genre of 'closet drama': plays written to be read only, and never intended for the stage. They had classical precedents: in the first century AD, the Roman philosopher Seneca wrote verse tragedies which were intended only to be read aloud, though they were fully dramatic in form. Similarly, a highly educated tenth-century German canoness, Hrotswitha of Gandersheim, wrote Latin comedies on Christian themes modelled on the works of Terence, which seem to have been intended merely for the pleasure of her immediate circle. In the early eighteenth century, Lady Mary Wortley Montagu seems never to have sought to have her play *Simplicity* staged, and many of the plays of Joanna Baillie, who is discussed below, though very well received in book form, were never produced on a stage.

The less courtly, more middle-class taste for sentimental drama in the second half of the eighteenth century produced some impeccably moralising and respectable women playwrights, such as Marianna Starke and Maria Barrell. Even so, it is noteworthy that Barrell's *The Captive* (1790), a sentimental treatment of the plight of debtors, was written while she herself languished in the King's Bench (the debtors' prison), with two children to support. Her prologue to the audience, which outlines her own pathetic state, is evidently a plea for sympathy and, in effect, a forestalling of criticism of her temerity in writing at all by showing herself in the character of a needy mother rather than of a vain and presumptuous female.[60] There were also women tragedians, notably Hannah More, best known as a moralist, but also quite a successful playwright. Brought up in Bristol, which boasted a very fine theatre (the Theatre Royal), she was stage-struck from an early age. Her first publication was *The Search after Happiness: A Pastoral Drama* (Bristol, 1773), which became a popular school play. Her first success on the professional stage was a tragedy, *The Inflexible Captive* (1774), a play on a Roman theme, the heroic resistance of Regulus, one of the heroes of the Republic. This was performed with great success in both Bath and Exeter in the year of its publication. She became friendly with the great actor-manager David Garrick, who wrote an epilogue for her *The Inflexible Captive*, and it was he who produced her great West End success, *Percy*, at Covent Garden in 1777. Its subject is an epic conflict between the great northern houses of Douglas and Percy in the twelfth century. It had a run of twenty-two nights (a long time, by contemporary standards), earned her about £600, and sold 4,000 copies in two weeks. Her final play, *The Fatal Falsehood* (1779), was much less successful, and she gave up writing for the stage. Her reasons were various. *The Fatal Falsehood* had involved her in the personal unpleasantness of a charge of plagiarism, which distressed her considerably. She also began to have increasingly serious doubts about the morality of writing for the stage. The dramatic code made honour and, in general, secular rather than religious motives the appropriate springs of action, and Hannah More began to find herself less and less happy at being forced into this stance, which was at odds with all her own most deeply held principles. Another Bristolian woman dramatist was the working-class poetess Ann Yearsley, discussed below, whose only play, *Earl Goodwin* (another drama set in early medieval England), was performed at the Theatre Royal, Bristol in 1789.

Frances Burney's attitude to dramatic writing was ambivalent. She wrote a series of plays between 1779 and 1782. The first was *The Witlings* (1779), a comedy satirising the bluestocking circles of Hannah More, Mrs Thrale and other educated women living in London, to which she herself had recently been admitted. Her comedy is unmalicious, but she was successfully persuaded by her father that public performance would be a joke in poor taste which would cause hurt and offence: Charles Burney was alarmed by his daughter's comedies (inexplicably so, to her mind) and successfully prevented any of them from appearing. One of her later comic plays, *Love and Fashion*, was accepted for performance at Covent Garden, but withdrawn by its author, partly but not entirely because of a family tragedy. She wrote to her father in distress, saying:

> to combat your – to me – unaccountable but most afflicting displeasure, in the midst of my own panics and disturbance, would have been ample

punishment to me, had I been guilty of a crime in doing what I have all my life been urged to, and all my life intended, writing a Comedy.[61]

The late comedies, *Love and Fashion, A Busy Day* and *The Woman-Hater* (1798–1802), are set in contemporary society. These plays aimed both at entertainment and at moral instruction, particularly in the ethics of true politeness. *A Busy Day* deals with the courtship between an upper-class man and a daughter of a *nouveau-riche* mercantile family. Both sets of relations behave appallingly (in this, the plot resembles that of Jane Austen's *Pride and Prejudice*), and the compatibility of Cleveland and Eliza is shown to depend on their personal qualities of kindness, courage and good sense. The play ends with a resounding moral, spoken by Cleveland:

> My Eliza... let me claim, from your true greatness of mind, a cool superiority to resentment against those who, forgetting that Merit is limited to no spot, and confined to no Class, affect to despise and degrade the natives of that noble Metropolis, which is the source of our Splendour, the seat of integrity, the foster Mother of Benevolence and Charity, and the Pride of the British Empire.[62]

– sentiments calculated to go down well with a London theatre audience. The comedies display her considerable gift for dialogue, and particularly for the accurate demarcation of social class in speech, and for the disjunction between characters' aspirations, whether to wit or gentility, and their actual qualities. The plays are also theatrically innovative: *The Witlings* opens in a milliner's shop, and the use of props, with actresses actually making up ribbon and lace confections as they speak, is considerably ahead of its time.[63]

Frances Burney, who had the example of her acquaintance Hannah More to encourage her, had a long-standing interest in the idea of writing for the stage. She was also interested in the money, not unreasonably. Her father saddened her by his completely negative reaction to her first comedy, and she was always reluctant to offend him. Thus it is not surprising that in her thirties, rather than give up dramatic writing altogether, she tried her hand at historical tragedies based on episodes from early English history, as the titles reveal: *Edwy and Elgiva, Hubert de Vere, The Siege of Pevensey* and *Elberta* (all written between 1788 and 1791). The immediate model for such a choice of subjects was More's *Percy*; more distantly, Shakespeare's historical plays. After her marriage, when she needed money, she consented (using her brother Charles as her agent) to let Garrick stage *Edwy and Elgiva* at Drury Lane, with Mrs Siddons in the role of Elgiva. The plot of this play deals with a secret royal marriage: though Edwy loves Elgiva, she is not a woman of suitably high status, and generally believed to be a concubine. She is stabbed at the instigation of St Dunstan, presented as a bitter, misogynistic moralist, and Edwy is killed in battle.[64] Although the plot does not lack for exciting episodes, the play was a disastrous flop. Frances Burney's great gift, well displayed in her novels and comic plays, was for the comedy of modern manners. Cumbering herself with tenth-century heroes and heroines and occasional stabs at historical verisimilitude cramped her abilities badly: it is a testimony to the prestige of this post-Shakespearean historical drama that she should have made several attempts at the genre.

Another very widely admired woman tragedian was Sir Walter Scott's friend Joanna Baillie (1762–1851), who published three volumes of *Plays on the Passions* in 1799, 1802 and 1812. Her aim was to write a paired comedy and tragedy on each of a series of ruling passions; the tragedies were sub-Shakespearean history plays, mostly based on the lives of notable characters in English history. Of the plays in this series the most highly regarded was *De Montfort*, in the first volume, a play about hate. Her protagonist De Montfort suffers from an irrational hatred for the amiable Rezenvelt, whom he has known since childhood; after being twice defeated by him in duels, he ends up murdering him. It was produced by John Kemble and Mrs Siddons (the greatest tragic actress of her day) in 1800, and was only moderately successful. Few of the *Plays on the Passions* were performed, and, in general, Baillie's work was regarded as literary, closet drama, rather than as plays for acting. Her most successful drama for the stage was an example of the Scottish Gothic tradition pioneered by her old friend Sir Walter Scott. This play, *The Family Legend*, was produced in 1810, with Mrs Siddons as the leading lady, first in Edinburgh, then in London, and was very well received. Its self-consciously Scottish status was emphasised, since Walter Scott wrote a prologue, and the only other internationally well-known Scottish novelist, Henry Mackenzie, wrote an epilogue. The play featured spectacular stage effects, and was a fundamentally more melodramatic concept than her earlier work.

The context for the successful theatrical activity of authors such as Hannah More, Frances Burney and Joanna Baillie is the smallness of the world of the London intelligentsia, and the rise of a number of remarkable theatrical talents who were judged to be acceptable company for ladies and gentlemen. David Garrick was personally welcome in the salons where Hannah More and Frances Burney talked with Mrs Thrale and Dr Johnson. The authors, therefore, were not sending their plays off to be read by strangers; still less were they expected to involve themselves in the actual process of staging. Garrick, as actor-manager, proprietor of a theatre, could and did take on work from his friends which he judged to have a reasonable chance of succeeding with the public; success by such means might encourage both authors and other managers to try a further venture. Despite the disaster of her tragedy *Edwy and Elgiva*, Burney's *Love and Fashion* was accepted for production by Thomas Harris of Covent Garden four years later. A little later in theatrical history, the remarkable family of the Kembles (actors, managers and scholars) played a similar role to Garrick's. The great tragic actress Mrs Siddons was not only a Kemble (sister of John); unlike most members of her profession, she was welcome in any lady's drawing-room since her manners were perfect and her morals well known to be beyond reproach.[65] Thus, the Kembles, male and female, also moved easily in the salons which welcomed intellectual women, which helps to account for the link between these professionals and Joanna Baillie; otherwise, it is hard to see how a woman from such a background could have made contact with the world of the theatre.

# Poetry

### A range of styles and talents

The principles of correctness and propriety subscribed to by writers of both sexes tend to make eighteenth-century poetry relatively hard to approach for the modern reader: the smoothness of surface texture and the tendency towards a highly formal and limited diction gives a misleading impression of sameness to a reader whose expectations of poetry are shaped primarily by nineteenth- and twentieth-century verse.[66] Eighteenth-century verse in general evinces a shift of taste in the 1740s: the earlier period is generally known as 'Augustan', and the phase from the 1740s to the Romantic revolution heralded by the publication of Wordsworth's and Coleridge's *Lyrical Ballads* in 1798 might reasonably be called the Age of Sensibility.

The splendid new Oxford anthology of eighteenth-century women poets by Roger Lonsdale does much to correct this general impression of smoothness and uniformity.[67] He prints more than 300 poems by a total of 107 eighteenth-century women in which it becomes clear that these women were prepared to write about virtually every subject under the sun (excluding pornography). There are far more humorous poems than one might have expected, and certainly more poems which baldly reveal unvarnished states of mind such as the heroines of fiction never seem to have experienced. The very talented Mary Jones (*d*.1778) wrote an amusingly splenetic 'Epistle from Fern Hill' (1750) about a tiresome visit to an extremely genteel hostess, who is driving her mad: she observes that the feeling is almost certainly mutual, since 'well-bred folks are ne'er so civil / As when they wish you at the devil'.[68] A Miss W—'s 'Answer' to Swift's unpleasant poem 'The Lady's Dressing-room' (1732), written in the same year, is still more of a surprise. A milliner calls on a male client with an unpaid bill, and is shown into his room to wait for him. This is part of what she finds:

> There on a block a wig was set
> Whose inside did so stink with sweat;
> The outside oiled with jessamine [jasmine],
> T'disguise the stench that was within.

And next a shirt, with gussets red,
Which Strephon slept in, when in bed;
But modesty forbids the rest,
It shan't be spoke, but may be guessed;
A napkin worn upon a head,
Enough, infection to have bred.

For there some stocks lay on the ground,
One side was yellow, t'other brown;
And velvet breeches (on her word),
The inside all bedaubed with t—d,
And just before, I'll not desist
To let you know they were be-pissed:
Four different stinks lay there together,
Which were sweat, turd, and piss, and leather.

There in a heap lay nasty socks,
Here tangled stockings with silver clocks,
And towels stiff with soap and hair,
Of stinking shoes there were a pair... [69]

And so on, and on, and on, with precisely the kind of coarse, robust
naturalism and unflinching eye for the sordid which is generally supposed to
be completely outside the range of eighteenth-century women writers.

Part of the social context for the quite large quantities of women's verse
which survive from this period is the developing periodical press. The
*Gentleman's Magazine*, founded in 1731, carried monthly poetry pages, to
which Anna Seward (1742–1809), among a number of others, was a regular
contributor. The *Monthly Magazine* was another such periodical: Anna
Laetitia Barbauld (1743–1825) published some of her best poems in it,
perhaps because her brother was literary editor. Elizabeth Carter published
in Samuel Johnson's *Rambler*, while Charlotte Lennox became editor of a
less successful venture along these lines, *The Lady's Museum*, which
produced eleven issues in 1760–1. All these journals, and several others,
welcomed contributions by women. The possible unsuitability of appearing
in print worried a few women, notably Ann Radcliffe, but it also still
worried some men (including Thomas Gray): the ideal of the poet
uncontaminated by consideration of the literary marketplace remained
strong. Women's verse was widely accepted and enjoyed in the eighteenth
century. The reason for its subsequent disappearance seems to be very
directly connected with the policies of two apparently all-inclusive editors,
Robert Anderson, in his *Works of the British Poets* (13 vols, 1772–5), and
Alexander Chalmers, in his *Works of the English Poets* (21 vols, 1810), who
decided to exclude women's poetry from their collections, as well as
anonymous poetry, and poets whose works had not already appeared in

convenient collected editions.[70] One possible reason for the exclusion of women is that these editors did not publish poems by living authors, and nearly all of the women who had dominated the literary scene of the 1770s and 1780s – women such as Hannah More, Anna Seward, Elizabeth Carter and Anna Barbauld – were still alive. These anthologies were enormously influential in creating a canon of English poetry; which gave the nineteenth-century poetess Elizabeth Barrett Browning the impression that there were virtually no female predecessors to whom she could look back.

One notable difference between Augustan poetry by women and by men, as Doody has noted, is women's marked preference for iambic tetrameter, rather than pentameter.[71] The associations of pentameter are epic and heroic, and even in the form of pentametric rhymed couplets (such as those of Pope), the shape of the line carries implications of authoritative public discourse. Where pentameter is used by eighteenth-century women, the context is often unusually public and declamatory: Elizabeth Carter's poem 'On the Death of Mrs Rowe' (1737), which is very consciously a tribute from one woman of letters to another, or the equally formal commendation, 'Verses to Mr Richardson, on His History of Sir Charles Grandison' (1753), by Anna Williams (1706–83).[72] Tetrameter, on the other hand, has associations which are comic, informal, relaxed and light: it was used by Samuel Butler in his long comic poem *Hudibras* (1662–78), and often by Swift and Gay. Another, equally informal, metre often used by these poets is the ballad stanza, with alternating tetrameter and trimeter lines; an elegant example is Anna Barbauld's mock-heroic poem 'The Mouse's Petition to Doctor Priestley Found in the Trap Where He Had Been Confined All Night' (1773; stanza 3):

> If e'er thy breast with freedom glowed,
>     And spurned a tyrant's chain,
> Let not thy strong oppressive force
>     A free-born mouse detain.

Many of the women poets of the eighteenth century aimed at gracefulness rather than grandeur: these light, unpompous, humorous metres served them well.

One of the most surprising things about eighteenth-century women's poetry is the amount of verse by working-class women which survives. The eighteenth-century vogue for natural, spontaneous, untaught peasant geniuses (none of these terms can now be used without irony: all were regarded as simply descriptive at the time) created a wide audience for Robert Burns and, later, John Clare, among others: they had been preceded by less well-remembered figures such as Stephen Duck, the thresher-poet. A variety of eighteenth-century women were marketed as self-taught geniuses, attracting considerable public interest, and also criticism. The washerwoman Mary Collier (*c*.1690–1762) published 'The Woman's Labour: An Epistle to Mr Stephen Duck' (1739) as a reply to the 'ploughman poet', who had the temerity to suggest that rural women were idle compared to their men. The subject is related to the whole genre of folk literature (the Scottish traditional poem, 'The Wife of Auchtermuchty', is an example) in which a man and wife change places; she finds his work quite straightforward, whereas he finds hers impossibly strenuous and difficult. The detailed description of a washerwoman's working day is an intriguing document for social history, though as poetry it is no more than neat and competent.[73] Janet Little (1759–1813), a Dumfries milkmaid, enlisted the help of Burns in publishing her *Poetical Works* by subscription, from which she made £50.[74] Another such poet, Elizabeth Hands (dates unknown), published a collection in 1789, which includes a comically satiric portrait of snobbish ladies' vulgar incredulity at the idea of a servant writing poetry:

'He, he, he,' says Miss Flounce: 'I suppose we shall see
An Ode on a Dishclout – what else can it be?'[75]

Such writers could expect condescension and impertinence from many of their patrons; but the subscription method of publishing – a list of sponsors was collected, and the book only published when a secure market was established – made it necessary to attract a patron to organise the subscription. In the case of Elizabeth Hands, the aim of the subscription was 'to make the remainder of her life comfortable to herself and family': since it attracted 1,200 names at five shillings each (£300), it must have succeeded in its aim.

The most impressive of these self-taught poets was Mrs Yearsley (1752–1806), a milkwoman from Bristol, married to a labourer and the mother of six, who used the pen-name 'Lactilla' ('the milky one'). Ann Yearsley was an independent-minded, proud woman, and an ambitious writer. Rather than warbling touching shepherdess ditties, she attempted large-scale work: the tragedy *Earl Goodwin*, mentioned above, a four-volume historical novel, *The Royal Captives* (1795), and a quantity of blank-verse poetry, including a poem of several hundred lines about Brutus – not the murderer of Caesar, but Brutus the Trojan, the legendary founder of Britain (an outline of the legend may be found in Edmund Spenser's *Faerie Queene*, Book II, Canto 10). The use of blank verse was in itself a token of literary ambition. The long poem 'Remonstrance in the Platonic Shade, Flourishing in a Height' (1796) is highly personal. It gives voice to her sense of vertigo at the boldness and freedom of her own thoughts, her identity as an aspirant poet. As an analysis of her own character, it does not in any sense aim to please: she states bluntly that she has gone beyond most women writers, and she fears the terrifying human cost which is being extracted from her:

...had my judgment reeled, my foot forgot
Its strenuous print, my inexperienced eye
The wondrous point in view; or my firm soul,
Made early stubborn, her exalted pride,
Though of external poor; the stagnant lake
Of Vice beneath, than Cocytus more foul,
Had oped its wave to swallow me, and hide
My frame for ever. This I saw: the year
Ne'er riped the corn, or strewed the yellow leaf,
But some too feeble maid, who in the morn
Ascended with me, lost her hold and fell,
Leaving the glorious plaudit of the wise
To rough laborious spirits. I attained
With wretchedness this summit... [76]

Note the classical reference (Cocytus is the river of the Roman underworld) and the Latinate syntax (for example the displacement of 'than' in the Cocytus clause): these difficult sentences are grammatically correct. She writes here slightly ahead of the Romantic movement, but seems to prefigure it in some ways: the assumption by the poet of priestly and visionary powers, the sublimity of her vision, are very out of tune with the work of other women poets of her time. In other ways, she looks back to the Augustans: the successful poem 'Addressed to Ignorance, Occasioned by a Gentleman's Desiring the Author Never to Assume a Knowledge of the Ancients' (1787) offers a flow of perversely witty classical allusion in a way which directly recalls Pope and Dryden. [77] Her writing is not, on any level, suitable to the Age of Sensibility in which she was writing.

Ann Yearsley demonstrably picked up a remarkable amount of learning, considering that she had no formal schooling at all. Her brother taught her to read, and her mother borrowed books for her when she was young. Her milieu in Bristol must have helped to make her work possible: it was an unusually lively and cultivated town, with bookshops, an excellent theatre, and an active community of intelligentsia, including Hannah More, Robert Southey and Joseph Cottle, many of whom went out of their way to help her.

The playwright Joanna Baillie was also a published poet. There is a tender warmth and humour in 'A Mother to Her Waking Infant' (1790), which observes the undoubted but 'unpoetical' fact that babies dribble ('[thy] little chin with chrystal spread'). The mother rhapsodises over her baby, but the sentiment is gently undercut by her noticing in the last stanza that the child is paying her no attention whatsoever. Some of Baillie's best poems are eclogues: loving, precisely focused vignettes of rural life, verbal equivalents of the Dutch genre paintings which were fashionable at the time, building a sense of the dignity and stability of family and village relationships.[78] Her writing is concerned with genuine feeling, simplicity and realism, in ways which suggest that her mind was moving in the same directions as Coleridge and Wordsworth's.

There is a memorable tartness in the brief poem 'The Humble Wish' (1726), by Arabella Moreton, who flourished in the first half of the eighteenth century, which ends:

Since this, I say, is every woman's fate,
Give me a mind to suit my slavish state.[79]

It is one of several poems in Lonsdale's collection which reflect directly on aspects of women's social position: a particularly well-represented theme is women's writing, and women's lack of access to formal education. Two particularly vehement examples are 'On Sir J— S— Saying in a Sarcastic Manner, My Books Would Make Me Mad' (1722), by Elizabeth Thomas (1675–1731),[80] and 'Hypatia' (1724), by Elizabeth Tollet (1694–1754).[81] The title of this last poem evokes a notorious example of the brutal suppression of educated women: Hypatia was a distinguished fourth-century mathematician in Alexandria, who was lynched by monks at the instigation of the bishop. It includes the lines:

Yet oft we hear, in height of stupid pride
Some senseless idiot curse a lettered bride.

Jane Cave's (1754–1813) poem 'Written a Few Hours Before the Birth of a Child' (1786) is an indication of the dignity and self-restraint of many eighteenth-century women poets, and also of the trials which they faced. Stanza 3 reads:

Come pain, or agony, or death,
  If such the will divine;
With joy shall I give up my breath,
  If resignation's mine.[82]

The 'if' in the last line of this stanza saves the poem from histrionics: she is aware that whatever the outcome of the hideous ordeal she faces at the hands of eighteenth-century obstetricians, she may not be able to hold fast to her best intentions. The last verse, in which the poet expresses the hope that if she dies, the baby will too, may read strangely now, but its grimness is explicable if one remembers that the fate of motherless babies was likely to be one of prolonged and pointless suffering (Jane Cave's husband was an Excise officer, and not wealthy).

Two poems by Scotswomen are still well known, both tear-jerkers. One is 'Auld Robin Gray' (1771), by Lady Anne Lindsay (1750–1825), a delicately stoic dramatic monologue by a Scottish peasant woman. The story is that her penniless lover went to sea to make his fortune; meanwhile, her family hit hard times, and Robin generously supported them. She was persuaded to marry him, and then, of course, Jamie came back from the sea to find her an old man's wife. It ends:

I gang like a ghaist, and I carena much to spin,
I darena think o'Jamie, for that wad be a sin.
But I will do my best a gude wife aye to be,
For auld Robin Gray, oh! he is sae kind to me.[83]

It is an excellent statement of the unsentimental uprightness of Scottish rural culture, in which duty and indebtedness must always outweigh romantic love.

The other poem that should be mentioned here is an example of that quintessentially Celtic genre, the lament for dead heroes (the earliest poem written in Scotland, *Y Gododdin*, written about 600 AD, is on this theme): 'The Flowers of the Forest' (1764), by Jane Elliot (1727–1805).[84] The tune, and the exquisite refrain-line, 'the flowers of the forest [the young men] are a' wede [weeded] away' pre-existed her poem, which was in effect built round them. The immediate theme is the catastrophic battle of Flodden, in the sixteenth century, but it could be any battle: the women of Scotland lamenting their lost lovers; the dreary loneliness and economic hardship which follows the loss of a generation of young men. It was published in David Herd's *The Ancient and Modern Scots Songs* (1769), and is still often sung in Scotland. Another eighteenth-century poem by a Scotswoman, *Hardyknute* (1719) by Elizabeth, Lady Wardlaw (1677–1727), a pastiche of ballad style, was widely admired for its vigour and pathos, extravagantly so by Scott, who quotes it frequently.

### Towards the Romantic movement

The new poetic style of William Wordsworth, Samuel Taylor Coleridge and other contemporaries was, to some extent, understood by its practitioners as an attempt to recover poetry from women: Wordsworth speaks in the Preface to his *Lyrical Ballads* of writing as 'a man speaking to men', and in a 'manly' style. John Keats, somewhat later, also said, according to a friend, that 'he does not want ladies to read his poetry: he writes for men'.[85] This is not to say, however, that women's poetry of the late eighteenth century is a literary cul-de-sac. Charlotte Smith is now better remembered as a novelist, but her sonnets were not only famous and widely read, they influenced the developing style of both Wordsworth and Coleridge, who saw her as the most distinguished modern exponent of this medium.[86] Another aspect of Charlotte Smith's poetical work which excited Wordsworth was her interest in nature and rural life, which he saw as a welcome contrast to the abstraction and artificiality of some of her contemporaries (this would also be true of Joanna Baillie). Ann Yearsley, whose writing is bold and original, though sometimes incoherent, and as unlike the 'loving stuff, about Shepherds and Shepherdesses; – & little lambs & all that'[87] associated with poetesses as it could possibly have been, moved in the same milieux in Bristol as Coleridge (Robert Southey, for instance, was a friend to both), and her writings may well have been known to Coleridge and Wordsworth. Keats also, despite the rejection of women's poetry implicit in the remark quoted above, admired the work of Mary Tighe, and drew on her poem *Psyche* (1811) for his own 'Ode on a Grecian Urn'.[88] The women poets of the eighteenth century had more to offer the Romantic revolution of the early nineteenth century than is now remembered.

NOTES

1 Jane Austen commented on Walter Scott (who was first known as a poet): 'Walter Scott has no business to write novels, especially good ones. – It is not fair. – He has Fame and Profit enough as a Poet, and should not be taking the bread out of other people's mouths. – I do not like him, & do not mean to like Waverley if I can help it – but fear I must' (quoted by Moers, *Literary Women: The Great Writers*, p.44). Walter Scott was also a major influence on the fiction of the Brontës – see W. Gérin, *Emily Brontë*, Clarendon Press, Oxford, 1971, pp.26–7.

2 *Collected Works of Katherine Philips*, ed. P. Thomas, pp.2–4.

3 *Eighteenth-century Women Poets: An Oxford Anthology*, ed. R. Lonsdale, Oxford University Press, Oxford, 1990, pp.468–9. This school was attended by 'Perdita' Robinson, actress, poet and novelist, who retained vivid memories of it.

4 'An Epistle to the Reader', printed in J. Goulianos (ed.), *By a Woman Writt: Literature from Six Centuries by and about Women*, New English Library, London, 1974, p.99.

5 See Thomas Sprat, *The History of the Royal Society of London, for the Improving of Natural Knowledge*, London, 1667, pp.40–4, 61–2, 111–15, especially p.113.

6 Virginia Woolf, *Three Guineas*, London, 1937, e.g. p.18. The relationship of gender and class here may not appear immediately obvious: if a conclusion may be drawn so far, it is this. The social contexts which appear to have fostered nearly every woman writer who has been discussed hitherto are united by their unconventionality. Thus, an unusually cultivated aristocratic family, a family in the middle rank of gentry declassed by the English Revolution, or Nonconformist families with their tradition of serious religious debate, all offered much the same opportunities to their female members. All these family types are recognisable as 'intellectual' in the twentieth-century sense. Outside these unusual families, the daughter of an eighteenth- or nineteenth-century legislator who would send his sons to university as a matter of course would hardly have more access to even rudimentary literary education than the child of an agricultural labourer. But it must be emphasised that this is not true either of Lowland Scottish culture, or of Gaelic-speaking Scotland and Ireland.

7 The literary pomposities of the period are heavy-handedly satirised by Richardson in *Clarissa Harlowe*, Vol. IV, letters 107 and 108, written in the character of a pompous and self-regarding young clergyman.

8 Moers, *Literary Women*, p.64.

9 See *Literary Women*, pp.173–210.

10 The only exceptions to this rule in an eighteenth-century context that are known to me are the first two novels of Charlotte Smith, *Emmeline, or The Orphan of the Castle* (1788) and *Ethelinda, or The Recluse of the Lakes* (1798). Spender, in *Mothers of the Novel*, p.221, comments that 'the entry of Emmeline and Ethelinda heralds the beginning of mature heroines in fiction'.

11 *Strictures on the Modern System of Female Education*, II, pp.13–14.

12 Jane Austen, Frances Burney, Maria Edgeworth, George Eliot and the Brontës are among the many women who hid their identities from the public.

13 J. Simons, *Fanny Burney*, Macmillan, London, 1987, p.19.
14 R. Halsband and I. Grundy, *Lady Mary Wortley Montagu: Essays and Poems, and Simplicity, a Comedy*, Oxford University Press, Oxford, 1977.
15 J. Spencer, *The Rise of the Woman Novelist: From Aphra Behn to Jane Austen*, Basil Blackwell, Oxford, 1986.
16 Spender, in *Mothers of the Novel*, pp.119–37, lists 568 novels by 106 women novelists working before Jane Austen. Pandora Press is in the process of reprinting a selection of these forgotten novels by obscure women writers.
17 Moers, *Literary Women*, p.144.
18 Spender, *Mothers of the Novel*, pp.91–3. Spender points out that she precedes Richardson in this respect.
19 *Mothers of the Novel*, p.197.
20 *Mothers of the Novel*, p.185.
21 Spencer, *The Rise of the Woman Novelist*, ch. 3: 'The Terms of Acceptance' (pp.75–103).
22 See J. Todd, *Sensibility: An Introduction*, Methuen, London and New York, 1986.
23 M.G. Jones, *Hannah More*, Cambridge University Press, Cambridge, 1952, p.190.
24 Simons, *Fanny Burney*, p.61, comments that, after the clandestine writing and publication of *Evelina*, her next novel was closely supervised: 'from start to finish, the composition of *Cecilia* was a struggle. Fanny Burney's progress, no longer confined to the relaxed privacy of her own room, was carefully monitored by the hawklike scrutiny of her father and Mr Crisp, ever watchful of the reputation of their protégée.'
25 *Westminster Review*, October 1856, reprinted in *British Women Writers*, ed. D. Spender and J. Todd, Unwin Hyman, London, 1989, pp.518–35.
26 *Camilla*, Bk IV, ch. 8. Similarly, in *Cecilia*, ch. 5, Cecilia finds, with regard to her lover, that, 'she began almost to fancy there was some fatality attending her acquaintance with him, since she was always sure of meeting, when she had any reason to wish avoiding him'.
27 There is an echo of this old function of the novel in the kind of pulp fiction, from Ian Fleming's James Bond books through to Shirley Conran and many others, which instructs its would-be upwardly mobile readers on the right labels, the right drinks ('shaken, not stirred'), where to go, what to say. This kind of writing is as much a guide to etiquette as Fanny Burney's presentation, through Evelina's mistakes, of correct behaviour in a ballroom.
28 In her journal, Burney recalls a conversation with Princesses Mary and Sophia, who had deplored radical tendencies in fiction:

> 'I now explained that *Politics* were, *all ways*, left out: that once I had an idea of bringing in such as suited me, – but that, upon second thoughts, I returned to my more native opinion that they were not a feminine subject for discussion.'

(Quoted by E. Figes, *Sex and Subterfuge: Women Writers to 1850*, Macmillan, London, 1982, p.47.)
29 *Camilla*, Bk IX, ch. 6.
30 In today's money, perhaps £3,000–£4,000: a lot of money, certainly, since it is a sixth of her father's annual income.
31 *Camilla* Bk II, ch.8; V, 8; V, 15; VII, 2.
32 It is found also in *Cecilia*, where a widowed mother denies herself and her daughters every convenience in order to lavish money on her only son – the remaining unmarried daughter comments, 'sums that would distress us for months to save up, could by him be spent in a day, and then thought of no more!' (ch. 4).
33 Littlewood, *Elizabeth Inchbald and Her Circle*.
34 What now seems an exaggerated respect for fathers was not peculiar to literary ladies, but was part of the whole structure of society in the seventeenth and eighteenth centuries. Jane Austen is the first major writer to express the possibility that fathers might be more stupid than their daughters.

35 Richard Edgeworth was himself a liberal thinker of considerable energy and dynamism, and an innovative educationalist. An admiring and deeply committed dramatisation of Richard Edgeworth's educational principles in action may be found in Maria Edgeworth's *Belinda*, ch. 8.

36 Though Byron, normally thought an exacting judge of female beauty, says that in 1813 she was 'a nice, unassuming Jeanie-Deans-looking body – and if not handsome, certainly not ill-looking'. Jeanie Deans was the unconventional heroine of Sir Walter Scott's *The Heart of Midlothian* (1818), described in ch. 9. This remark of Byron's is the first half of a comment on Edgeworth quoted below (see note 43).

37 S.M. Gilbert and S. Gubar, *The Madwoman in the Attic: The Woman Writer and the Nineteenth-century Literary Imagination*, Yale University Press, New Haven and London, 1984, p.150.

38 Figes, *Sex and Subterfuge*, p.27.

39 Johnson, *The Rambler*, IV (31 March 1750), quoted in M. Butler, *Jane Austen and the War of Ideas*, Clarendon Press, Oxford, 1975, p.20.

40 The occasion of this fear is another of Edgeworth's broadly humorous episodes: Lady Delacour is challenged to a duel by a sort of female rake called Harriot Freke (again, the name is significant), and her pride will not permit her to decline a challenge. The duel does not come off, but the ladies agree to fire into the air as a formal gesture. Lady Delacour has never handled a gun before, and the recoil bruises her breast very severely (ch. 4). Medical theory of the time held that cancer could be produced by bruising, but although her fears are ultimately proved false, she is certainly left with some kind of chronic problem which causes her a great deal of physical pain. The incident modulates in a characteristic way, from farce to near-tragedy.

41 Spender, *Mothers of the Novel*, p.287.

42 E. Inglis-Jones, *The Great Maria*, Faber, London, 1959, p.113.

43 Figes, *Sex and Subterfuge*, p.26.

44 Littlewood, *Elizabeth Inchbald*, p.123.

45 C.F. McIntyre, *Ann Radcliffe in Relation to Her Time*, Yale University Press, New Haven, CO, 1920, pp.4–5.

46 Spender, *Mothers of the Novel*, p.239.

47 Moers, *Literary Women*, p.131.

48 *Eighteenth-century Women Poets*, pp.466–8.

49 We find the same characteristic in Maria Edgeworth, another subscriber to *Camilla*. In her *Belinda*, published five years later than *Camilla*, the cynical but good hearted Mrs Delacour, who has just been telling Belinda that she really must buy two extremely expensive sets of clothes for court, says, as Belinda sighs, 'A silver penny for your thoughts! ... You are thinking that you are like Camilla, and I like Mrs Mitten [*sic*]' (ch. 5). She goes rattling on to the effect that novel reading for young ladies is extremely dangerous – yet in the episode referred to, a knowlege of the novel would actually help Belinda to stay within the bounds of the funds available to her, especially since the rules of conduct of the time predisposed girls, like Camilla and Belinda, to trust the judgment of older people like Lady Delacour and Mrs Mittin rather than rudely to oppose them. In the end, Belinda does not buy the dresses, though for rather complex reasons.

50 It is a further mark of John Thorpe's awfulness that he criticises *Camilla* by reference to Fanny Burney's life: her marriage to a French emigré. This is a frequent impertinence in the treatment of women writers, and one which they have usually found it hard to forgive (see Moers, *Literary Women*, pp.144–5).

51 Gilbert and Gubar, *The Madwoman in the Attic*, pp.107–8.

52 Russ, *How to Suppress Women's Writing*, p.71.

53 Butler, *Jane Austen and the War of Ideas*, p.165.

54 Gilbert and Gubar, *The Madwoman in the Attic*, p.160, collects together some of the most significant of these scalding moments of personal shame leading to increased self-knowledge.

55  Butler, *Jane Austen and the War of Ideas*, pp.154 and 162.
56  Incidently, this scene is one of many which indicates Austen's debt to Burney. In Burney's *Cecilia*, Mrs Delville is successful in parting her son and Cecilia by appealing to the pride of the family name. Lady Catherine is a parody of Mrs Delville, and the scene is clearly at least reminiscent of that in the earlier book – though Elizabeth is made of sterner stuff than Cecilia. In the same book, we find a relationship between Cecilia and a simple young protégée, both as it turns out in love with Mr Delville, of which the Emma–Harriet Smith–Knightley triangle in *Emma* is reminiscent in the same way.
57  J.W. Bowyer, *The Celebrated Mrs Centlivre*, Duke University Press, Durham, NC, 1952, pp.183 and 218.
58  Printed in *The Female Wits*, pp.328–87.
59  Bowyer, *The Celebrated Mrs Centlivre*, pp.246–9.
60  Todd, *Sensibility: An Introduction*, p.41.
61  Doody, *Frances Burney: The Life in the Works*, p.287.
62  Fanny Burney, *A Busy Day*, ed. Tara Ghoshal Wallace, Rutgers University Press, New Brunswick NJ, 1984, p.148.
63  This play, still unpublished, is described at some length in Doody, *Frances Burney*, pp.66–98.
64  Described in Doody, *Frances Burney*, pp.179–81.
65  The reverence with which Mrs Siddons was regarded both in and after her time is represented in, and by, Dinah Maria Craik's 1856 novel, *John Halifax, Gentleman* (ch. 6).
66  Doody, *The Daring Muse: Augustan Poetry Reconsidered*, offers a reading of eighteenth-century poetry which emphasises its bold, experimental aspects.
67  *Eighteenth-century Women Poets*.
68  *Eighteenth-century Women Poets*, p.164.
69  *Eighteenth-century Women Poets*, pp.130–4.
70  *The New Oxford Book of Eighteenth-century Verse*, ed. R. Lonsdale, Oxford University Press, Oxford, 1984, p.xxxvi.
71  Doody, *The Daring Muse*, pp.240–4.
72  *Eighteenth-century Women Poets*, pp.167, 241–2.
73  *Eighteenth-century Women Poets*, pp.171–3.
74  *Eighteenth-century Women Poets*, pp.453–5.
75  *Eighteenth-century Women Poets*, pp.425–6.
76  *Eighteenth-century Women Poets*, pp.392–401, at pp.397–8.
77  Discussed by Doody, *The Daring Muse*, pp.130–1.
78  *Eighteenth-century Women Poets*, pp.429–45.
79  *Eighteenth-century Women Poets*, p.105.
80  *Eighteenth-century Women Poets*, pp.40–2.
81  *Eighteenth-century Women Poets*, pp.99–100. Another poem of Elizabeth Tollet's, pp.101–2, a sonnet 'On the Prospect from Westminster Bridge, March 1750', is an interesting comparandum to Wordsworth's famous sonnet on the same view, written in 1802: Tollet's declarative, historically conscious poem illustrates very neatly the difference between the classical mode of the eighteenth century and the Romantic mode which succeeded it.
82  *Eighteenth-century Women Poets*, p.376.
83  *Eighteenth-century Women Poets*, pp.277–8.
84  *Eighteenth-century Women Poets*, p.265.
85  For these and other quotations on this subject, see *Eighteenth-century Women Poets*, pp.xl–xli.
86  Charlotte Smith, *Elegiac Sonnets* (1789), reprinted by Woodstock Books, Spelsbury, Oxford, 1992. For her influence, see, for example, *The Prose Works of William Wordsworth*, ed. A.B. Grosart, London, 1876, III, pp.151 and 507, and S.T. Coleridge, *Sonnets from Various Authors*, Bristol, 1796, p.1.

87 A dry remark by Charlotte Smith about her own sonnets, and publishers' expectations, in a letter of 1806 to her publisher, quoted in R.P. Turner, *Charlotte Smith (1749–1806): New Light on Her Life and Literary Career*, University of Southern California PhD, 1966, p.98.

88 Mary Tighe, *Psyche, with Other Poems* (1811), reprinted by Woodstock Books, Spelsbury, Oxford, 1992. See E.V. Weller, *The Poems of Mary Tighe, with Parallel Passages from the Work of John Keats*, Century, New York, 1928.

# Chapter 4

# The nineteenth century

## Culture and society

### The social environment

From the time of Jane Austen onwards, the contribution of women to English literature becomes increasingly significant. A woman of the Victorian era, unlike a woman of the Regency, could look back to a whole tradition of women's writing, some of which had won both wide popularity and critical acclaim, and which was, moreover, chastely respectable in style and content.[1] The rigidly blameless lives of Mrs Hannah More, Jane Austen, Maria Edgeworth *et al*, together with the high moral tone of their fiction, did much to relieve the aspirant women writers of the later nineteenth century from the fear that to write at all might be perceived as unchaste, unladylike, and unsuitable for their social position. Women had been writing romances and novels since the early seventeenth century, and in the eighteenth century, more than half of all novels written and published were by women.[2] The significance of the change does not lie in a sudden appearance of a number of women writers, but in the fact that there was a substantial quantity of the works of their predecessors around which could neither be dismissed as intellectually inadequate nor as morally dubious.

It is in the time of Jane Austen herself that we can see a new preoccupation with morality and social organisation. In Jane Austen's earlier works, *Sense and Sensibility* and *Northanger Abbey*, the idleness or otherwise of the leading male figures is seen as a matter affecting only themselves. In *Mansfield Park*, *Emma* and *Persuasion*, the landowning gentleman comes to be justified in his position by his managerial efforts on behalf of the community as a whole. The complete mental and physical idleness of Mr Woodhouse and Sir Walter Elliot is not condoned, but implicitly contrasted with the vigorous efforts of Mr Knightley, who spends at least as much time with William Larkins and Robert Martin as he does with Emma and her acquaintances, and with the various naval heroes in *Persuasion*, who have not only risked their lives in battle for their country, but have brought naval principles of organisation and alert self-discipline to their retirement in the country. Social analysis is not Jane Austen's preoccupation, but it is clear that the power to do good or ill within the community to which one belongs is something which mattered more and more to her as she grew older. In this, she is a woman of her time. Evangelicalism became an increasingly significant force in English society in precisely the period spanned by her writing: 'in the first two decades of the nineteenth century it became effective as a powerful upper-middle-class pressure group directed towards reforming abuses and combating vice.'[3]

The trend towards social analysis which began in Jane Austen's time increased as the century wore on, partly because society was, in fact, changing extremely fast. This is the century of the Industrial Revolution, of the shift of economic weight from landholding to capital, of the shift of population from country to city, and the shift of employment from agricultural labour to urban working-class employment in factories. Since so much had changed, so quickly, it was inevitable that a questioning of social structures should follow. The new manufacturing industry concentrated the mass of the population in the new cities of the Midlands, such as Manchester, Birmingham and Sheffield, but there was no social mechanism to deal with fluctuation in the demand for employees. The result was the 'Hungry Forties', in which the urban poor suffered acutely from the vagaries of international trade.

### A changing reading public

Other factors were at work to change the shape of the reading public of nineteenth-century Britain: although universal education did not move towards becoming a reality until Forster's Elementary Education Act of 1870, the literate public was vastly increased from its eighteenth-century level, partly through the efforts of the new, religiously non-conformist charity schools. In answer to this spread of literacy, many cheap publications of an improving and socially stabilising kind were produced (probably the earliest writer to see the size of the potential market for this type of writing was Hannah More). Further advances in printing technology made the mass-marketing of tracts possible, and also allowed commercial publishers to satisfy an ever increasing demand for inexpensive reading material in such series as Murray's 'Family Library' and Colburn and Bentley's 'Novels'.

The commercial success of these and many other series goes some way to creating a nineteenth-century canon, both in terms of content and (equally important) in terms of format. In effect, the commercial judgment of the British publishing-houses in creating libraries of 'standard authors' produced a situation in which many nineteenth-century women writers were to flourish. At the same time, this standardisation caused many works of the recent past, unorthodox in sentiment or physical format, to disappear from view.

**Literary themes and concerns**
In this new climate of moral earnestness and social flux, the nature of fiction, both male and female, changed significantly. Courtship and marriage, the lives of a few young people coming to terms with themselves and each other, the now traditional focus for the novel, continued to hold their place. But increasingly, the doubts and decisions of the heroes and heroines are set against a carefully defined social context, a panoramic background against which they may have individual or metaphoric significance. Another notable trend in Victorian fiction is towards the historical novel. Whereas Frances Burney delighted in setting her heroines in the up-to-the-minute world of fashionable society, reproducing the catchwords, conversational styles and slang of the *ton,* many Victorian writers, from George Eliot and Emily Brontë to William Makepeace Thackeray, preferred to set their fictions in the past. This is in part a question of perspective. Social panorama was irrelevant to the writers of the Regency, therefore they had no reason to be uneasy about setting their novels in the present. George Eliot preferred to deal with the social problems of the past, which had been resolved by time, rather than with the much more problematic crises of her own decade, which included, of course, the increasingly vociferous demands of women for a decent education and freedom from legal and social disabilities. She could hardly have created a Maggie Tulliver or a Dorothea Brooke of the 1860s and 70s (*The Mill on the Floss* was published in 1860, *Middlemarch* in 1871–2) without making her an overt feminist – and Eliot was profoundly unwilling to jeopardise her unique position in Victorian culture by allying herself in any way with the Victorian women's movement.[4]

This attitude of George Eliot's, even given that by the 1870s she enjoyed a highly authoritative status, is a testimonial to the continued difficulties, even in the new moral climate outlined earlier, of the woman writer versus the culture in which she lived. George Eliot's position depended on her singularity, as the position of acceptable women writers often does. To permit herself to be associated in the public mind with women's concerns at large would drag her down rather than elevating the position of the others – a justifiable fear which she demonstrably shares with such notable late twentieth-century novelists as Doris Lessing. The context for such a fear of identification with women's causes is the often astounding statements of blank prejudice and *ad feminam* criticism which survive from the Victorian era. One J.M. Ludlow, writing a review of Elizabeth Gaskell's *Ruth* in the *North British Review* in 1853, declared that only mothers ought to write novels, thus disposing on principle of Jane Austen, Maria Edgeworth and Frances Burney, to say nothing of the Brontës and George Eliot:

...what is to become of the women who remain unmarried, and yet have gifts such as fully qualify them to do good service in literature? Gently, and with all reverence must we tell them – Endeavour to find for your gifts other employments...Because you have leisure, which the wife and mother has not, spend that leisure upon others...To you belongs the daily working, the drudgery of all charitable institutions...

This is particularly insidious as a dismissal, since very few women writers of any real ambition or achievement in the eighteenth and nineteenth centuries were married, or mothers.

The Poet Laureate, Robert Southey, wrote a notoriously discouraging letter to Charlotte Brontë: 'literature cannot be the business of a woman's life, and it ought not to be.' Nineteenth-century criticism tended to cope with unquestionably talented writing by such a woman as George Eliot by claiming that she had a 'masculine mind'. She quite evidently had no such thing, though it is certainly true that she quietly appropriated an unhurriedly omniscient mode of story-telling and an unabashed proclamation of the larger symbolic significance of the story she told, which was at the time a masculine rather than a feminine mode of discourse. Thus, in a society which was nearly as sensitive to the difference in masculine and feminine speech-patterns as is twentieth-century Japan, George Eliot's style caused unease and puzzlement. The nearest thing to a feminist heroine that she ever permitted herself, Maggie Tulliver, responds with sharp covetousness to her first sight of all the books in her brother's tutor's study – 'How I should like to have as many books as that!' – and is promptly slapped down by her brother. This rare introduction by George Eliot of a scene which points to women's lives sometimes being too small for them is described by an anonymous reviewer for the *Dublin University Magazine* as one where 'the woman's hand is unmistakably shown, and the lack of true perspective becomes most palpable.'[5] The phrase 'lack of true perspective' in the quotation above is worth noticing. Perspective, by definition, is the view from a particular standpoint. Movement in any direction will cause a shift in perspective. And Virginia Woolf has this to say of women and the novel:

When a woman comes to write a novel, she will find that she is perpetually wishing to alter the established values – to make serious what appears insignificant to a man, and trivial what is to him important. And, for that, of course, she will be criticized; for the critic of the opposite sex will be genuinely puzzled and surprised by an attempt to alter the current scale of values, and will see in it not merely a difference of view, but a view that is weak, or trivial, or sentimental, because it differs from his own.[6]

All this Dublin reviewer is saying, then, is that women's perceptions do not count, and ought not to be expressed, an assertion which has an emotional, not a logical basis.

# The novel

## Mary Shelley

Mary Shelley (1797–1851) is one of the earliest women novelists of the nineteenth century, and very much an anomaly among the highly respectable women writers of her time. She was pregnant by sixteen, and eloped with another woman's husband. She was a second-generation feminist, the daughter of Mary Wollstonecraft, who wrote *A Vindication of the Rights of Woman,* and the inadvertent cause of Wollstonecraft's tragic death from puerperal fever a few days after Mary's birth. Mary Shelley published seven novels, but the one which has brought her lasting fame is her first, *Frankenstein; or, The Modern Prometheus* (1818). This was not the first science fiction to be written by a woman, an honour which probably goes to Margaret Cavendish's *The Description of the New Blazing World* (1666), but it is a uniquely powerful one. The story of a scientist who creates a monster which ultimately destroys him has proved an extraordinarily potent modern myth, which informs, among other things, the terms of our current debates about nuclear power and test-tube babies. Mary Shelley was the first to raise, in a focused literary form, the question of whether the powers of the scientist should be limited by moral considerations. In its own century, Frankenstein's nameless creature was more easily seen as a symbol of working-class revolt, evoked as such by George Canning, Foreign Secretary in 1824, and by Elizabeth Gaskell (*Mary Barton,* ch. 15).[7]

It has been easy for critics of women's writing to see it as naïve and spontaneous. Mary Shelley's novel was not, as the critic Mario Praz once insultingly said, 'a passive reflection of some of the wild fantasies which were living in the air round her', and neither was it an unconsidered, direct response to her ghastly experience of maternity. Although it is the result of an intensely personal meditation on the creation of life and the responsibilities owed by parents to their children, it is also a reasoned and tightly focused summary of two generations of radical European thought, in particular Rousseau's notion of the intrinsic virtue of the noble savage, and the subsequent debates about the relationship of the individual to society. Mary Shelley was as capable of mediating experience through her literary inheritance as any of her male contemporaries. It may be stressed that very few of the adaptations of this work for any medium do any kind of justice to its qualities.

*Frankenstein* is not Mary Shelley's only work of speculative fiction. Her much later work, *The Last Man* (1826), is also an extrapolation from contemporary society, set in the year 2073. It begins with the abdication of the last monarch of Britain, and ends with a plague that wipes out the entire population of the earth. The plot displays her imaginative range as a political thinker; her handling of the political repercussions of this universal disaster are confident, and carry conviction. Different types of people react in very different ways to the approach of death: some seek pleasure while they still can; others relapse into despair, turn to God, or remain manipulative to the last. This is not so much a novel about individual character, as about the range of human possibility.

Another aspect of the life and work of Mary Shelley which sets her apart from most other women writers of her time was her unusual involvement with male intellectual and creative circles. Rather than associating with other women writers, she was part of the circle of radical thinkers which included her father, William Godwin, her husband, Percy Bysshe Shelley, and her friends Lord Byron, Samuel Taylor Coleridge and Leigh Hunt. The only other woman writer of note who was at all connected with the Godwins' circle was Dorothy Wordsworth (1771–1855), whose private *Journal,* written between 1798 and 1803, is a masterpiece of description from nature, and the quarry from which her brother William drew material for some of his best-known poems (including 'Daffodils'). However, William Wordsworth and his sister had passed out of William Godwin's life before Mary was of an age to benefit by the association; and the literary ladies personally known to Godwin, like Mrs Inchbald, refused to go near the scandalous Mary Wollstonecraft, or later, her daughter, so as not to sully their own reputations.

By contrast, such writers as Jane Austen, Maria Edgeworth and Mary Brunton were completely detached from the currents of radical and metropolitan intellectualism, but assiduously read one another's works, corresponded, and took incidents, aspects of plot and character from one another's writing. Thus, *Frankenstein,* though it is one of the most widely known works to have been written by a nineteenth-century Englishwoman, remains outside the tradition of women's writing.

### Harriet Martineau

The period between the end of the writing careers of Maria Edgeworth and Jane Austen and the rise of Mrs Gaskell, the Brontës and George Eliot was a fallow one for women's writing, apart from the independent figure of Mary Shelley. It is perhaps for this reason that Harriet Martineau (1802–76) achieved considerable success with her only novel, *Deerbrook* (1839). She was already famous by then for her non-fiction, best-selling *Illustrations of Political Economy* (1832–4), and continued to write as an immensely successful journalist for the rest of her life. Her novel focuses on the relationship between two sisters, one more beautiful, the other more attractive in character. Their relationship is delicately balanced, especially since the beautiful Hester has always tended to be jealous of her sister, with whom her own husband, Mr Hope, had fallen in love initially before marrying Hester. The complicated human relationships are set against the social, and particularly the economic, structure of the community as a whole, and thus the sufferings of individuals are carefully set in context. The novel follows Jane Austen's fictional prescription, in dealing with two or three families in a country village, but its earnest informativeness and concern with exploring the financial, as well as emotional, springs of action mark it as plainly the product of a later era.

### Elizabeth Gaskell

Elizabeth Gaskell (1810–65) is one of the first major women writers to combine her literary career with the duties of a respectable wife and mother. Anything but a social radical, as far as her expressed views went, her justification of her own and Charlotte Brontë's writing was characteristic of herself and her era:

> When a man becomes an author, it is probably merely a change of employment to him. He takes a portion of that time which has hitherto been devoted to some other study or pursuit...and another merchant or lawyer, or doctor, steps into his vacant place and probably does quite as well as he. But no other can take up the quiet, regular duties of the daughter, the wife, or the mother, as well as she whom God has appointed to fill that particular place: a woman's principal work in life is hardly ever left to her own choice; nor can she drop the domestic charges devolving on her as an individual, for the exercise of the most splendid talents that were ever bestowed. And yet she must not shrink from the extra responsibility implied by the very fact of her possessing such talents. She must not hide her gift in a napkin [a reference to Luke 19:20]; it was meant for the use and service of others. In an humble and faithful spirit must she labour to do what is not impossible, or God would not have set her to do it.[8]

This is a mid-Victorian statement of what is sometimes now referred to as the myth of the superwoman, but the serene, if stern, religious faith which underlies it gives it at least a more coherent rationale than that of the twentieth-century version. It is also an effective answer to J.M. Ludlow, quoted a few pages back. Mrs Gaskell's statement of individual moral responsibility for the proper use of one's own gifts has moved a considerable distance from earlier women novelists' concern about the propriety of venturing into print. Moreover, the sense that the proper subject-matter for women writers should be strictly and narrowly delimited, deeply felt by the nineteenth-century critical establishment, is repeatedly flouted by all the great women writers of the era. Elizabeth Barrett Browning wrote definitively to a shocked reader of Harriet Beecher Stowe's *Uncle Tom's Cabin* (1851–2), the anti-slavery epic which in the eyes of many lighted the fuse of the American Civil War:

Is it possible that you think a woman has no business with questions like the question of slavery? Then she had better use a pen no more. She had better subside into slavery and concubinage herself, I think, as in the times of old, shut herself up with the Penelopes in the 'women's apartment', and take no rank among thinkers and speakers.[9]

It is not a point of view which Frances Burney, or even Jane Austen, would have felt herself able to adopt. We are a long way from the idea of two inches of ivory as the suitable ground for women's writing. Respectable, religious Mrs Gaskell, who is now mostly remembered for the quite astonishingly innocuous, sub-Austen village comedy of *Cranford* (1851–3), also wrote on working-class Communism and the conflict of labour and capital, social injustice, urban misery, prostitution and unmarried motherhood (particularly in *Mary Barton* (1848) and *Ruth* (1853)). Her descriptions of the conditions of life in the Manchester slums leave nothing to the imagination once one understands the Victorian vocabulary; when she speaks of 'heaps of ashes' in the street, she means human excrement, and would be so understood; similarly 'he had opened a door, but only for an instant; it led into a back cellar, with a grating instead of a window, down which dropped the moisture from pigsties, and worse abominations' (*Mary Barton,* ch.6) needs little effort of the imagination, for all the colourless choice of words. Mrs Gaskell was not a sheltered, housebound lady lacking in direct experience. Her direct knowledge of the lives of the poor probably exceeded that of Dickens, who also wrote vividly and movingly on their sufferings. As the wife of a Unitarian minister in Manchester, it was her business to go about the city and see what could be done to relieve suffering, which brought her into direct confrontation with the worst Manchester had to offer.[10] When *Mary Barton* first came out, anonymously, it was praised by the *Athenaeum* for its tough and fair-minded exposition of class conflict and its understanding of the roots of proletarian resistance. Once the book was known to have been written by a woman, the tone of critical comment changed; the love story which is one strand of her narrative became the main focus, and the political analysis was suddenly found to be emotional and lacking in objectivity.[11]

*North and South* (1854–5) follows *Mary Barton* in being concerned with the roots of class conflict. Its other aim, as the title expresses, is to promote understanding between the people of the rural South of England, and the industrial North. The heroine, Margaret Hale, is forced to move to a dirty, cotton-spinning industrial city, and takes with her a full set of Southern English prejudices. She becomes deeply sympathetic to the troubles of the working-class community, and clashes with the industrialists, particularly the stubborn, hot-headed John Thornton. Politically opposed, the pair are temperamentally compatible, and after the various roots of social conflict have been carefully and sympathetically explored, they are brought together, a symbol of a more humane and less exploitative relationship between workers and industrialists, and of increased mutual understanding between North and South.

Mrs Gaskell's most daring book, the one which caused her the most trouble with her contemporaries, is *Ruth,* the story of an unmarried mother. Mrs Gaskell loads the scales of sympathy in favour of her heroine to an extent which to the modern reader is almost comic. Ruth is lively, innately virtuous, very young, motherless, and 'yields' to her upper-class seducer in a way which removes all possible blame which the reader might attach to her and transfers it to him. However, in the mid-nineteenth century, the world at large agreed with the censorious Mr Bradshaw, who employs Ruth as a governess until he discovers that she is not married, a fact which to his mind makes her a completely different creature, long though he has known her:

> 'Oh, Mr Bradshaw! Ruth was not depraved, and you know it. You cannot have seen her – have known her daily, all these years, without acknowledging that!'...
>
> 'I saw her daily – I did *not* know her. If I had known her, I should have known she was fallen and depraved, and consequently not fit to come into my house, not to associate with my pure children.' (Vol. III, ch. 3)

It is hard to realise now that Mrs Gaskell was making a courageous and unusual stand in endorsing such views, but she was. Single motherhood can never be easy, but English law governing illegitimacy used to be vengeful and punitive to an extent which it is now almost impossible to imagine. Single mothers were not tolerated: in the seventeenth and eighteenth centuries, an unmarried pregnant girl could be hounded out of her home and across the country, because the financial responsibility for a bastard fell on the parish where the child was born, so each set of officials naturally tried to get rid of the girl before it was too late. Though implementation in practice gradually relaxed, this treatment of unmarried mothers remained law until the 1950s.[12]

The vengeance of the law was not directed against unmarried mothers to the same extent in the mid-nineteenth century (though 'the workhouse' still loomed before them), but the vengeance of society most assuredly was. Where Mrs Gaskell may have caused even more offence, however, is in her stout insistence that the unmarried father's guilt is as great as his partner's. At the beginning of the century, Jane Austen's *Sense and Sensibility* includes the romantic Willoughby who is discovered, as the story progresses, to have seduced and abandoned a girl (ch. 31). This is glossed over, even by the sensible Elinor, once she actually sees him again: 'Willoughby, in spite of all his faults, excited a degree of commiseration for the sufferings produced by them' (ch. 45). In this early work, Austen is still accepting the social mores of the Regency; and it is Willoughby's self-inflicted sufferings which are the object of Elinor's commiseration. Upright

Mrs Gaskell, on the other hand, makes it quite clear that anything which is a sin for a woman is a sin for a man – though, of course, sin is something perceived by the eyes of God, for which the sinner must answer at the Last Judgment; and crime or misdemeanour, which are human categorisations, are identified and punished in this world. Ruth and her lover have both sinned, but she has committed a social crime, and he has not.

## The Brontës

Charlotte Brontë and Elizabeth Gaskell were personal friends. Mrs Gaskell is only now attaining adequate recognition of her achievement as a novelist. By contrast, not only has Charlotte Brontë become a standard author, but the Brontë family story has become a literary legend (largely created by Mrs Gaskell's biography of Charlotte) as compelling as that of Byron; the story of three doomed, consumptive geniuses immured on the Yorkshire moors with their wastrel brother – like all legends, its relationship to historical reality is somewhat tangential.

The Brontës (Charlotte, 1816–55, Emily, 1818–48, Anne, 1820–49) struck a new note in English literature with the passion of their writing and the stark violence of their plots. All three deal intensely with aspects of women's experience, their writing richly textured with details at once symbolic and sensual (as, for instance, the use of the colours red and white in both *Wuthering Heights* and *Jane Eyre*). Their virginal heroines are neither passive nor sexually frigid, and the strength of their feelings about the men they encounter inevitably brought upon their authors accusations of 'coarseness'.

One aspect of female fantasy which is particularly significant to both Emily and Charlotte Brontë is the extreme attractiveness of a man who is capable of seeing the heroine not merely as a sexual being (though that is important), but as anarchic, dangerous, savage and powerful. It is not delightful, they tell us through the structure of their narratives, and sometimes explicitly, to be persistently trivialised and regarded as both less and more than human. Emily and Charlotte Brontë are the classic exponents of this need to be recognised. Edward Rochester, in *Jane Eyre* (1847), discerns an elemental fire in the slight, pale, demure figure of his bastard ward's young governess. Heathcliff and Catherine, in *Wuthering Heights* (1847), recognise one another's qualities from the start, though Catherine allows herself to be seduced, in a reversal of conventional assumptions, into respectable marriage and ordinary middle-class feminine standards, and suffers and dies for it, just as Mrs Gaskell's Ruth suffers for her transgression of the conventional moral code. The peculiar attraction of dark, ugly, exasperating M. Paul in *Villette* (1853) is that he sees Lucy Snowe, so quiet and pale that other people are barely capable of registering that she even exists, as a true scarlet woman, sensual, sexual, proud and dangerously intellectual. How deeply and truly flattering to find that one's satanic individualism, one's wayward, unspoken rejection of the social cult of maidenly self-abnegation should be so clearly visible to this man's discerning eye.[13] Thus, Jane Eyre, Catherine Earnshaw and Lucy Snowe are all in a position to look one particular man in the eye, as an equal, to address him, in Baudelaire's phrase, as 'mon semblable, mon frère'.[14] The egalitarian relationship of brother and sister was the natural mode for all the Brontës, whose much-loved brother, Branwell, had in happier days participated fully with them in their communal fantasy-life of stories and drama. In Charlotte's case, the free association of equals fought in her mind with the equally significant but hierarchical relationship of teacher and pupil. Emily and Anne, however, had no equivalent pull towards hierarchic relationships. Anne Brontë's second novel, *The Tenant of Wildfell Hall* (1848) (which Charlotte disapproved of),[15] gives us a heroine who is older, more experienced (in every sense, including the sexual), and wealthier than the man who loves her, thereby effectively reversing the novelists' by now traditional paradigm of older man and younger girl. Issues of hierarchy are simply irrelevant between wolfish Heathcliff and Catherine – 'Nelly, I *am* Heathcliff', says Catherine (ch. 9).

'[Her] mind contains nothing but hunger, rebellion, and rage', wrote Matthew Arnold of Charlotte Brontë in 1853.[16] This was a statement of the moral outrage generated by all three of the Brontë sisters, one of the many voices which cried out in condemnation of their savage and 'unfeminine' writing. In our own century, since feminist criticism, at least, has come to value the capacity to generate outrage very highly, such remarks have changed their significance from positive to negative. 'Rage' and 'subversion' have become as much unthinking clichés for the appropriate qualities of women's writing, as 'modest purity' was in the last century. It makes no more sense to claim that women ought always to be angry than to claim that they ought never to be angry. Another problem for feminist criticism is the tenet that women should maintain, at all times, an acute consciousness of gender. But to lay down what all women ought to do is inevitably inimical to individual talent.

Emily Brontë is the least obviously feminist of the three sisters, even though she can hardly be faulted for not 'confronting her rage'. Her thought is androgynous, since she was not (in her writing, or her remarkable life)[17] engaged with the petty and degrading warfare of contemporary social intercourse between the sexes. *Wuthering Heights* inhabits the territory of the ballad (a genre which had become by the nineteenth century the possession of marginalised groups: women, regional working-class communities and travellers); it is a strange, repetitive story of heredity and environment re-enacted in two generations, showing the destructive effect of Heathcliff, a figure very much in the tradition of Milton's Satan, on an otherwise hermetically enclosed world of isolated minor Yorkshire gentry. Although, in *Wuthering Heights*, Linton does effectively break the spirit of his savage bride, Catherine, showing that Emily Brontë was quite aware of the terrible power exercised even by weak men over strong women, the focus of the novel is elsewhere. The unexpected message of *Wuthering Heights* is that escape is always possible. Catherine escapes from Linton into death, which is presented here, and again with Heathcliff himself, as a perfectly straightforward option – indeed, it is one Emily Brontë took herself.[18] Death, for Catherine and Heathcliff, may be merely the resort of a captured tiger, but it is a resort none the less. Conventionally feminine Isabella Linton leaves Heathcliff after her marriage to him, in defiance of the law and social convention. In the next generation, Cathy and Hareton escape Heathcliff's malign and destructive power through their love.

Not the least achievement of the sisters is the expansion of the territory of the English novel, not only in terms of character (readers of *Wuthering Heights,* for instance, are required to take uncultivated dialect-speakers entirely seriously), but in terms of narrative mode and range. *Wuthering Heights* is perhaps the purest product of the intense, introverted fantasising world of the Brontës' childhood in a remote Yorkshire parsonage, in which the three girls, with their only brother Branwell, influenced each other's literary development almost to the exclusion of all outside models in the production of obsessively visualised otherworldly sagas of passion, politics and betrayal.

*The Tenant of Wildfell Hall* is the only overtly feminist novel produced by any of the three. Though it is structurally flawed, it is an eloquent argument against patriarchal control of women, and a devastating indictment of the principles of education for boys which allowed them to grow up completely self-indulgent and at the mercy of their own uncontrolled passions. Helen Huntingdon, the heroine, takes her child and leaves her husband to his drinking and whoring, not only for her own sake, but for the sake of her son's future, earning her living subsequently as a professional painter. This removal of a son from his father's control was a very bold step indeed. A writer contemporary with the Brontës, Caroline Norton, was separated from her husband, and denied all access to her children by him, which caused her agonising grief and anxiety. Being made of stern stuff, she initiated a feminist movement for reform of the law, and succeeded in getting the Infants Custody Act passed in 1839, giving mothers against whom adultery had not been proved the right to the custody of children under seven, and access to older ones. Anne Brontë, in introducing this theme, is boldly declaring herself as a subversive and anti-establishment thinker.

Charlotte Brontë was less extraordinary in her outlook than Emily, who was one of the few people in history who actually lived according to the slogan of the American Revolution, 'give me liberty or give me death'.[19] Most people, and certainly most women, have found some way of reconciling themselves to living with some degree of dependency.[20]

Anne, though better able than Emily to deal with the outside world, was deeply feminist and egalitarian in her views, if we may judge from her published work. Charlotte, however, found the fundamental assertion of self which is so remarkable a feature of *Jane Eyre* – 'Do you think [says Jane, addressing Rochester], because I am poor, obscure, plain, and little, I am soulless and heartless? You think wrong! – I have as much soul as you, – and full as much heart!' – complicated by the need, her own and Jane's, to look up to a man, and call him 'master'. The eponymous heroine of *Jane Eyre* emphasises an ambiguity: she withholds her assent. Before Charlotte Brontë gives her a name, class or age, we are introduced to her sense of herself as a person under siege, fighting back against a powerful and hostile world. Yet in Charlotte Brontë's novel *Shirley* (1849), she claimed to have drawn a verbal portrait of Emily, who had died in the previous year. To anyone who has read Emily Brontë's own writings, this is almost as unexpected as Jane Austen's statement that *Mansfield Park* was to be about ordination.[21] Some incidents in the story of Shirley Keeldar were taken from Emily's life, notably Emily's resolutely branding herself with a hot iron after having been bitten by a dog suspected of rabies.[22] But we have no excuse from any incident of Emily's known life, or from her surviving writing, for thinking that she ever yearned to live under the protection of male authority. In fact, M. Heger, who taught both Emily and Charlotte, and knew them well, commented that Emily 'should have been a great navigator' and commented on 'her stubborn tenacity of will, which rendered her obtuse to all reasoning where her own wishes, or her own sense of right, were concerned.'[23] Yet Charlotte's heroine ends up insisting on being dominated by her older, wiser tutor-lover, and chirping winsomely, 'Will you be good to me, and never tyrannise?' (ch. 36); and it is only too plain that Charlotte has shifted ground from the memory of Emily as she was, to Emily as she would have liked her to be. She once said of her younger sister, 'Emily is not quite so tractable or open as I could wish...with profound and never-shaken esteem, it is a small thing that they should vex us occasionally by, what appear to us, unreasonable and headstrong notions.'[24] In *Shirley,* she revised the character of a beloved but 'unreasonable' and 'headstrong' sister who desired liberty above every human good, into the far more familiar model of a proud Kate who was just waiting for the right Petruchio: a tameable shrew.

On the other hand, Charlotte Brontë's *Villette* is remarkable for experiment with narrative and a much more radical subject-matter. The strange, abrupt story is told by a narrator who is distracted and depressed, at times actually hallucinatory. A crucial episode in the novel is Charlotte's ambivalently admiring portrait of the great actress Rachel (under the name of Vashti), which celebrates the actress's incisive power and commanding will to self-expression, though Vashti/Rachel's polar opposition to the expected character of the nineteenth-century woman is ambiguously acknowledged by identifying her with Satan – 'Fallen, insurgent, banished, she remembers the heaven where she rebelled' (ch. 23). Satan, a figure who was still seen very much in the light of Milton's extraordinarily powerful characterisation in *Paradise Lost* (1667), was a tragic hero as well as an embodiment of evil, and important as such to both Charlotte and Emily Brontë. This dangerous Vashti, then, is specifically set against the 'pulpy', formless femininity whose sole *raison d'être* is the physical flesh – Peter Paul Rubens and 'all the army of his fat women'. It is therefore significant that Lucy Snowe herself, later on in the novel, is forced not only to take part in a play, but to act the role of a man.

### Dinah Craik and Geraldine Jewsbury

Two other, very different, novels of the mid-nineteenth century are of lasting interest: the best-selling *John Halifax, Gentleman* (1856), by Dinah Maria Craik (1826–87), and *Zoë* (1845), by Geraldine Jewsbury (1812–80). The plot of *John Halifax* was extremely topical in the great days of new-made wealth from manufacturing industry. Its subject is a 'self-made man', first seen as a literally penniless fourteen-year-old, who achieves substantial wealth and marriage to a girl of a much higher social class entirely by means of his innate qualities of nobility, honour, self-discipline and hard work. The main theme of the novel is that John Halifax's moral qualities are those of a 'true gentleman' (the qualification is frequently insisted on), and that his upward social mobility is in a direct way the seeking of his proper level in society. This meritocratic thesis was evidently a very acceptable one to the novel-reading public. Another attractive feature of the novel is its strong regional flavour. It is set in Gloucestershire, and without sounding like a guide-book, Dinah Craik is delicate and precise in her evocation of a very specific landscape.

*Zoë* is a very different type of novel. Its heroine, like that of Elizabeth Barrett Browning's long poem *Aurora Leigh,* is identified at the outset as a free spirit by her Anglo-Greek parentage: in the nineteenth century Greece carried strong connotations of intellectual freedom and liberty. Like Aurora, Zoë receives a boy's rather than a girl's education, confirming her independence of mind. Another clue to the way that the author wishes us to regard her is provided by her name: 'zoe' means 'life' in Greek. Her story is juxtaposed with that of an English Catholic priest, Everhard Burrows, whose spiritual crises are based on Jewsbury's own. Zoë and Everhard fall in love, though Everhard's vows prevent him from declaring himself. The novel is ahead of its time in its treatment of religious, moral and philosophic issues, and was strongly criticised for its indecency when it first came out: its integration of a plot based on the life of a woman with consideration of much wider issues provided a useful model for George Eliot's philosophical fiction.

## George Eliot

The most respected of all nineteenth-century women novelists is George Eliot (1819–80). She achieved a unique position of moral authority in her own lifetime, despite the scandal of her sharing her life with G.H. Lewes, to whom she was not married. She is unusual among Victorian women writers (though she shares this quality with Elizabeth Barrett Browning) in being formidably and exhaustively well educated. She was a translator, journalist, essayist and editor long before she became a novelist. Her deep familiarity with continental scholars and philosophers – David Friedrich Strauss, Ludwig Feuerbach, Benedict de Spinoza – placed her among the intellectual élite of her day, which gave her a considerable advantage in wringing an uncondescending respect from male critics.[25] However, she owed a great deal as a novelist to the writings of other women. As Gillian Beer comments:

> We tend to overlook the creative importance of writers who are no longer much read; perhaps that is why the urgency of George Eliot's response to [Geraldine] Jewsbury and [Fredrika] Bremer has been ignored. Their novels concentrated George Eliot's attention on problems crucial in her own art.[26]

Women's writings create yardsticks, models and precedents for their successors, particularly their female successors. Jane Austen could not have written as she did without Frances Burney and Mary Brunton before her. George Eliot, in turn, struck off at a tangent from Jane Austen's *Emma*, which Lewes had made her read, to create *Adam Bede* (1859). Hetty Sorrel, in the same novel, who is seduced and abandoned, would not have been written as she was had not George Eliot had a revisionary impulse towards Mrs Gaskell's *Ruth*. Hetty is a much more ordinary girl than Ruth, with none of her predecessor's saintly qualities. She invites her own destruction in a way that Ruth does not, and hence is very much more realistic. It is only fair to Mrs Gaskell to add that George Eliot, when *Adam Bede* was published, was still sheltering behind a masculine persona, so the cool, detached, Thackeray-like worldly wisdom with which she anatomises the unfortunate Hetty did not strike painfully upon the public consciousness; whereas Mrs Gaskell, writing as a woman, had to withstand severe criticism for her imprudence.[27] George Eliot also read Charlotte Brontë with attention, and many other women novelists besides. In addition, she read a great deal of non-fictional writing by women, feminist and otherwise, notably by Harriet Martineau, her journalist rival, and Barbara Bodichon, her friend. The 'Woman Question' pervades *Middlemarch*, albeit somewhat indirectly. The distinctive character of George Eliot's fiction derives from its measured, meditative, authoritative style, and the imperative demands made by the unhurriedly omniscient narrator for an enlargement of human sympathy on the part of the reader.

Dull, ordinary people, leading dull, ordinary, provincial lives are presented in their passionate individuality. She is scrupulous in engaging the reader's awareness that unattractive or unsympathetic characters, though they may be thwarting the path of the heroine, are themselves struggling with the complexities of life, and fully capable of suffering. The dreadful Mr Casaubon, a sterile, peevish, dried-up pedant, is still given a claim on the reader. Chapter 29 of *Middlemarch* (1871–2) begins as follows;

> One morning, some weeks after her arrival at Lowick, Dorothea – but why always Dorothea? Was her point of view the only possible one with regard to this marriage?…In spite of the blinking eyes and white moles objectionable to Celia, and the want of muscular curve which was morally painful to Sir James, Mr Casaubon had an intense consciousness within him, and was spiritually a-hungered like the rest of us.

This shifting of emphasis away from the young people who, as always, form the pivot-points of the narrative, and towards an awareness of the whole human landscape within which they are set, is George Eliot's great contribution to the development of the English novel. Her religious and philosophical interests underlie her construction and treatment of character, but they are expressed by the action, rather than merely intruded.[28] Her didactic intentions, though expressed mostly through humdrum characters and undramatic incident (there are exceptions, such as the fate of Hetty Sorrel in *Adam Bede,* and the flood in *The Mill on the Floss* (1860): both these are early works) were central to her fiction.

*Adam Bede* was suggested by Harriet Beecher Stowe's second anti-slavery novel, *Dred* (1856), which Eliot had enthusiastically reviewed for the *Westminster Review*: 'why', she enquired, 'can we not have pictures of religious life among the industrial classes in England, as interesting as Mrs Stowe's pictures of religious life among the negroes?' It might not occur to a modern reader of *Adam Bede* that its chief interest was as a picture of working-class religion, but this clearly formed a large part of Eliot's intention.

*Silas Marner* (1861) is an unusual novel in that sexual love plays a very subordinate part in the plot, which turns chiefly on religion, parenthood and the effect of society on the individual. In a sense, it is Eliot's most feminist novel: the thesis that attending to the daily care of a little child is a medium for spiritual and human growth is a very unusual one. The hero, Silas Marner, is a handloom linen weaver, which was a conspicuously lonely and isolated way of life. Having been driven by a false charge of theft out of the little religious sect in which he was brought up, he seeks no further social contact, but becomes an embittered recluse and a miser. His final point of despair is reached when his gold, his only consolation, is stolen – in fact, by the squire's wicked son. The lives of the squire's family, at the head and in the heart of the local community of Raveloe, and the completely isolated Silas are strangely intertwined, for Silas finds and adopts the older son's unacknowledged daughter, whose mother died while attempting to bring the child to Raveloe through the snow. Silas, thus unexpectedly a single parent, cares for the child devotedly, and finds himself gradually forced to join the life of the village in the interests of his adopted daughter Eppie. Even his gold, ultimately, is found and restored to him. Meanwhile, Eppie's real father, who has no children by his legitimate and acknowledged marriage, attempts to reclaim his child; but she refuses to leave Silas, and marries a working-class man. One strand in the novel is the transforming power of unselfish love; another is the effect of environment on character. Silas's very emotional openness and vulnerability make his unjust expulsion from his sect an intolerable blow; once he has a responsive object to love, the natural sweetness of his character reasserts itself. Eppie's natural father believes that he could reclaim the child at any time, since she is genetically of his stock; in fact, since she is brought up in a poor weaver's cottage among village folk, her habits of speech and thought are those of a working-class girl.

The later *Felix Holt the Radical* (1866) is, like Mrs Gaskell's *North and South,* a political novel, contrasting the perceptions of characters in different social positions. Its radical and reforming hero, Felix Holt, attempts to convince the labouring classes by his own example that education and independence are the keys of personal contentment and social justice. He is contrasted with the fundamentally decent but far less high-minded Harold Transome, owner of the local estate, who stands for Parliament, and sees no objection to undermining the democratic process by recognised, though not entirely honourable, forms of bribery and corruption. The novel as a whole raises a series of questions relating to the dichotomy between law and justice, personal morality and social convention. The heroine, Esther Lyon, is faced with a choice between the emblematic lives of these two men, and ultimately chooses Felix, honour and poverty.

George Eliot's last great novel, *Daniel Deronda* (1876), was written out of her consciousness of the position she had achieved as a moral arbiter in English society, with the conscious intention of emulating Harriet Beecher Stowe's awakening of the American public conscience on the subject of slavery. She wrote to Mrs Stowe to tell her so. The subject she chose for this assault on public complacency was Zionism and English anti-semitism. It is characteristic of the expectations which readers bring to the work of women writers that most people (readers and professional critics alike) have tended to hurry over the story of Daniel Deronda himself and the whole Jewish side of the plot, and to follow F.R. Leavis in believing that the novel is, or should be, essentially about Gwendolen Harleth.[29] Gwendolen's story is certainly gripping, in a relatively conventional way, as the ill-educated, self-willed proud beauty is pressured by her mother's need for financial support into marrying a wealthy sadist whom she believes, from his respectful behaviour as a suitor, that she will be able to manage. Grandcourt, her husband, is without doubt one of the nastiest characters in fiction, and one of the very, very few from whom George Eliot withholds all sympathetic involvement. We are thus put in a difficult ethical position when we find ourselves breathing a sigh of relief as Gwendolen passively allows him to drown before her eyes. By contrast, the interwoven story of Deronda's gradual rediscovery of his Jewish roots cannot by its nature offer the reader the same kind of excitement. In one of her periodic ascensions of the prophetic tripod, George Eliot attempted magisterially to weld the two halves together in the reader's interest; she was concerned to account for the propriety of introducing the story of a frivolous and historically insignificant girl into her great canvas of major international events:

> What, in the midst of that mighty drama, are girls and their blind visions? They are the Yea or Nay of that good for which men are enduring and fighting. In these delicate vessels is borne onward through the ages the treasure of human affections.                      (ch.11)

In the judgment of posterity, the apology should have been directed the other way, partly because the insistence on high moral seriousness in fiction which was made in the 1860s and 70s has been eroded by subsequent generations. The personal and political were, in her understanding, necessarily interwoven.

George Eliot's awareness of the cramped social and intellectual life of contemporary Englishwomen took her in a direction different from the Brontës' passionate avowals of spiritual equality. Her religious sense led her to see the spiritual depth which can be the unexpected good of a physically circumscribed life. Thus, the complete failure of Maggie Tulliver in *The Mill on the Floss,* or Dorothea Brooke in *Middlemarch,* to lead lives at all commensurate with their abilities is not seen as entirely negative. The figure of Antigone, from Greek myth, is referred to several times by George Eliot. Antigone, caught in a terrible family conflict, heroically renounced her own chance of marriage and future happiness in order to bury her brother, an action which condemned her to death. Dorothea Brooke is referred to as 'a sort of Christian Antigone – sensuous force controlled by spiritual passion' (ch. 19); Mirah Lapidoth in *Daniel Deronda* identifies with Antigone (ch. 32); and Maggie Tulliver is genuinely forced to a choice between the conditional and censorious affection of her brother, and the ardent affections of two separate lovers. On every occasion of trial, her loyalties remain with her brother. George Eliot has in all these instances used the ancient Greek figure of Antigone as a device to articulate the tensions between women's social or familial constraints and their human aspirations in her own time.

## Margaret Oliphant and Frances Trollope

The Brontës and George Eliot were hard acts to follow. The next generation of women writers was less distinguished, and essentially derivative in its aims and achievements. Jane Eyre was the mother of many daughters; Mr Rochester was the father of many sons.[30] A notable characteristic of the end of the Victorian period is an ever-greater market for novels, and an increasing number of women writing successfully for money. Margaret Oliphant (1828–97) struggled valiantly to support herself, her children and her nephews. Her 'Carlingford' books, in particular, are well observed and very entertaining, but she was debarred from attempting any more ambitious writing by the sheer speed at which she was forced to write. Kirsteen (1890) is one of her most interesting novels. It takes the very Scottish plot of the poor but intelligent boy who goes south to make his fortune, and constructs it round a girl, who remains single, becomes a successful couturier, and leads a happy and contented life. By Mrs Oliphant's time, a writer of competent potboilers could make a perfectly reasonable living out of it, far better than by governessing or needlework, and less unpleasantly. Another noteworthy woman who wrote entirely for money is Frances Trollope (1780–1863), mother of the novelist Anthony Trollope, whose embittered dissection of 1830s America in her travel book Domestic Manners of the Americans (1832) earned her not only notoriety, but also 600 much-needed pounds. The insatiable demands of the circulating libraries for new fiction on tried-and-true patterns created a plethora of competent, professional and unambitious writing. Mrs Trollope followed up her first success with more than twenty completely undistinguished novels on a variety of subjects, ranging from high society to slavery (her anti-slavery novel, Jonathan Jefferson Whitlaw (1836), preceded Uncle Tom's Cabin by fifteen years). Charles Reade, a novelist who gave English literature its first heroine who is a woman doctor (in A Woman-Hater (1877)), complained that his books were not distributed by the all-important small circulating libraries: 'they will only take in ladies' novels. Mrs Henry Wood, 'Ouida', Miss Braddon – these are their gods.'[31]

## Sensationalist writers

Mrs Henry Wood (1814–87), 'Ouida' (1839–1908), Rhoda Broughton (1840–1920) and Mary Braddon (1835–1915) dominated the fiction market. The end of the century is characterised by a growing sexual explicitness, a gradual loosening of the iron bands which constrained a Maggie Tulliver. It became increasingly possible for a fictional character to have some sexual experience outside wedlock without having to die for it. The sexual disgust experienced by a woman in Gwendolen Harleth's position, married to a man she detests, is expressed more and more frankly. The novels of 'Ouida' (Marie de la Ramée) were considered notoriously outspoken and immoral in their day. The heroine of Rhoda Broughton's Cometh Up as a Flower

(1867) speaks bitterly of her revolting husband: 'has he not every right to kiss my face off if he chooses, to clasp me and hold me and drag me about in whatever manner he wills, for has he not bought me?…for so many pounds of prime white flesh, he has paid a handsome price on the nail.'[32] There is nothing here about the glories of feminine self-abnegation; the best Nell hopes for is that horrid Sir Hugh will go and bother the cook instead – she can at least give him notice and leave if she dislikes it.

Mrs Henry Wood's *East Lynne* (1861) deals with an equally titillating situation. A young mother of three, more sinned against than sinning, elopes with a cad, and subsequently returns in disguise as governess to her own children, one of whom is dying of tuberculosis. Mrs Wood adheres firmly to the convention that a single mistake by a woman leads to a lifetime of remorse, expiation and the torments of conscience: 'she had found herself plunged in an abyss of horror, from which there was never more any escape; never more, never more' (Part XI). The reader's position with respect to the heroine is an interesting one: one is clearly intended to sympathise with Lady Isabel, young, aristocratic, beautiful and unlucky, and to maintain one's sympathy throughout the second half for her maternal love; equally clearly, one is intended to condemn her for leaving her husband. Thus the reader, secure in her or his own possession of the moral high ground, is invited to a more or less sadistic position of positively enjoying the suffering experienced by the unfortunate Lady Isabel.

Probably the most readable of these sensational novels by Victorian women writers is Mary Braddon's *Lady Audley's Secret* (1862). Her heroine, a past-mistress of the manipulation of her image, deserts her husband, marries bigamously, deserts her child, pushes her first husband down a well, thinks of poisoning the other, and sets fire to a hotel. It is moot which of the many things she has to hide is the 'secret' of the title. Male novelists complained of the new style of heroine who 'cometh up as a flower or throweth her husband down a well', but the books sold just the same. Lady Audley inverts the clichés of generations. The dainty, demure blonde is the villainess; the little governess is the bigamist. We are encouraged to side with the heroine, for all her villanies, and yet, of course, vice cannot triumph. Mary Braddon's solution is to have Lady Audley confess (in her ultimate stratagem?) that she is subject to hereditary insanity, and therefore not responsible for actions which to the most uninstructed eye appear motivated by intelligent self-interest. She ends her days, however, in a comfortable private lunatic asylum on the Continent, rather than on the gallows. The plea of lunacy is the only possible way out for this exuberantly wicked heroine, for whom there seems no obvious parallel later than Aphra Behn's Isabella in *The Nun, or The Fair Vow-Breaker* (1697), a sympathetically treated bigamist who murders both of her husbands within twenty-four hours (though Isabella confesses, and is executed). By contrast Mary Braddon maintains the possibility of sympathy for her heroine by ensuring that she is never actually guilty of shedding blood, regardless of her intentions. This school of writing was given its death-blow by a masterpiece of unintentional comedy, Daisy Ashford's *The Young Visiters* (1919). Daisy Ashford (1881–1972) wrote the story of Ethel and Mr Salteena when she was nine, and her innocent attempt to manipulate the conventions of the sensational novel is inimitably charming:

> I shall put some red ruge on my face said Ethel because I am very pale owing to the drains in this house.
> You will look very silly said Mr. Salteena with a dry laugh.    (ch. 2)

Daisy Ashford, sadly, never wrote an adult novel. Her talent was precocious: a large part of the charm of *The Young Visiters* lies, of course, in its naïveté, but it also shows a genuine gift for blocking out a shapely, coherent story.

### Mrs Ward
The sensational novelists did not dominate the fiction market unopposed. The enormous Victorian appetite for novels of ideas, which had made George Eliot a major public figure, also made a publishing phenomenon out of lesser, but equally serious and didactic novelists. Dinah Craik's *John Halifax, Gentleman,* which went through edition after edition, has already been discussed. An even more successful best-selling writer was Mary Ward (1851–1920), always known by her husband's name as Mrs Humphry Ward. Mrs Ward was the granddaughter of Thomas Arnold, the enormously influential headmaster of Rugby School, a niece of the poet Matthew Arnold, and herself a tireless campaigner for the underprivileged, whose most notable achievement was the creation of a national system of education and training for the mentally handicapped. Her most significant novel, *Robert Elsmere* (1888), was a runaway popular success, which sold almost a million copies in the author's lifetime, was translated into many foreign languages, and was the focus for the development of the first international copyright agreement.

*Robert Elsmere* appears an unlikely best-seller to late twentieth-century tastes. It fictionalises the dynamic religious, educational and social conflicts of the nineteenth century in the likeable and sympathetically treated person of Robert Elsmere, who becomes an energetic, intelligent and effective Anglican parson married to a woman of sincere but somewhat narrow-minded and scrupulous piety, but who is forced out of the Church by his intellectual convictions. Since the Church represents his source of status, income and employment, as well as a major part of his relationship with his wife and the centre of his spiritual life, this is a major step for him. The difficulties created by Elsmere's intellectual growth and progress away from conventional Christianity for himself and his wife, Catherine, miserably torn between passionate love of her husband and her sense of her religious duties, is treated with a tender and sympathetic insight worthy of George Eliot herself. It is plain that the novel is fundamentally a vehicle for its intellectual and moral messages, but Mrs Ward successfully brings her complex and essentially abstract material to some kind of life; her study of character is convincing in its earnestness, and she varies the narrative with love-interests, social comedy, and sketches of a wide variety of human types, from Elsmere's mercurial and somewhat fantastical Irish mother, whose character is subtly related to Elsmere's own, to the brilliantly talented and wayward Rose, Catherine's young sister, the depressive and fastidious intellectual, Langham (Elsmere's Oxford tutor), and a whole gallery of country people and urban artisans, some comic, some treated with the deepest seriousness.

The novel, technically inadequate though it is in many respects, was devoured by contemporary readers. William Gladstone, the ex-Prime Minister, described it in a private letter as 'a tremendous book', and it was deeply admired by, among others, Henry James, the painter Edward Burne-Jones, and Leo Tolstoy, who, astonishingly, admired Mrs Ward more than any other living novelist. The warmth of Tolstoy's reaction may suggest something of the special quality of *Robert Elsmere*: like the Russian novelist's *War and Peace,* it combines an interest in very large issues with a minute concern with the individual, the details of ordinary life in a wide variety of social milieux, and the portrayal of changing intellectual consciousness, with the development of ideas in a changing environment as well as physical action. Like *War and Peace,* it is also very long. Mrs Ward's frantic publishers persuaded her to prune it at proof stage so as to fit it into the standard three volumes of the nineteenth-century novel, but it is still extremely bulky.

Mrs Ward functions as a reminder of how difficult it is to sort literature into eras. Her range of interests, and the style of her mind, make her a natural successor to George Eliot (or even to Hannah More, eighty years earlier); yet she was chronologically a contemporary of D.H. Lawrence, and was still writing at the time of the First World War. Her writing did not progress: in her later years, she became a kind of literary dinosaur, unaware that she had been superseded by an entirely new way of perceiving and writing. Her later books include physical details of the modern world, such as motor-cars and telephones, but the minds and interests of her characters remain resolutely nineteenth-century. Thus, it is her earliest work, where she is genuinely reflecting the mood of an era, which is the most worth reading.

**Towards the Modernist era**

In some ways, the period between about 1890 and the First World War has a flavour of its own, transitional as it is between the Victorian era and

Modernism; more sceptical and irreverent, more sexually explicit, and more interested in experimental forms of writing. For example, George Egerton (1859–1945; her real name was Mary Dunne) wrote two collections of powerful short stories, *Keynotes* (1893) and *Discords* (1894), with cover designs by Aubrey Beardsley, dealing in a newly realistic mode with sexual trauma, infanticide and other dangerous subjects. At the same time, and in the same milieu, Ada Leverson (1862–1933), Oscar Wilde's closest female friend (and one of the few friends of either sex to offer him unhesitating support after his release from prison), wrote a series of sparkling society comedies which, like Wilde's own plays, conceal considerable depth of feeling and understanding beneath their brilliant and epigrammatic surface. Her three best novels, known collectively as *The Little Ottleys* (1908–16), deal with the same cast of characters, and centre on the deteriorating relationship between a self-absorbed and stupid man and his highly intelligent and attractive wife. All, ultimately, ends happily, with Edith Ottley in a position to marry the man who has adored her for years, and the appalling Bruce leaving for America with a woman as unappealing as himself. In the hands of a lesser writer, the Ottleys' story would simply be depressing; as it is, Ada Leverson's humour, energy and flair for expressing two or three meanings at once through the nuances of civilised conversation make it a worthy monument to the sophisticated society of *fin-de-siècle* London.

Another genre of the end of the century was the novel of rural life. The greatest names here are the very popular Constance Holme (1881–1955) and Mary Webb (1881–1927). They look back, ultimately, to Emily Brontë's *Wuthering Heights,* as romantic fiction tended to lean on the plot of *Jane Eyre,* though in a slightly different way: it was not the plot of *Wuthering Heights* which attracted imitators, so much as the atmosphere of volcanic passion within a small group of poor, unfashionable country people. The ultimate parody of this genre was *Cold Comfort Farm* (1932) by Stella Gibbons (1902–89), which has contrived to render its originals almost unreadable:

'Well, mother mine,' he said at last, 'here I am, you see. I said I would be in time for breakfast, and I have kept my word.'

His voice had a low, throaty, animal quality, a sneering warmth that wound a velvet ribbon of sexuality over the outward coarseness of the man.

Judith's breath came in long shudders. She thrust her arms deeper into her shawl. The porridge gave an ominous, leering heave; it might almost have been endowed with life, so uncannily did its movements keep pace with the human passions that throbbed above it.                    (ch. 3)

Mary Webb's *Precious Bane* (1924), which broke new ground by making its heroine physically deformed (she has a hare lip), but still capable of attracting a man, is probably the best of these stories of elemental rural passion.

## Anglo-Irish writers

Another area of growth and development in English writing at the very end of the Victorian period was Anglo-Irish literature. Oscar Wilde, Bernard Shaw and W.B. Yeats were three brilliant Irish writers of this period, but the most important woman was Lady Augusta Gregory (1852–1932). She formed part of a literary group concerned to reawaken Ireland to a sense of its own past glories, literary and historical. She was the patroness of W.B. Yeats and J.M. Synge, among others, but she was also a woman of considerable literary gifts in her own right. Her career as a playwright is discussed at the beginning of the section on twentieth-century drama, but before she became a playwright, she was already an able translator from Irish. Her *Cuchulain of Muirthemne* (1902) is a sensitive and lively version of the greatest epic of ancient Ireland, deftly toning down grotesque or sexually explicit details which would have made a literal version unacceptable to a late nineteenth-century audience, while retaining much of the spirit and character of the original text. Her presentation of the real literature of medieval Ireland in a highly readable and accessible English, based on the dialect of contemporary Irish country people near her home at Coole, was not the least of her achievements in reviving an Irish cultural identity. A comparable figure is Lady Charlotte Guest (1812–95), the translator of the national epic of Wales, the *Mabinogion* (which appeared among her Welsh translations between 1838 and 1849): the fact that Charlotte Guest's daughter Enid Layard was Lady Gregory's oldest and closest woman friend, whom she had known for years before she began writing herself, may represent a genuine connection between the two women.[33]

The remarkable collaborations of the two Irishwomen Edith Somerville (1858–1949) and Violet Martin (1862–1915) – the pen-name of the latter being 'Martin Ross' – deal with the Ireland in which Lady Gregory lived, but their intentions and focus are entirely different. Although they are skilful in rendering Irish country speech, they focus their attention rather on the Big House, the Anglo-Irish society which was in decline throughout their writing careers. Their most popular works are the *'Irish R.M.': Some Experiences of an Irish R.M.* (1899), *Further Experiences of an Irish R.M.* (1908) and *In Mr Knox's Country* (1915). In these collections of comic episodes, an Englishman, Major Yeates, is made a Resident Magistrate in rural Ireland, and finds that he is not only cheated by the Irish, but outgeneralled by the Anglo-Irish gentry. In the course of the three books, he comes to understand the ways of the country, through a career of hunting, horse-trading, and the occasional administration of justice to a culture whose notions of equity are foreign to his own. Most of the comedy arises from the interaction of cultures with different priorities (Irish, Anglo-Irish and English are observed with accuracy and affection throughout), and there is much of the 'social embarrassment' comedy of the conventional Victorian comic novel. The tone throughout is relaxed, tolerant and genial. There are no hints of gathering political conflict, although the great houses are shown in the full shabbiness of grand decline.

The range of the works of Somerville and Ross goes beyond the comic: *The Real Charlotte* (1894), which many consider their masterpiece, draws on the Irish Gothic tradition of Sheridan LeFanu. The tone is sombre and the feeling of the decline of the Ascendancy is all-pervasive. *The Silver Fox* (1898) is a serious account of the conflicts arising from the development of rural Ireland, incorporating remarkably skilful and unobtrusive elements of the supernatural. After the death of Violet Martin in 1915, Somerville continued to write, aided, as she asserted, by spiritualist communications from her collaborator. The chief work of this period is *The Big House of Inver* (1925), a chronicle of the final decline of an Anglo-Irish family, strongly reminiscent of that earlier masterpiece of Irish women's writing, Maria Edgeworth's *Castle Rackrent*.

# Drama

## The theatrical scene
The Victorian era was a bad time for playwrights. In the early period, theatres grew bigger and bigger, and what filled them was melodrama: a large-scale spectacle in which words played a less and less significant part (the main descendant of this type of theatrical show is the Christmas pantomime). The theatres catered principally for a working-class audience; many middle-class people, under the influence of the Evangelical movement, were doubtful about the morality of going to the theatre at all, and the kind of shows that were put on did nothing to reassure them. In the 1860s, the melodramas and farces of the early Victorian period increasingly gave way to smaller-scale, more naturalistic drama aimed at enticing the middle classes back into the theatres, and working-class entertainment was provided by the music halls. Another factor which controlled English drama was that the theatre was heavily censored. The Lord Chamberlain (the master of the sovereign's household) had had legal power to interfere with potentially seditious or treasonable drama since the sixteenth century. This was ratified by Act of Parliament in 1737, but considerably toughened and extended by the Theatres Act of 1843, which stipulated that all new plays had to be sent to the Lord Chamberlain for consideration, with a two-guinea fee for reading. The presentation of an unlicensed play would cause the theatre to be closed down. A play could be rejected for performance on the vaguest of grounds, whenever the Lord Chamberlain 'shall be of the opinion that it is fitting for the Preservation of Good Manners, Decorum or

of the Public Peace' to do so. This quite obviously militated against innovative, questioning or socially critical drama; and indeed, the increasingly adventurous theatre of the 1890s and later saw endless battles between dramatists and the Lord Chamberlain's office.[34] The novel was not subject to the same restrictions, so it is not surprising to find that the adventurous themes addressed in Victorian fiction are not reflected in an equally daring Victorian drama, and that the most original writers of fiction, whether male or female, were not attracted to the stage.

## Madame Vestris: a theatrical impressario

Before the 1860s, it is very difficult to associate any original development in drama with women. The one fascinating exception is Madame Vestris (1797–1856). She first appeared on the stage in 1817, and was an unquestionable star, the object of hysterical adulation by press and public alike. Having conquered London, she spent a few years in Paris, and returned more or less able to make her own terms. Madame Vestris rose to fame as a sex symbol: her legs in particular were regarded as faultlessly perfect, and she was expected to display as much of them as possible by taking male roles. However, she was also a talented singer and actress, who resented this focus on her body, and she therefore used this adulation, and the enormous salary it brought her, to start her own company, realising that her only chance of being treated as a serious actress was by working for herself. Thus, she became one of the first actress-managers.[35] This was a very large-scale undertaking. In the Covent Garden season of 1839–40, she had a total of 684 employees on her payroll.[36] Her first venture into management was to lease the Olympic Theatre in 1831, and set about creating a more refined style of theatre which did not depend on the display of female legs.[37] Madame Vestris also wrote a play of her own, *Woman*. She asked the famous actor-manager Macready to produce it, which he was unwilling to do, unless the major speeches of the leading lady were transferred to the leading man. This is an insight into the priorities of the actor-managers such as Macready and Henry Irving who dominated much of Victorian theatre: they selected plays on the basis of the dramatic possibilities of the leading male role, which they would be taking themselves.[38] Madame Vestris was virtually unique in being a woman with such a fanatical following of her own that she was in a position to challenge the actor-manager's authority.

Madame Vestris was a dramatic innovator. Her theatres, first the Olympic, then Covent Garden, which she and her second husband, Charles Mathews, ran from 1839 to 1842, and finally the Lyceum which they ran till 1855, pioneered a new style of sophisticated light entertainment. She was closely involved with the new movement towards realism in drama, naturalistic, historically accurate costumes and set design. Her theatres pioneered the 'box set' which was the physical environment for the new illusionism of the Victorian theatre, first introduced at the Olympia in 1832. The style of play which she favoured was economical and deftly managed, elegant, charming and relatively subtle. Most of these adjectives are no longer seen as terms of praise in the theatre, but in the context of their own era, the graceful comedies and extravaganzas of the Vestris–Mathews management represented the first move towards a new, tasteful theatre capable of attracting an educated audience, thirty years ahead of its time.

## Victorian playwrights
A number of women wrote more or less professionally for the stage in the early Victorian period. Catherine Boaden, for example, had four plays put on between 1825 and 1832, while two more were published in Cumberland's twenty-five-volume *British Theatre* (1829). Mrs Catherine Gore (1799–1861), also known as a writer of frothy novels about high society of the kind George Eliot most disliked, produced thirteen plays between 1831 and 1840 before retreating to the novel after some less than successful efforts. She had some gift for witty dialogue, and her *Quid Pro Quo* (1844), a comedy set in high society, is a testimony that some attempt was still being made to provide comedies suitable for fashionable and educated people. Some women better known in other fields also wrote plays: Felicia Hemans (see below, pp.124–5) was partially successful with a tragedy, *The Vespers of Palermo,* which was staged both at Covent Garden and at Edinburgh in 1823, and Mary Russell Mitford (1787–1855), better known as an essayist, also wrote six tragedies, of which one, *Rienzi* (1828), received both public and critical acclaim.

The small (500–800 seats), comfortable theatres which were built in the 1860s to house bourgeois, 'cup-and-saucer' dramas gave opportunities to women writers. These theatres were designedly places of family entertainment, where respectable women could go; and the kinds of plays which were suitable for such audiences were as much within the technical grasp of professional women writers as the novel designed for family reading. A number of novels by women, Mrs Henry Wood's *East Lynne* (1861, adapted in 1866), for example, and Mary Braddon's *Lady Audley's Secret* (1863, adapted twice in the same year), were rewritten for the stage, and were extremely popular (the show-stopping line from *East Lynne,* as the disguised runaway wife grieves over her deserted child, 'Dead! and never called me "mother"', became a cliché in its own right).[39] The adaptors were mainly anonymous, penny-a-line hacks paid by the theatres (though the prolific playwright and actor-manager Dion Boucicault adapted Mrs Gaskell's *Mary Barton* and 'Lizzie Leigh' as *The Long Strike*, in 1866), and whether women were among their number would be hard to discover. The Edwardian playwright Cicely Hamilton records, 'it was advisable to conceal the sex of [a play's] author until after the notices were out, as plays which were known to be written by women were apt to get bad reviews';[40] thus plays actually written or adapted by women may well have appeared under men's names. One mid-Victorian adaptation has a woman's name attached: *Trotty Veck* (1877), an adaptation by Mrs Charles Calvert of Charles Dickens's Christmas story, *The Chimes*; the name was evidently changed to prevent confusion with the well-known vehicle for the star actor Henry Irving, *The Bells* (1871).

Women's writing of any quality only returned to the theatre when the public rediscovered an appetite for a more intellectual type of drama in which the author maintained much more control over the whole presentation, which will be discussed in the next chapter. The tyranny of the actor-managers, and the formulaic, male-centred drama which resulted from this, meant that women with something to say (as distinct from women merely trying to make a living) were far more likely to write fiction. However, plays by acknowledged women authors did continue to appear in the later nineteenth century. Lady Dufferin's *Finesse, or Spy and Counter Spy*, was staged at the Haymarket in 1863, and Sidney Frances Bateman (who also wrote a comedy called *Self* (1868) ) had *Geraldine, or The Master Passion* put on at the Adelphi in 1865.

In the 1870s, Mary Braddon, whose novel *Lady Audley's Secret* had been successfully adapted as a play, tried her hand at a play of her own – *Griselda*, which appeared in 1873. She later published two comedies, *Married Beneath Him* and *Dross, or The Root of Evil*, both in 1882. Mrs S. Lane's *Taken from Memory*, Miss J. Evelyn's *A Crown for Love* in 1875, the American Kate Field's *Extremes Meet* in 1877, and two plays by Emma Schiff, *The Rights of Women* (1871) and *The Twin Sisters* (1870), were other women's plays of the 1870s. Mary Braddon, as a best-selling novelist, was clearly a good risk for a theatre management, as was Lady Dufferin, whose status as a titled lady offered the public the enticing hope that her play would give them an insight into life in high society.

Mary Braddon's *Griselda* is an example of what went to make a successful play in the 1870s. It was based on Chaucer's story of Patient Griselda, and played as a medieval costume drama. It was preceded by Byron's *Manfred* and followed by W.G. Wills's *Mary Queen o' Scots*, which suggests that the management of the Princess's Theatre had invested in an all-purpose spectacular set representing bits of a medieval castle. The production was extremely lavish: as an extra touch of luxury, the programmes were perfumed by Charles Rimmel (Rimmel's was then an up-market perfume and cosmetic house). *Griselda* was very well received, and ran for three months. Press reviews focus on the sumptuous magnificence of the costume and appointments, the graceful pathos of the plot, and the smoothness of Mary Braddon's versification. The lines which brought down the house were in response to a suggestion that the Marquis is seeking a divorce:

God made us one, and if the Pope can part us,
God and the Pope must be antagonists!

This clearly appealed strongly to the generally chauvinist and anti-Catholic English audience; moreover, the spectacle of a noble woman hugging the chains of her appalling marriage to a husband who puts her through daily psychological torture was equally well calculated to get a positive response.

Another successful woman playwright of the 1880s was Mrs Oscar (Aimée) Beringer, author of *Tares* (1888) and *A Bit of Old Chelsea* (published 1905). The gulf between the highly professional work of this type of playwright and the new drama of the 1890s is illustrated by Mrs Beringer's courageous decision to arrange a matinée performance of a play by Ibsen, *The Pillars of Society*. Just before it went on, she was stricken by terror at its possible effects on its audience, and fell back on the methods of her own type of drama: she asked a well-known and popular actress to come on at the end and do a comic monologue. George Bernard Shaw, who was an eyewitness, commented:

> It was as if some good natured pagan, coming into a cathedral at high mass, and seeing a number of people looking very grave, had tried to cheer them up with a comic song. [41]

Mrs Beringer's failure of nerve suggests why this era of women's drama has been forgotten: it aimed at nothing more than undemanding entertainment for middle-class audiences, and was not calculated to rock any boats. Few of these plays can have been published, though some may have survived in manuscript, and their authors are mostly extremely obscure. [42] But what this list of authors implies, regardless of the literary quality of their work, is that there has never been a generation when women stopped writing for the theatre. If these writers were mostly humble providers of sensational melodrama, undemanding comedy and cliché-ridden tragedy, so were their brother hacks. The importance of these names is in demonstrating that continuity is not completely lost: there was never a point after 1662 when it would have been possible to tell an aspirant young woman playwright that women never wrote for the stage, and therefore should never begin to.

An earlier woman playwright who continued to be performed was Susannah Centlivre. Mrs Centlivre's *The Busy Body* was performed at the Haymarket in 1844 and staged again in 1871 (when it was appreciated by the audience, but not by the critics) and *The Wonder: A Woman Keeps a Secret* was personally requested by Queen Victoria (who was, on this occasion, amused) in 1840, and staged again in 1862. [43] The survival of Susannah Centlivre's work, mysteriously disengaged from the evil reputation of the seventeenth-century female wits, must be directly connected to the simple fact that the roles of Marplot and Sir Felix offer magnificent opportunities for bravura performances by the male lead. But though there is no Victorian woman playwright whose output, in either quantity or quality, could challenge that of Dion Boucicault or Arthur Wing Pinero, it would be a mistake to assert that the drama had become a completely male business.

The authors of the 'new woman' and suffragette plays of the 1890s were accused of morbidity, unwholesomeness, and many other vices, but it was not possible for their critics to take the line that women could not, and did not, write for the theatre.

# Poetry

### Felicia Hemans and Jean Ingelow

Felicia Hemans's (1793–1835) verse is transitional between women's poetry of the eighteenth century and that of the Victorian period. In some ways, her work is technically quite advanced. She appreciated the virtues of the dramatic monologue as a literary form some years in advance of Tennyson and Browning, though she did not attempt the colloquial rhythms which characterise the monologues of Browning. In a purely commercial sense, she was a very successful poet, one of the few women in the history of English literature to have been able to support herself and her children by writing verse. Her work concentrates on giving the public what it wants, and is interesting, therefore, in what it reveals about public taste. Her poetry is roughly comparable in its thematic range with the novels of Sir Walter Scott, focusing to a very great extent on stirring incidents in medieval, biblical and ancient history, or in the lives of Indian braves, chamois-hunters, crusaders, Italian maidens and other picturesque individuals. What this eclectic variety of people have in common is that they may be deemed to experience simple, direct and heroic emotional reactions. Her best-known, and much parodied, poem 'Casabianca' (1828) ('The boy stood on the burning deck') is by no means an unfair representation of most of her work. It is based on a historical incident: the thirteen-year-old son of the admiral of the *Orient* stayed at his post in the Battle of the Nile after the ship had caught fire, and died when it exploded. This offers a simple lesson in the virtue of obedience for the reader's consideration, and the potential horror of the event is absorbed by the intensely genteel vocabulary, so that the poem reads essentially as a dramatised moral point.[44] Her *Records of Women* (1828) displays a variety of heroines: the heroic mother is particularly well represented. She also includes Joan of Arc in the portrait gallery, and at the end of this poem suggests her disquietude with the concept of the woman whose emotional energies are not focused on husband, children or parents:

> Oh! never did thine eye
> Through the green haunts of happy infancy
> Wander again, Joanne! – too much of fame
> Had shed its radiance on thy peasant name;
> And bought alone by gifts beyond all price –
> The trusting heart's repose, the paradise
> Of home, with all its loves – doth fate allow
> The crown of glory unto woman's brow.[45]

This is, in effect, a dark warning to aspirant women. Joan is not held up as an example, but as a tragically suffering figure – not because she was burnt at the stake (Felicia Hemans expected her heroines to be able to stand any amount of mere physical pain), but because she has transcended the domestic world which offers the only possibility of happiness.

Mrs Hemans's successor as a popular poet was Jean Ingelow (1820–97), whose poems expressed some suspicion of marriage (she remained single) but firmly upheld woman's status as 'the angel in the house' nonetheless. Perhaps her best poem is 'Divided' (1863), which describes how a couple start walking on either side of a little streamlet which gradually gets wider and faster until it irrevocably divides them: the symbolism is obvious, but effective.

### Elizabeth Barrett Browning

The most significant woman poet of the nineteenth century, whose position nearly equalled that of George Eliot herself, was Elizabeth Barrett Browning (1806–61). She is now known mostly for the series of love-poems addressed to her husband (Robert Browning), *Sonnets from the Portuguese* (1844, 1850), but much of her work was highly political, in the grand Victorian tradition of moral seriousness. She wrote poems on slavery, including 'The Runaway Slave at Pilgrim's Point' (1850), which deals boldly with the rape of a black woman by white men, and 'A Curse for a Nation' (1860), which exploits to the full her prophetic and Sibylline status as a distinguished woman poet.[46] She wrote poems, such as 'The Cry of the Children' (1844), on the miseries of the industrial working class, and she wrote political poems connected with the liberation of Italy, where she and Robert Browning settled after their marriage. In other words she, like George Eliot, consciously took on the burden of a vocation to speak of, and to, a much larger world of feelings and ideas than the merely personal and domestic.

Her long, blank verse poem, or verse novel, *Aurora Leigh* (1857) conflates characteristics of the two genres, possessing as it does the long, discursive, circumstantial plot of a novel, and the two-dimensional, symbolic characters and minimal dialogue proper to an epic poem. *Aurora Leigh* was shocking to the sensibilities of its first readers. Aurora, a young writer, boldly sets herself up in a room of her own to write for a living, an unimaginable step for the guardians of public morality. At the end of a complex plot, the heroine takes a working-class girl with an illegitimate baby into her home; again, a highly improper action, as upper-class virgins such as Aurora were supposed to protect their own purity by resolutely shunning seduced women. *Aurora Leigh* was considered shocking in many different respects. The heroine was dangerously emancipated, the whole enterprise of creating this gigantic poem unwomanly in the first place, the plot involved dangerously sexual themes of seduction and rape, and even the language was 'coarse', at least according to the *Dublin University Magazine* (which also, incidentally, favoured George Eliot with the most hostile review of her entire career). Elizabeth Barrett Browning's language is certainly remarkable for its vigour and immediacy. Here she is, for example, on her villain, Lady Waldemar, Aurora's rival, in full evening dress:

> ...How they told,
> Those alabaster shoulders and bare breasts,
> On which the pearls, drowned out of sight in milk,
> Were lost, excepting for the ruby clasp!
> They split the amaranth velvet-bodice down
> To the waist or nearly, with the audacious press
> Of full-breathed beauty...                    (Bk V, lines 618–24)

This is remarkably effective in conjuring up Lady Waldemar. It is her pearl necklace, not her cleavage, which dips down to her waist, but the syntax, and the use of 'full-breathed', which brings with it the association of full breasts, creates a triumphantly opulent image which hovers, like Lady Waldemar's bodice, barely within the bounds of decency. Amaranth, by the way, is purple.

The issue of 'coarseness', with which practically all English writers of any merit (even Jane Austen) have been charged at one time or another, was attacked at its true root by Elizabeth Barrett Browning, arguing against William Thackeray's rejection of one of her poems:

> has paterfamilias, with Oriental traditions and veiled female faces, very successfully dealt with a certain class of evil? What if materfamilias, with her quick sure instincts and honest innocent eyes, do more towards their expulsion by simply looking at them and calling them by their names?[47]

In short, it was not in the interests of women as a class, but in the interests of men as a class, that respectable ladies were forced by social pressure to reject, ignore or pass over sexually victimised women.

## Christina Rossetti
The other great English woman poet of the Victorian period is Christina Rossetti (1830–94). Her best-known poem, set to music and used as a Christmas carol, is 'In the Bleak Midwinter' (before 1872). She was the sister of Dante Gabriel Rossetti, the painter and poet, but, unlike her brother, she wrote as a deeply committed Christian. Like 'Orinda' a century before, she focuses with a particular intensity on relationships between women. *Goblin Market* (1862), which is sometimes wrongly thought to be a poem for children, turns on the fervent love of one sister for another, and on adolescent sexuality. She writes with the most exquisite formal and technical control of the English language, which has contributed to making

her work appear, to a twentieth-century taste, more bloodless than it actually is. Much of her poetry deals with confinement and isolation, as, for instance, in her long poem, 'A Royal Princess' (1861). Few would now guess from its title that this was a campaigning poem, written as a contribution to a fund-raising book intended to relieve distress among the Lancashire millworkers of whom Elizabeth Gaskell wrote so eloquently. The princess, who is the narrator, is almost paralysed by depression and boredom, amid the stately pre-Raphaelite luxury of her surroundings:

> All my walls are lost in mirrors, whereupon I trace
> Self to right hand, self to left hand, self in every place,
> Self-same solitary figure, self-same seeking face.

She comes to realise, in her powerlessness and isolation, that her father is a tyrannical and oppressive ruler of his people and not just of herself. The word 'alone' echoes through the poem, as the unfortunate princess, insulated as far as possible from political, social and human realities, strains her ears for news of the real world. The people, like the Parisian mob at the time of the French Revolution, ultimately storm the gates and fire the palace, and the princess determines, instead of accepting the defence mounted by her father and his troops, to go down to the mob at the gates with her lap full of gold and jewels, and to offer herself in a purely personal act of atonement: the first truly significant act of her expensively trivial life, and, as she fully recognises, probably the last.

## Emily Brontë

The three Brontë sisters also wrote considerable quantities of poetry, much of it in connection with their extensive cycles of fictional histories, and some of it of considerable power. Emily Brontë in particular wrote memorably assertive lyrics, rejecting, for instance, in the poem which begins 'Often rebuked, yet always back returning / To those first feelings that were born with me' any form of influence, social or religious, which might in any sense overshadow or influence her individual vision. The poetic elements in *Wuthering Heights* partially prepare us for poems which are as fine as they are individual. Emily Brontë might be seen as a part of the visionary tradition which includes William Blake and Gerard Manley Hopkins. In her religious poems there is no conventional piety, but an aspiring certainty born of intense personal experience:

> Though earth and man were gone,
> And suns and universes ceased to be,
> And Thou were left alone,
> Every existence would exist in Thee.
>
> There is not room for Death,
> Nor atom that his might could render void:

> Thou —— THOU art Being and Breath,
> And what THOU art may never be destroy'd.
>
> ('No Coward Soul is Mine', 1848)

Perhaps her most haunting poem is 'The Vision' (1845). The setting is the familiar wintry moorland of Haworth and of *Wuthering Heights*; it is evoked with an intensity beyond that even of the novel. The female speaker is awaiting, with hushed certainty (mirrored by the sure movement of the lines), an other-worldly visitant: the 'angel nightly tracks that waste of frozen snow'. An apparition is hinted in the last stanzas, verses as haunting as they are individual in nineteenth-century poetry:

> What I love shall come like visitant of air,
> Safe in secret power from lurking human snare;
> What loves me, no word of mine shall e'er betray,
> Though for faith unstrained my life must forfeit pay.

> Burn then, little lamp; glimmer straight and clear –
> Hush! a rustling wing stirs, methinks, the air:
> He for whom I wait, thus ever comes to me,
> Strange Power! I trust thy might; trust thou my constancy.

## Minor poets of the late nineteenth century

The end of the nineteenth century produced only one or two poets whose work lasted beyond their time. One was Charlotte Mew (1869–1928), who was possessed of a small and horrid talent for expressing, in both poetry and prose, renunciation, repression and captivity. Her most famous poem, 'The Farmer's Bride' (1916), is a dramatic monologue spoken by a well-meaning man whose very young wife has been so traumatised by his sexual demands that she literally cannot bear to see him or speak to him. Despite its wooden and somewhat cliché-ridden form, the poem, and the collection of the same name, struck a chord with many readers, including Virginia Woolf. Other women poets of this period include Alice Meynell (1847–1922), whose poetry is religiously sincere but stylistically unenterprising and intellectually trivial, and Frances Cornford (1886–1960), whose gift for the evocation of mood in simple words, sometimes reminiscent of R.L. Stevenson's *A Child's Garden of Verses* (1885), is seen in her late poem 'From a Letter to America on a Visit to Sussex: Spring 1942' (*Collected Poems*, 1954):

> How simply violent things
> Happen, is strange.
> How strange it was to see
> In the soft Cambridge sky our Squadron's wings,
> And hear the huge hum in the familiar grey.

The nineteenth century · 129

NOTES
1 Sir Walter Scott was not ashamed to admit a debt to Maria Edgeworth in an end-note to his *Waverley*, and Thomas Babington Macaulay and Samuel Johnson both spoke highly of Fanny Burney.
2 Spender, *Mothers of the Novel*, p.118.
3 Butler, *Jane Austen and the War of Ideas*, p.163.
4 George Eliot was approached by Emily Davies, the founder of Girton College, Cambridge, in 1876, but even the cause of women's higher education, though Eliot had spoken movingly of the limited education available to a Dorothea Brooke, failed to elicit much of a positive reaction from her. See D. David, *Intellectual Women and the Victorian Patriarchy*, Macmillan, London, 1987, pp.177–8.
5 *George Eliot: The Critical Heritage*, ed. D. Carroll, Routledge & Kegan Paul, London, 1971, pp.145–53, p.148.
6 V. Woolf, *Women and Writing*, Women's Press, London, 1979, p.49 (written in 1929).
7 Canning said of the West Indian slave, as emancipation was debated in the House of Commons, 'to turn him loose in the manhood of his physical strength, in the maturity of his physical passion, but in the infancy of his uninstructed reason, would be to raise up a creature resembling the splendid fiction of a recent romance'. Quoted by M. Butler, in *The London Review of Books*, 5 May 1988, pp.12–13. Gaskell, in *Mary Barton*, commented that 'the actions of the uneducated seem to me typified in those of Frankenstein, that monster of many human qualities, ungifted with a soul, a knowledge of the difference between good and evil…why have we made them what they are; a powerful monster, yet without the inner means for peace and happiness?'
8 E. Gaskell, *Life of Charlotte Brontë*, repr. Arthur Dobson, Bradford, 1968, pp.315–16.
9 Moers, *Literary Women*, p.140 – see also p.14.
10 Gaskell also, of course, had access (of a sort) to contemporary social analysis: 'with a struggle and a fight I can see all Quarterlies 3 months after they are published. Till then they lie on the Portico table, for gentlemen to see. I think I will go in for Women's Rights.' (Moers, *Literary Women*, p.82.)
11 Spender, *Mothers of the Novel*, p.164.
12 Compare Aphra Behn's novel, set in the London of her own time, *The Adventure of the Black Lady* (1684), in which the heroine, Bellamora, has come up to London to bear an illegitimate child, having been raped by her lover. As if she did not have troubles enough, she is actually in trouble with the law. The bailiffs of the parish are alerted to her existence and state, and they promptly rush in to send her to a House of Correction (i.e. to prison), and her child to a parish nurse. Bellamora, who had pinned her last hope on secrecy, does the only thing she can, which is to marry her baby's father in the nick of time, though she is disgusted by him (Hobby, *Virtue of Necessity*, p.97).
13 In a later and more cynical generation, the heroine of Sylvia Townsend Warner's *Lolly Willowes* (1926) dedicates herself to the devil as a witch, out of the profound conviction that no other being in the universe is remotely interested in understanding her.
14 Baudelaire's address to his reader was taken up by T.S. Eliot, in *The Waste Land*, 1. 76.
15 Charlotte Brontë, *Biographical Notice of Ellis and Acton Bell*, printed in the Penguin Classics edition of *Agnes Grey*, ed. A. Goreau, Harmondsworth, 1988: 'The choice of subject [of *Wildfell Hall*] was an entire mistake. Nothing less congruous with the writer's nature could be conceived. The motives which dictated this choice were pure, but, I think, slightly morbid.'
16 Gilbert and Gubar, *The Madwoman in the Attic*, p.337.
17 On which see Gérin, *Emily Brontë*. Her life was distinguished by an absolute lack of compromise, and an unfaltering insistence on personal freedom.
18 Her brother Branwell's funeral was the last occasion on which Emily left Haworth parsonage. She caught a cold at his funeral, and managed, by systematic self-neglect, to die within three months. Her life seems to have been bound up with Branwell's, as her heroine Catherine's was bound up with Heathcliff's.

19 The conclusion of a speech by the American lawyer, Patrick Henry.
20 Emily Brontë's poetry expresses thoughts utterly at variance with the conventional aspirations of a young girl:

> Riches I hold in light esteem
> And Love I laugh to scorn
> And lust of Fame was but a dream
> That vanished with the morn –
>
> And if I pray, the only prayer
> That moves my lips for me
> Is – 'Leave the heart that now I bear
> And give me liberty.' (1841)

21 For the first assertion, see Gaskell, *Life of Charlotte Brontë,* ch.18; for the second, Moers, *Literary Women,* p.70.
22 Gérin, *Emily Brontë,* p.154.
23 P. Beer, *Reader, I Married Him,* Macmillan, London, 1974, pp.114–16.
24 Goreau, introduction to *Agnes Grey,* p.30.
25 The librarian of Harvard wrote to his wife about a meeting with George Eliot in 1873: 'She has a power of *stating* an argument equal to any man; equal to any man do I say? I have never seen any man except Herbert Spencer, who could state a case equal to her. I found her thoroughly acquainted with the whole literature of the Homeric question; and she seems to have read all of Homer in Greek, too, and could meet me everywhere. She didn't talk like a bluestocking – as if she were aware she had got hold of a big topic – but like a plain woman, who talked of Homer as simply as she would of flat-irons' (quoted by Beer, in *Reader, I Married Him,* p.42). This letter raises in rather an acute form the problem of the tone in which even the most brilliant of women may be permitted to speak of intellectual matters. George Eliot seems to have been particularly good at soothing alarmed male sensibilities.
26 G. Beer, *George Eliot,* Harvester, Brighton, 1986, p.45.
27 *George Eliot,* pp.73–4.
28 See R. Ashton, *George Eliot,* Oxford University Press, Oxford, 1983, pp. 15–17.
29 See F.R. Leavis, *The Great Tradition,* Chatto and Windus, London, 1948, pp.47–82; and J. Miller, *Women Writing about Men,* Virago, London, 1986, pp.22–3.
30 P. Thomson, *The Victorian Heroine: A Changing Ideal, 1837–1873,* Oxford University Press, Oxford, 1956, pp.37–56 (on governess-heroines), and Showalter, *A Literature of Their Own: British Women Novelists from Brontë to Lessing,* Virago, London, 1978, pp.139–43 (on virile and saturnine heroes).
31 *A Literature of Their Own,* p.157. Reade's feminist sympathies are commented on by Thomson, in *The Victorian Heroine,* pp.82, 106 and 151–2. Reade reversed traditional priorities in sympathetically portraying women whose brains made up for their lack of virtue.
32 *A Literature of Their Own,* p.174.
33 E. Coxhead, *Lady Gregory: A Literary Portrait,* Macmillan, London, 1961, p.37.
34 K. Tynan, 'The Royal Smut-Hound,' first published in 1965, and reprinted in M. Wandor, *Look Back in Gender: Sexuality and the Family in Post-war British Drama,* Methuen, London 1987, pp.73–85. See also J.R. Stephens, *The Censorship of English Drama, 1824–1901,* Cambridge University Press, Cambridge, 1980.
35 Still earlier the Opera House (the King's Theatre in the Haymarket until 1737) had been managed from 1773 to 1778 by two women: Frances Brooke, a playwright, and the actress Mary Anne Yates.
36 W.W. Appleton, *Madame Vestris and the London Stage,* Columbia University Press, New York, 1974, p.128.
37 Charles E. Pearce, *Madame Vestris and Her Times,* Stanley Paul & Co., London, 1923, p.276.

38 A comedy called *Woman* which was put on at the Queen's Theatre in 1835 may be Vestris's play: it is listed as anonymous in Allardyce Nicoll's handlist of early Victorian plays, Vol. II of *A History of Early Nineteenth-century Drama, 1800–1850*, Cambridge University Press, Cambridge, 2 vols, 1930.

39 It did not in fact appear either in play or novel in quite this form: the play version is 'Oh, William! wake and call me mother once again! My child is dead!' (quoted in Harry Blamires, *The Victorian Age of Literature*, Longman, Harlow, 1988, p.150).

40 C. Hamilton, *Life Errant*, J.M. Dent, London, 1935, p.60.

41 J. Holledge, *Innocent Flowers: Women in the Edwardian Theatre*, Virago, London, 1981, pp.25–6.

42 They are not mentioned either in the *Oxford Companion to the Theatre*, or *The Feminist Companion to Literature in English*.

43 Bowyer, *The Celebrated Mrs Centlivre*, pp.115–16 and 190.

44 *The Poetical Works of Felicia Dorothea Hemans*, Oxford University Press, Oxford, 1914, p.396.

45 *Poetical Works*, p.263.

46 It would be wrong to assume that eighteenth-century women never wrote on such themes: anti-slavery poems were written by Helen Maria Williams, Hannah More and Ann Yearsley, in response to the Slave Bill of 1788. But Elizabeth Barrett Browning herself was not aware of this aspect of eighteenth-century women's poetry.

47 Moers, *Literary Women*, p.156.

# Chapter 5

# The modern era

## Women in a changing world

### The new century

Victorian England, and certainly Victorian literature, were both less static, and less stable, than many people now suppose. It was a time of violent social change and questioning, which saw the creation of the modern industrial and political world, and an entirely new sense of the rights of hitherto marginalised groups. The nineteenth century witnessed the beginning of the fight for reproductive rights – contraception, abortion and so on – and campaigns to improve the social and legal position of women; all of which, naturally, affected the nature and scope of women's writing. Just as significantly, by the end of the nineteenth century, it was possible for a determined girl to work for a university degree alongside her male contemporaries, competing in the same examinations and marked at the same standard – ending the long tradition of intellectual *apartheid* which marks women's access to learning from the eighth century to the nineteenth. The result of this is that twentieth-century women write more like twentieth-century men than like earlier women.

It was, of course, the late Victorian atmosphere of increasing moral and social uncertainty which led guardians of social morality and national morale, both official (such as Queen Victoria herself) and unofficial, to make the confident and complacent pronouncements which we associate with the era. Writers and thinkers of the late nineteenth century were forced to declare their colours one way or another. What nearly all of them had in common was a persistent optimism that the human condition could be improved, though of course the various recipes for Utopia were completely incompatible. Another characteristic aspect of Victorian thinking was that literature *mattered*; that a work would either improve its readers or deprave them. It was not only George Eliot who took her moral influence over the lives of her readers deeply seriously. There is an element of conscious propaganda in the works of many other novelists of this era, from Charles Dickens to Mrs Humphry Ward.

The difference between the Victorian and the modern outlook may be illustrated by the comment of one great novelist on another – Virginia Woolf, writing a warm, laudatory and perspicacious review of George Eliot:

A scrap of her talk is preserved. 'We ought to respect our influence,' she said. 'We know by our own experience how very much others affect our lives, and we must remember that we in turn must have the same effect on others.' Jealously treasured, committed to memory, one can imagine recalling the scene, repeating the words, thirty years later and suddenly, for the first time, bursting into laughter.[1]

The old queen died in 1901, which was in one sense the end of an era. But if there was a single event which ushered in the modern period, it was not the turn of the century, nor the death of Victoria, but the 1914–18 war, in which the carnage of millions of young men produced an unprecedented level of bitterness among survivors of both sexes, and an outcry against the tragic and futile waste of it all. There was a revulsion at the Victorian dream that people could be made better than they were, and the whole concept of character and motivation was overturned by the psychological researches of Freud and Jung and the literary innovations of James Joyce, Dorothy Richardson and Virginia Woolf.

Psychoanalysis is one of the salient facts which separates us from the Victorians. In the context of an increasingly secularised society, a vulgarised and trivialised version of Freud's theories has come to hold something of the explanatory force which was once allotted to evangelical Christianity. The concept of the unconscious – and in particular of the unconscious motivations which prompt acts apparently arbitrary or bewildering even to their perpetrators – became increasingly fashionable in the 1920s, as it still is. The significance of sexuality as part of the continuous fabric of existence, and the analysis of what it means to be a sexual being, were other aspects of this new interest in the workings of consciousness, increasingly exploited by writers. The fact that James Joyce's *Ulysses* (1922) and D.H. Lawrence's *Lady Chatterley's Lover* (1929) were prosecuted for obscenity suggests that they were presenting new ideas, and that is usually a challenging and disturbing thing to do.

An equally courageous, though less distinguished, novel of this period is Radclyffe Hall's (1880–1943) *The Well of Loneliness* (1928), which was also prosecuted for obscenity. It presents a similar challenge to the status quo by dealing publicly with female homosexuality, from a sympathetic standpoint.[2]

It is a plea for the human dignity of lesbian women, and hence deserves respect as a historical document. It is difficult now to find *The Well of Loneliness* anything but innocuous, and also to see quite why the establishment found it so threatening, since Stephen Gordon (the heroine) suffers as much as the most vindictive moralist would wish. But what is perhaps most significant is the way that the trial of *The Well of Loneliness* for obscenity, like the trial of *Lady Chatterley,* showed how far some of the most respected contemporary writers had moved from the moral orthodoxies of previous generations. Virginia Woolf and E.M. Forster were among the distinguished novelists who publicy testified to the book's sincerity of purpose, while admitting in private that it was not, as a novel, particularly good.[3] Radclyffe Hall could, at times, write much better, and did so in *The Unlit Lamp* (1924), her book on the 'surplus spinster', which is a sombre and agonising account of the total contempt in which the lives of middle-class women were held in her own time. It is an unusually frank and perceptive analysis of the terrible power of *self*-limitation: the assimilation of the views of more powerful people, with consequent loss of one's personal identity. Hall's courageous stand, and her consequent martyrdom at the hands of the self-appointed guardians of public morality, inspired few, if any, imitations. For example, the writer and garden designer Vita Sackville-West (1892–1962), the creator of Sissinghurst, had a number of female lovers, among whom were Violet Trefusis and Virginia Woolf. All three of these women wrote novels which directly reflect their love-affairs with one another, and in each case, the work is a *roman à clef* in which the sexes have been 'normalised' – though in Virginia Woolf's *Orlando* (1928), the boldest of the three (and by far the best novel) the Vita-figure, Orlando, is immortal, and belongs to both sexes by turns.[4]

## Changes in culture and education

Another characteristic of the modern period which marks it off from the nineteenth century is the supersession of a system of common cultural referents by a widening, less and less homogeneous concept of culture. This is so to a great extent because the late twentieth century has become increasingly self-conscious about élitism, and culturally more complex than any previous century. A book such as this written in the late nineteenth century would have been able to assume that the reader was a white middle-class Christian, and almost certainly familiar with a whole range of writing from the hymns of Keble to the novels of Charles Dickens. No such assumption can now be made. The existence of a common culture made life considerably easier for writers, since they could expect references to be picked up, but it had the negative effect of excluding the viewpoints and experiences of many categories of people from the official culture represented by magazines, novels and social legislation. Resentment at this was felt in the Victorian era and earlier, and is often expressed by women writers, for example in *The Mill on the Floss,* in which Tom Tulliver assumes that the algebra and Latin with which he is tormented are beyond his sister's capacity, though she is intellectually far more capable than he, and that her mind is necessarily undeveloped because she has not learned these things. Later on, sitting over Tom's books, Maggie thinks, 'Latin, Euclid and Logic would be a considerable step in masculine wisdom – in that knowledge which made men contented, and even glad to live...And so the poor child...began to nibble at this thick-rinded fruit of the tree of knowledge...feeling a gleam of triumph, now and then that her understanding was quite equal to these peculiarly masculine studies' (Bk IV, ch. 2). Education no longer makes judgments about what is appropriate on grounds of sex, nor does it confine all boys to a single and very narrow path of appropriate learning: the arts and sciences have progressed so far that it is now literally impossible for one person to encompass the whole range of his or her culture. While there is considerable evidence that gender stereotyping still affects the choices make by boys and girls, the process whereby children are manoeuvred into making culturally appropriate decisions is now one of deflection rather than actual coercion. A girl who wants to study structural engineering or astrophysics, or a boy who wants to train as a nurse, may experience opposition of various more or less subtle kinds, but the girl will not be refused a place on a university course on grounds of her sex, which is a considerable advance on the position a hundred years ago.

The history of English education is naturally profoundly relevant to the history of English literature. The development away from the polarised educational experiences of Maggie and Tom Tulliver, from his formal study of Latin and mathematics, and her unfocused, home-based education, to the varied opportunities open to both sexes which we now take for granted has wrought many changes in the way people write, as well as in the way they think about writing. The cultural hegemony of Latin, Greek and mathematics was broken at the end of the nineteenth century; what is particularly relevant to English literature is that departments of English, and professors of English literature, were created at this time in all British universities except Oxford and Cambridge (which eventually followed suit). This professionalisation of the study of English has naturally led to a more self-conscious attitude in its creators. The early twentieth century was also the age of a vastly expanded publication of older literary texts, in expensive scholars' editions, and also in cheap popular series such as Everyman. For the first time, English literature from the time of Chaucer to the modern day became easily and generally available: for example, the works of Aphra Behn were edited in 1915 by Montague Summers, after two centuries of total obscurity. Many writers of the twentieth century have studied English at university; some, such as David Lodge and A.S. Byatt, even teach it. Even those twentieth-century writers who did not go to university, like Virginia Woolf, tend to show in their work an awareness of critical theory and of the importance of literary criticism, as well as a much greater knowledge of the whole body of English literature than their predecessors. Writing has therefore become a more self-conscious activity, aware of an audience of professional judges as well as of the buying public.

The effect of all this on creative writing has naturally been considerable. The omniscient narrator is vanishing, and fragmented texts are wholly acceptable. There is an increasing appreciation of the many different ways of telling a story, or expressing a truth. Realism, or verisimilitude, is increasingly understood as merely another set of conventions, and so being 'true to life' has become less and less important to either writers or readers. Writers play games with their characters, exploiting the fictionality of fiction: fables and fantasies, writing about writing, books about books.

# The novel

## Virginia Woolf

Virginia Woolf (1882–1941) has achieved a curious position within English culture. She is unquestionably the best-known English woman writer of the twentieth century, the only really well-known female member of the so-called 'Bloomsbury group' of writers and painters, and the first major English novelist to write from a position of overt and committed feminism. Yet the combination of various factors, notably the considerable scholarly and popular interest in disentangling the social, sexual and literary relationships of the Bloomsburyites, and Virginia Woolf's own tragic history, which included sexual abuse in childhood, a lifelong struggle with depression, and ultimately, suicide, have meant that many readers are more interested in her life than her fiction. It is fairly clear that Virginia Woolf's first novel, *The Voyage Out* (1915), was in some ways a cathartic piece of writing, confronting, in a highly symbolic form, the fear of male sexuality which was a legacy of the abuse she suffered in childhood. This explains some of the puzzling aspects of the novel: the heroine's violent reaction to an unsought and unexpected kiss from a relative stranger, and the aura of fear and nightmare which hangs about her reactions to her harmless fiancé, who is in no sense sexually predatory. But although knowledge of this background helps to explain *The Voyage Out,* it does not explain it away. The novel is far more than a distorting mirror of its creator's emotional life: it interweaves themes of sexual politics, the uniqueness and loneliness of individual perceptions, the analysis of relationships between older and younger people of the same sex, and social observation. It also shows in its style and structure a characteristically Woolfian interest in telling a story through minute and sharply observed physical details which express a character or a state of mind. Rachel, the heroine, describes her aunts with the words:

> 'They are small, rather pale women,' she began, 'very clean. We live in Richmond. They have an old dog, too, who will only eat the marrow out of bones...They are always going to church. They tidy their drawers a good deal.'
> (ch. 11)

The chosen details express an extremely narrow and confined life, but not a discontented one, lived with a rigid regard to the personal proprieties, but, as the obviously loved and indulged dog bears witness, not without warmth. The novel as a whole is intricate and satisfactory on this basis, and should be read on such terms. Rachel – solitary, obsessive, musical – is unable to come to terms with the life laid out for the daughter of a wealthy father around the turn of the century, or with marriage, which would trap her even more absolutely in a life irrelevant to her human aspirations – 'she wanted many more things than the love of one human being – the sea, the sky' (ch. 22). Her death, from undiagnosed typhoid, cuts across the traditional narrative pattern of girls settling down and coming to terms with their lives, but is the nearest thing to a happy ending possible for this particular heroine. Like Catherine Earnshaw in *Wuthering Heights,* she chooses death.

Part of the reason for readers' difficulties with Virginia Woolf is the explicit modernism of her style. Realism, the dominant style of nineteenth-century novels, is in itself highly artificial, and follows a set of agreed conventions. It is as much a product of a particular social context as the demand for highly finished 'truth to nature' in the visual arts. But as writers became more interested in fictionality, and in showing the reader how their reactions were being manipulated, they alarmed much of their audience, as have contemporary painters of abstracts, and composers of atonal music. Thus, readers approaching Virginia Woolf's novels in the expectation, or hope, of plot, character or narrative structures being developed in the way that pre-First World War writers would have developed them, have been disconcerted and alienated. Reading Virginia Woolf's life into her fiction may be related to this fear of fictionality as such: the demand for a single layer of meaning which can be directly related to 'real life'. In *To the Lighthouse* (1927), for instance, Mrs Ramsay, wife and mother, seductive though Woolf makes her, is ultimately as flawed and one-sided a creature as her husband who is more obviously unsympathetic. Her understanding of the traditional wifely role includes the necessity of providing false reassurance for her husband's genuine fears of creative and intellectual inadequacy. Although this is a marriage of love as well as dependency, Mrs Ramsay finds, like Dorothea Brooke when she marries Casaubon, that false, or ignorant, praise only fuels the anxiety it temporarily assuages, and enmeshes Mr Ramsay further in a cycle of dependence and arrogance.

Virginia Woolf's views are never simple. Traditional society, and patriarchal attitudes, seemed to her to have failed very badly, dehumanising men and women in different ways. She moved through traditional patterns of behaviour, as represented by the Ramsays, towards a much more androgynous ideal, represented in *To the Lighthouse* by the painter Lily Briscoe. Woolf's honesty has confused many readers, since the lives of her Lily Briscoes are in many ways sad and difficult, and the lives of her Mrs Ramsays in many ways rich and fulfilling. Striking out at an angle from the expectations of any culture will inevitably create tensions, difficulty and guilt, while to do what is expected is generally to reap the benefits of social and familial approval. Virginia Woolf is fully aware of the advantages of cultural conformity, but the goal sought by Lily Briscoe is of a quite different kind to the contentment of the dependent woman: joy rather than happiness.

Virginia Woolf is also at times a very playful writer. The most conspicuous examples of this are her biography of Elizabeth Barrett Browning's dog, *Flush* (1933), and *Orlando* (1928), a celebration of Vita Sackville-West. These are not funny books, on the level of plot or language, but they are witty and comic in their structure. *Flush,* as the biography of a spaniel, is the prose equivalent of a mock-epic like Pope's *The Rape of the Lock,* devoting a surface of serious and even scholarly enterprise to a comically minor subject. Since the author is Virginia Woolf, even *Flush* raises serious questions, to do with love and emotional dependence, within its light-hearted exposition of a dog's life and times. *Orlando* is more complex. It is an anti-novel, mock-epic in tone. The Writer's Preface, as writer's prefaces do, names all kinds of debts:

> I have had the advantage – how great I alone can estimate – of Mr Arthur Waley's knowledge of Chinese...no one can read or write without being perpetually in the debt of Defoe, Sir Thomas Browne, Sterne, Sir Walter Scott, Lord Macaulay, Emily Brontë, De Quincey, and Walter Pater, – to name the first which come to mind.

This is not spoof in the sense of pure invention: Waley was indeed the greatest English translator of Chinese alive, and Sir Thomas Browne, for one, was certainly read and valued by Woolf. But there are no Chinese references whatsoever in *Orlando*; and the juxtapositions of 'literary influences' in the list above – as well as the absolutely un-Woolf-like tone of didactic authority in 'no one can read or write without' – go to show that her writing is parodic rather than serious. Orlando, the bisexual hero, flourishing between 1500 and 1928, is bored to death by the great men of the past with whom he/she associates – he/she is perverse, androgynous and defiantly him/herself. The actual sex-change which takes place is treated in the mode of fantasy rather than science fiction, that is, it just happens; and Woolf, in mischievous allusion to Jane Austen's 'let other pens dwell on guilt and misery. I quit such odious subjects as soon as I can' (*Mansfield Park,* ch. 48), skips over the details with the words 'let other pens treat of sex and sexuality; we quit such odious subjects as soon as we can'. In both cases, the author is explicitly asserting the right to direct the reader's attention within the novel, a form of authorial control which came naturally in the nineteenth century, but which a modernist writer like Woolf cannot use without irony.

Woolf is the first woman writer of the twentieth century to feel and express the urgent need for a woman writer to identify a woman's tradition in writing. The irony of this is that she is one of the first examples of the confluence of men's and women's culture. As the daughter of Sir Leslie Stephen (author-editor of the *Dictionary of National Biography*), she was a part of the milieu which was professionalising English literature; and she delighted in the academic rediscovery of almost forgotten writers like Aphra Behn and Sir Thomas Browne, participating with gusto in the creation of new literary canons. The experimental qualities of her own writing inevitably owed much to the men she associated with: there is no woman writer of a generation earlier able to provide the sort of stimulus which Frances Burney offered Jane Austen and Maria Edgeworth. Although the worthy Mrs Humphry Ward was intellectually respectable, she was valueless as a stylistic mentor. It was the American Henry James (1843–1916) who was the most influential model and exemplar for early twentieth-century experimental writers, both male and female. Woolf's search for female literary models involved patient hours of research in the British Museum, and was the logical outcome of her feminist position: her male literary models, who included, apart from Henry James, William Shakespeare and the (male) authors of classical Greek tragedy, profoundly shaped the character of her mind and her art in ways which sprang directly from her cultural milieu.

**Contemporaries of Virginia Woolf**
Virginia Woolf was not the only widely read woman writer of her generation, just as Bloomsbury was not the only centre of English literary culture. The loose coalition of variously connected writers (mostly poets), English and American, for whom Ezra Pound was a central figure, received equally critical attention. It included James Joyce, T.S. Eliot, D.H. Lawrence and Amy Lowell, and was thus, again, a field of endeavour in which men and women worked side by side. The best-known of the modernist women writers active in England were Katherine Mansfield (1888–1923), who wrote stories; the poet and novelist H.D. (Hilda Doolittle, 1886–1961), an American who spent much of her working life in London; and Dorothy Richardson (1873–1957). Katherine Mansfield came from New Zealand, and her work, like that of the innovative Australian novelist, Christina Stead, has the analytic quality of someone who has had to come to terms with English culture rather than simply growing up in it. In her tragically short life, Katherine Mansfield confined herself to the writing of lapidary short stories and her famous journal, rather than embarking on the longer form of the novel. The stories deal with moments of perception, of comprehension, often profoundly negative. She shows the women in her stories as humiliated and destroyed by life, rather than as fighting through its horrors to self-knowledge or even emotional independence. Virginia Woolf, who spoke with distaste of Katherine Mansfield's 'callousness and hardness' is fundamentally more optimistic. Her own fiction offers her characters many and diverse possibilities of happiness. Katherine Mansfield

was, however, extremely important to Virginia Woolf, who wrote in her diary on hearing of Mansfield's death: 'I was jealous of her writing – the only writing I have ever been jealous of...probably we had something in common which I shall never find in anyone else.'[5] This comment, in both its positive and negative aspects, brings out the importance to a woman writer of measuring herself specifically against other contemporary women. Katherine Mansfield might be 'my rival', in the same diary entry, but she was also the person written for: 'mon semblable, ma soeur'.

Another female member of the literary circle which included D.H. Lawrence was Catherine Carswell (1879–1946), who wrote two novels, *Open the Door* (1920) and *The Camomile* (1922), and a number of works of criticism, including a study of Lawrence, *The Savage Pilgrimage* (1932), which is her best-known work. She gave the manuscript of *Open the Door* to Lawrence to read, receiving his *Women in Love* in exchange, and each criticised and modified the other's work. At one point in the 1920s, they seriously considered collaborating on a novel to be set in Scotland; the sketch of the plot for this novel eventually emerged in a completely different form as Lawrence's *The Plumed Serpent*. Her imaginative sympathy with Lawrence's approach to writing is evident at many points in *Open the Door*: its heroine, Joanna, suffers a series of essentially unsatisfactory relationships with men before uniting herself with one who shares her own commitment to life rather than death, just as Lawrence's heroine, Constance Chatterley, in *Lady Chatterley's Lover,* makes a number of mistakes before finding a man she can truly respond to. The first indication that Joanna will ultimately come to love Lawrence Urquhart comes when she finds how well he dances:

> From the outset he caught Joanna up into something of his own dignity, winning her surprised acknowledgment. Then, as the reel progressed, she began to lose all sense of identity. Every moment she became less herself, more a mere rhythmical expression of the soil from which they both had sprung...Beneath the candid darkness of Lawrence Urquhart's face, soon she was no more than a field of barley that swings unseen in the wind before dawn. (ch. 2)

Carswell also shares with Lawrence an exceptionally vivid and precise ability to evoke landscape.

May Sinclair (1863–1946) first made her name with a relatively simple novel (her fourth), *Divine Fire* (1904), about a poet, Rickman, who renounces easy popularity in favour of intellectual integrity and truth to his own vision, and, through this self-denial, wins not only happiness, but the love of a beautiful woman and public recognition for his work. Sinclair's commitment to psychoanalysis and women's suffrage led her away from such conventional writing into a more hard-edged exploration both of human personality and of feminist politics. Her novel *The Three Sisters* (1914) combines both interests: the Cartaret sisters are the daughters of a patriarchal clergyman, and are all attracted to a young doctor, but they are three very different psychological types. The novel is thus used to explore the interaction of character and environment, and was perhaps suggested by her 1912 biography of the Brontë sisters. Two later novels, *Mary Oliver: A Life* (1919) and *The Life and Death of Harriet Frean* (1920), are also psychological novels, which give particular attention to the relationship of mother and daughter, then a relatively unexplored area: both are bleak accounts of the crippling effects of convention on women's lives.

Dorothy Richardson stands almost entirely outside the literary cliques and coteries of the 1920s. She was engaged, throughout her life, in the writing of a sort of twentieth-century epic, known collectively as *Pilgrimage*. The first volume, *Pointed Roofs*, came out in 1915. She was an independent working woman on a small salary (she had no training for any career, and was employed as a dentist's secretary), living in rented rooms in London, one of the new generation of working girls whom Virginia Woolf praised and admired, able to make their own rules, and to experiment sexually without becoming social outcasts. The main subject of Richardson's work is not so much her heroine's life and times, as her heroine's consciousness, the evolution of a single individual in the context of the experiences of her life. The texture of *Pilgrimage* is of a flow of impressions: Miriam's enormous openness to the world around her, which goes so far as to threaten to drown her own personality beneath the flood of sensual stimuli provided by the world: 'the human demand, besieging her wherever she is, for an inclusive awareness, from which men, for good or evil, are exempt,'[6] and similarly, 'views and opinions are masculine things...women are indifferent to them really...women can hold all opinions at once, or any, or none. It's because they see the relations of things which don't change, more than things which are always changing' (*Pilgrimage*, Vol. III). These comments between them provide a novelistic credo, expressing her commitment to difference, to a radical new way of writing based on a consciously feminine aesthetic. This in turn means that the volumes of *Pilgrimage* are a prolonged and subtle meditation on what it means to be a woman in the twentieth century. She was convinced that men and women speak different languages, but whereas women are bilingual, and have come to terms with the dominant, and alien, discourse of men, men are not only unable to speak women's language, they have never had any reason to attempt to understand it, or indeed to value it. Her writing thus explores the literary processes which create and re-create gender and identity.

Another 1920s novel which explores issues of gender, through the unexpected context of an adventure story, is *Moonraker* (1927), by F. Tennyson Jesse (1888–1958). *Moonraker* is a 'boy's book', superficially in the swashbuckling tradition of R.L. Stevenson's *Treasure Island* and J.

Meade Falkner's *Moonfleet*; in fact, it extends and subverts its genre in a number of ways. It is set in 1801, and the narrator, Jacky, runs away to sea, where he becomes the friend and companion of Captain Lovel, a female pirate (modelled on real-life female pirates such as Anne Bonny and Grania O'Malley). Captain Lovel is a strong and decisive character who represents a way of being female which does not involve weakness. The story also subverts the usual assumptions of such tales by making Jacky's other hero the great black general, Toussaint L'Ouverture, whom he is able to assist in his fight against slavery.

**Writers of the 1930s**
Since most novelists' work is produced over a span of forty years or even longer, identifying writers with particular decades is a difficult exercise. However, writers do tend to come to maturity and public recognition at a specific historical moment, and with hindsight, it is often possible to see why a particular group was acclaimed by the critics at a particular time. The Modernist experimentation of the 1920s was followed in the 1930s by reaction. In the decade leading up to the Second World War, the novel of ideas, or the novelistic expression of contemporary moral dilemmas, regained some of the ground which it had held in the late nineteenth century. As Europe gradually moved towards war, the battle-lines between socialist, particularly Communist, ideologies and various forms of Fascism were reflected in the work of contemporary writers and thinkers, together with other aspects of the nature of the modern industrialised state and the relationship of the individual to society. Whereas the didactic purposes of late nineteenth-century literature had focused mainly on issues connected with religion, 1930s literature was political.

One of the liveliest and subtlest commentators on the politics of her time was Rebecca West (1892–1983), novelist and journalist. She was an active suffragette from the age of fifteen, and her interests remained political rather than introspective throughout the 1920s: she was thus well placed to respond as a mature writer to the new interests of the 1930s. Her first novel, *The Return of the Soldier* (1918), foreshadows some of her later interests in its concern with the human costs not only of the First World War, but also of the gracious life of the Edwardian upper classes, on which many writers looked back with simple nostalgia. The narrator, a cousin of the soldier whose return is awaited, believes at the outset that she and her sister-in-law have created the nearest possible thing to a perfect life for their much-loved Chris, only to find that as a result of his war wound his unconscious needs cause him to forget the last fifteen years of his life, which included his marriage, as an unbearable mistake. At twenty, he had been passionately in love with a working-class girl, who at thirty-five is physically ruined by the squalor and poverty of her life, but is spiritually whole, sane, and a woman not only happy in herself, but dynamically good: the creator of happiness in those around her. The narrator thinks, bringing her to see him for the first time since their youth, as the car comes into Baldry Court:

> Surely she must see that this was no place for beauty that has been not mellowed but lacerated by time, that no one accustomed to live here could help wincing at such external dinginess as hers...But instead she said, 'It's a big place. How poor Chris must have worked to keep it up.'
>
> (ch. 4)

The priority of human or spiritual values over the essential emptiness of mere possession expressed in this novel is one which Rebecca West returned to many times in her later writings. Another issue which is clearly apparent in the novel is her feminism. The working-class Margaret Grey has been worn out physically by a life of drudgery; the narrator, a spinster hanger-on, has been chronically under-employed; and Chris's wife Kitty is an expensively useless objet d'art, spoiled, entirely self-centred, and unhappy. A clue to her personality is given by her little dog, bought for ornament, ignored once it had gone out of fashion, but picked up and cuddled by her when she happens to be in need of comfort herself (ch. 6). The reason for the existence of women like Kitty as the vehicles of conspicuous consumption is spelled out clearly:

> it is their civilising mission to flash the jewel of their beauty before all men, so that they shall desire it and work to get the wealth to buy it.
>
> (ch. 6)

Another writer of the same period who shares some of the same concerns is Naomi Mitchison (b.1897). Much of her fiction is set in the distant past which, like Rebecca West (who wrote a study of St Augustine), she found a stimulating approach to an analysis of the present. Two important novels of the 1930s, *The Corn King and the Spring Queen* (1931) and *The Blood of the Martyrs* (1939), are directly related to contemporary issues. Writing as a socialist, she used *The Corn King* to explore a wide variety of social structures, from the relative anarchy of tribal life to various forms of democratic, oligarchic and imperial rule, and also to examine different philosophies of power and the way in which the 'haves' are able to contain and control moves towards a more democratic society. *The Blood of the Martyrs* is set in a community of Christians in Rome at the time of Nero, in 55AD, when the emperor and his advisers used the Christians, then a somewhat suspect lower-class sect, as scapegoats for the release of social tensions. The mobilisation of popular hatred against inoffensive Christians, and the position of the Emperor Nero as the symbol of a collective Roman fantasy of power, bear a direct and obvious relationship to the destruction of European Jewry and the rise of Hitler to power at the time when Mitchison was writing.

Both these novels, in keeping with their author's socialist principles, avoid creating a single central figure. The complex structure of *The Corn King* presents the reader with three characters from the primitive community of Marob (Erif Der, her husband and her brother), four from Sparta (the king, his wife, his lover and his lover's fiancée), two Greek philosophers, and a complex gallery of supernumeraries, rather than focusing on a single thread of events, or a single personality. Similarly, *The Blood of the Martyrs* interweaves the stories of all the people, mostly slaves, who form the small Christian community at the heart of the novel, rather than allowing the deracinated British prince, Beric, to crowd his fellow-seekers off the stage.

Many critics agree that her masterpiece is *The Bull Calves* (1947), a novel which raises too many issues for summary treatment. It is a historical novel which transcends almost all other attempts at the genre, with remarkable scholarly notes and a useful attempt to invent an orthography for Lowland Scots speech. The motive force for its composition was the death of a twentieth-century child, to which her oblique creative response was to chronicle a few eighteenth-century days in the life of her ancestors. Against a background of persecution and fear in the wake of the last mainland rebellion against English domination of Britain, her ancestors, some historical, some invented, play out a history of Scotland which ends in the affirmation of the primacy of the intuitive, the sensual and the unconventional.

Another writer concerned to analyse the state of modern Europe was Stevie Smith, poet and novelist (1902–71). Stevie Smith understood and analysed the specific sins of the over-intellectual, the abstract thinking which cripples emotional response, the pride and, above all, the anger. Her remarkable novel *Over the Frontier* (1938) is a Faustian allegory of a proud, independent and clever woman who is seduced in wartime by a shrewd Intelligence officer into selling her soul to that ultimate male hierarchy, the army. The irresistible bait which tempts Pompey, Smith's heroine and alter ego, into becoming a highly successful officer is the opportunity to express, as she has never expressed it before, her passionate anger and contempt for a world which threatens to trap and circumscribe her. Of her other two novels, *Novel on Yellow Paper* (1936) is an earlier episode in Pompey's life, and *The Holiday* (1949) is entirely separate.

The importance of the past as a tool for analysing the present is clear in the work of other women writers of this period. Sylvia Townsend Warner (1893–1978) was highly educated, an accomplished linguist and translator, and a distinguished musician and musicologist. Her work in these various fields is characterised by relentless intelligence and intellectual curiosity which enable her to think her way convincingly into the remarkably diverse historical and social settings of her major novels: *Lolly Willowes* (1926; upper-class English society on either side of the First World War), *Summer Will Show* (1936; Paris in the revolution of 1848), *After the Death of Don*

*Juan* (1938; an operatic evocation of aristocratic eighteenth-century Spain), and *The Corner that Held Them* (1948; an obscure East Anglian convent in the fourteenth century). These novels are united by their passionate sympathy for all the oppressed, all those who suffer at the hands of others. Many of her heroines are women who successfully escape from the power of their oppressors. In *Lolly Willowes,* the spinster aunt of an oppressive upper-middle-class family suddenly asserts her identity after years as an unnoticed domestic encumbrance by moving to an obscure village in the country and taking up the serious practice of witchcraft, justifying this move by her conviction, based on years of family life and conventional religion, that the devil is the only remaining personage who might be prevailed on to perceive her as a fully human being. In *Summer Will Show,* an English gentleman's wife escapes from the Jane Austenesque constraints of English country existence to the Paris revolution of 1848 and a profoundly loving relationship with her husband's ex-mistress, a Jewish demi-mondaine of Russian origin called Minna. This book plays in interesting ways with women's narrative techniques. The opening section, set in England, is a homage to the eighteenth-century Mothers of the Novel. The first Parisian section is a spell-binding tale, by Minna, of her and her family's sufferings in the Russian pogroms, contrasting the previous narrative with the art of the peasant story-teller. The plot rests on the differences between Sophia and Minna, in experience, character and nature, and on their profound similarities as women in a man's world. Sophia soon discovers that her wealth and social position were entirely dependent on her husband's consent, but just as Minna, as a child saved from death by a priest, refused to relinquish her Jewish identity, Sophia will not buy back her way of living from a husband at the price of her self-respect. Nearly all Sylvia Townsend Warner's writings share an interest in the nature of women's resistance to the rigid structures imposed on them, sometimes comic, or covert, sometimes radical. *After the Death of Don Juan,* in clear reference to the events of the Spanish Civil War in the 1930s, contrasts the essentially futile preoccupations of the aristocrats within the castle (who are the characters from Mozart's opera *Don Giovanni*) with the very real sufferings and political vitality of the peasants at the gates.

Rose Macaulay (1881–1958) is another writer who shared the preoccupation with the political destiny of Europe characteristic of this period, and also its equally characteristic interest in the position of women. A third, less common field of interest for her is in Christianity. Her early novel *Dangerous Ages* (1922) focuses specifically on the position of women, a twenty-year-old, two sisters, one in her later thirties and one of forty, their sixty-year-old mother and eighty-year-old grandmother. The unmarried woman in her thirties is traditionally at a dangerous age; the novel makes it clear that of these women, only the oldest of the women, who at eighty has more or less outlived her conflicts, has achieved serenity. The youngest woman is sure that she will be able to juggle the demands of love and work; her mother, after rearing her family, is trying (unsuccessfully) to return to her medical studies, broken off for marriage and motherhood; her grandmother, widowed and alone after a lifetime of doing her duty as a wife and mother, is completely empty of significance to herself. Rose Macaulay's last and best-known novel, *The Towers of Trebizond* (1956), is a very different book, in which the heroine travels in the wilds of Turkey with her aunt, a priest called Father Chantry-Pigg, and a camel. The aunt and the priest share a preoccupation with converting the Turks to Anglo-Catholicism; the heroine is powerfully drawn towards the certainties of orthodox religion, but unable to yield to its pressures because of her passionate love for a married man which she is unable to repudiate. This plot allows Rose Macaulay to present a kaleidoscope of people, events and moods: she writes with evocative sensuality about food and landscape; there are patches of political and theological argument; and the aunt is both sublime and ridiculous, in the manner of the great Victorian lady travellers.

Not all writers of this period, of course, shared the same methods and preoccupations. Ivy Compton-Burnett (1884–1969) took a path which was completely independent of her contemporaries, in terms of both style and content. The archetypical Compton-Burnett novel, whatever the time of its writing, is set in a large upper-class English family around the turn of the century. She once said, 'I do not feel that I have any real or organic knowledge of life later than 1910.' Her preference for expressing almost the entire content of her novels in direct speech links her with the earlier experimental novelist Ronald Firbank: the effect is not unlike reading the script of a play for radio, in which the individuality of the voices and the relevant background information are established only by what is said, with a bare minimum of stage directions. The novels make considerable demands on the reader's concentration, since speech is frequently left unattributed, and pages of dialogue may occur without its being noted that some person who should not have overheard is actually in the room.

In terms of content, the classic Compton-Burnett plot is a highly stylised and abstract treatment of the uses and abuses of power, exploring the interaction between a man who holds all available forms of power, money, moral authority, social standing, legal control, and his powerless underlings. These patriarchs, following Lord Acton's famous dictum that power corrupts, and absolute power corrupts absolutely, are atrocious, self-pitying tyrants. For example, Horace Lamb in *Manservant and Maidservant* (1947) is a monster of pathological miserliness and cruelty who drives his eleven- and twelve-year-old sons to such a pitch of desperation that they seize an opportunity to attempt his murder. He also whines, 'has none of you any sympathy except with children and servants?' (ch. 2) when he finds that an action of notably mean-spirited self-righteousness does not meet with the general approval he feels it deserves.

The defence of the financially and socially helpless underlings, wives, children, poor relations and servants, against the intolerable demands of their masters, is in their use of language – irony, ambiguity, and a persistent refusal to say what they know is expected and desired. For example, Horace Lamb appeals emotionally to his sons:

> 'You know in your hearts that nothing base has ever come from me.'
> There was silence.                                              (ch. 10)

Similarly, Miles Mowbray, in *A Father and His Fate* (1957), puts clumsy pressure on his family to surrender the last vestiges of their independence to his all-devouring ego, and is outraged when he does not succeed:

> 'My Audrey, do you love your father? You are my Cordelia, you know.'
> 'Then you know the risk you are taking.'
> 'Yes, that is sure to be said. And so I am left without a word. That is what would happen to me. I did not expect anything else. Always some excuse to leave me high and dry, a forgotten hulk on the strand! Well, I am learning to suffer it. I expect nothing...'                (ch. 1)

In all her novels, Compton-Burnett presents the bleak, claustrophobic horror of the patriarchal family as it was before it was eroded by various forms of social change and individual opportunity. She intensifies the impression she desires to create by refusing to anchor her characters in space or time through making reference to any outside events or phenomena whatsoever: the result is that the characters, like those in Sartre's influential play *Huis Clos* ('No Exit') (1944), seem suspended in an eternal limbo. The result is the blackest of black comedies, dealing with the subtlest expressions of mental cruelty and the will to power.

### Post-war and contemporary fiction

The trend of English fiction since the end of the Second World War in 1945 has been away from the highly political, consciously European interests of many writers of the 1930s. To some extent there has been a return to the Modernist tradition of stylistic experimentation, an increased interest in sexuality, fantasy, and the fictionality of fiction.

Rosamond Lehmann's (1903–90) *The Weather in the Streets,* published in 1936, includes an episode in which the heroine, entangled in an unhappy affair with a married man, becomes pregnant and has an abortion. This is handled with the utmost delicacy: her state of mind, as she attempts to sell the only valuable thing her lover has given her (a ring), is described at some length, then the next section begins ' "Stay where you are, Mrs Craig," he said softly. "There now. Quite comfy? That's right. Don't worry. All over"' (Part 3, vi-vii). Nonetheless, the novel upset many critics, and many readers, when it was first published. By contrast, in writers of the 1960s and later, the more sordid details of sexuality, abortion, contraception, venereal disease and so on, are often treated with exhaustive, clinical accuracy. For example, Nell Dunn (b.1936) became well known for two books, *Up the Junction* (1963) and *Poor Cow* (1967), in which she examines with journalistic detachment the lives of young working-class London women, including their sexual experiences, and many other women writers such as the American novelist and poet Erica Jong (b.1942) have pursued erotic explicitness still further.

Rosamond Lehmann's later novels include *The Ballad and the Source* (1944): not a war novel, but one which addresses a subject of interest to many women writers, a child's attempt to understand the complexities of the adult world. At ten, the narrator Rebecca finds herself drawn to the glamorous, elderly Mrs Jardine. She is unable to understand the dislike many people, including even Mrs Jardine's own granddaugher, feel for the old lady: a long tale of betrayal and misjudgment unfolds, gradually and indirectly, through the conflicting perceptions of four very different characters. Another writer who explores similar problems of perception and identity is the Anglo-Irish Elizabeth Bowen (1899–1973). *The Death of the Heart* (1938), for instance, chronicles the impact of a sixteen-year-old illegitimate female orphan on a sophisticated, somewhat rigid group of middle-aged Londoners. Portia, whose viewpoint is central to the novel, intuitively understands some things about the family she has entered only too well; other things, of course, she does not understand at all. Her desperate need to be loved and accepted for herself is the touchstone against which the tired evasions and suppressions of the adult world are shown up as second-rate: 'a sort of secret society about nothing, keeping on making little signs to each other' (Bk 3, ch. 6). Later novels, notably *The Heat of Day* (1949), reflect the peculiarly intense, uncertain lives of Londoners enduring the Blitz.

Olivia Manning (1908–80) is a very different kind of novelist. Her most characteristic preoccupation is with discontinuity of experience, between people of different ages and backgrounds. Her first novel, *The Wind Changes* (1937), drew on her Anglo-Irish family background, and dealt with the fight for Irish independence, from the viewpoint of an uncomprehending and apolitical young woman, but all her other novels were written in the post-war period. *The Doves of Venus* (1955) is particularly concerned with the difference between the perspectives of people of different generations. The very young heroine, Ellie, has a conversation with Tom, perhaps fifty years her senior, in which the difference of their outlook is made plain:

'When I was eighteen it seemed we were reaching the Golden Age. Horror, cruelty, injustice – all those things were being left behind.'

Ellie's view is very different:

'Hydrogen bombs…they're a sort of insurance against getting old and not marrying and having no money and perhaps dying alone of starvation in a basement, the way old people do. I just tell myself: 'Don't worry, we'll all be dead long before that happens.'     (Part 2, vi)

Olivia Manning's best-known works are the Balkan and Levant trilogies, a sequence of six novels written between 1960 and 1980, dealing with the same couple, Guy and Harriet Pringle. They represent a considered, distant view of the war, as experienced by a specific individual, comparable in seriousness to Rebecca West's *Black Lamb and Grey Falcon,* though, of course, radically different in format, Olivia Manning had some training as a painter, and this is reflected in her work by her remarkable power to evoke scenes by means of specific, sharply focused detail. The novels form a precisely observed, enormously detailed testimony to the texture of life on the edges of the great European conflict.

One innovative novel of the 1960s which stands completely outside the themes of the other writers mentioned so far is *Wide Sargasso Sea* (1966) by Jean Rhys (1894–1979). Having written a series of shrewdly ironic novels before the Second World War chronicling the misadventures of pathetically passive chorus-girls and kept women in beautiful prose, she dropped out of sight so completely that she was generally believed to be dead. The publication of *Wide Sargasso Sea* brought her triumphantly back to life in the perceptions of the reading public. The novel is very much part of the women's tradition in English writing which is a prolonged, revisionary quarrel with one's predecessors, since it interrogates Charlotte Brontë's *Jane Eyre* from the perspective of almost the only person in it presented entirely without sympathy: Bertha Mason, Rochester's insane first wife. It is, of course, a study of madness, alienation and helplessness, familiar themes in the writing of Jean Rhys, and indeed, in much of women's writing. The unfolding of a dissociated inner consciousness in the form of an interior monologue draws on the practice of the Modernists, Dorothy Richardson and Virginia Woolf: the content of the novel stresses the alienation experienced by white West Indians, a subject entirely outside Charlotte Brontë's interests and experience, and the ways in which Rochester's actions and character contribute to the increasing madness of his wife.

A novelist whose concerns bear some relationship both to the group of politically conscious 1930s writers discussed earlier and to Ivy Compton-Burnett's concern with the more intimate forms of evil is Muriel Spark (*b*.1918). Her best-known novel, *The Prime of Miss Jean Brodie* (1961), set in the early 1930s, deals not with a father and his family, but a teacher and her pupils. Miss Brodie presents herself to her favoured group of pupils as a dictator, a Mussolini, or even 'Providence' or 'God'. In apparently seeking to extend the perceptions and moral range of her pupils, Miss Brodie is in fact seduced by a need to use them to enhance her sense of her own importance. The cool, dispassionate tone of Muriel Spark's writing, like that of Ivy Compton-Burnett, allows the comic aspects of her monstrous creations to be perceived in addition to a sense of the havoc they spread around them. Spark's Catholicism leads her, in the opinion of some critics, to attempt to overburden the novel with a moral and spiritual superstructure which it is too slender to support. Despite this, it is likely to be amongst her most enduring works: as a portrait of a particularly idiosyncratic city (Edinburgh) in a decade of change (the 1930s) it has an almost uncanny accuracy and power of evocation.

Similar preoccupations with power and morality are found in her other novels, as are powerful evocations of place. *Memento Mori* (1959) and *The Girls of Slender Means* (1963) offer two visions of London. The former concerns itself with a group of distinguished elderly intellectuals troubled by threatening telephone calls from Death itself; the latter with the scattered lives of a group of career girls lonely in London, living in a hostel of suffocating gentility. Again the preoccupations with an enclosed society and with personal morality and spirituality are dominant. *The Mandelbaum Gate* (1965) is set in Israel and Jordan, in divided Jerusalem, a city which becomes an involved metaphor for the 'Heavenly City' which is absent on earth but alive and accessible in the minds of individuals.

*The Abbess of Crewe* (1974) is an apparently lightweight work which returns to the preoccupations of the earlier novels: enclosed female community and use and abuse of power. It is a travesty (in every sense of the word) of the political events which led to the downfall of President Richard Nixon in the USA: in an enclosed convent, a ruthless and aristocratic nun (incidentally, with a distinguished degree in English Literature) organises a system of electronic surveillance and espionage to secure her election as abbess of her convent. The juxtapositions in the book are thought-provoking: an easily abused technology and the power that comes with it are set against the unchanging spells of the Church offices and the English poetry which the Abbess murmurs instead of her devotions. It is, as with *The Prime of Miss Jean Brodie,* a book of puzzling tone: an essentially lightweight novel is being used to carry the weight of apparently serious political and moral reflection.

Another interest of her more recent novels is youth remembered from middle age. *Loitering with Intent* (1981) is about a young woman, Fleur, writing her first novel, while working for a sinister baronet, Sir Quentin Oliver. She finds that her writing and his life resonate disastrously until it becomes unclear whether life is imitating art or vice versa. She and her novel survive (though Sir Quentin does not) with the assistance of the baronet's mother, a spirited nonagenarian. *A Far Cry from Kensington* (1988) pursues similar themes. Its subject, Mrs Hawkins, works in publishing in the early 1950s, and so the technical business of writing is as much a part of the narrative as it is in *Loitering with Intent.* Young Mrs Hawkins is immensely fat, serene and self-confident. Looking back on herself from the 1980s, actually a much happier woman, she is able to present the ironic distance between the perceptions which people had of her, those she had of herself, and the ways in which she defended herself from her own unhappiness and uncertainty. Her basic honesty and integrity enable her to survive the malicious hatred of Hector Bartlett, a hack writer whom she had described, with appallingly felicitous accuracy, as a *pisseur de copie*. She refuses to retract this phrase, because it is true; and though he succeeds in getting her sacked from two consecutive jobs and attempts to destroy her by black magic, her unshakable ability to distinguish between truth and nonsense enables her to hold herself together, and indeed, to achieve genuine personal happiness. Religion is subtly but pervasively a force in these novels. Although Mrs Hawkins is quite unconcerned about the difference between Anglo-Catholicism and Roman Catholicism, faith is a solid and substantial element in her life, which enables her to deal clear-headedly with manifestations of evil and chaos such as Hector Bartlett and his Radionics Box. These novels are also quietly subversive of the thesis that young people are happy, and the middle-aged and old entangled by evasion and compromise. Instead, they are about discovering happiness when one is old enough to understand and appreciate it. *Loitering with Intent* ends with the sentence:

> And so, having entered the fullness of my years, from there by the grace of God I go on my way rejoicing.

In addition to her novels, Muriel Spark has written poetry and studies of Mary Shelley and the Brontës, clearly demonstrating her awareness of a tradition of women's writing, a tradition from which she diverges in many ways: she writes much *about* women, but with a curious detachment, a long perspective.

The writing of Iris Murdoch (*b*.1919) is deliberately cerebral and formal, influenced, sometimes overtly, by her non-fiction writing as a professional philosopher. Many of her novels are centred on the viewpoint of a male character. She once commented on this tendency, as follows:

> about writing as a man, this is instinctive...I think I want to write about things on the whole where it doesn't matter whether you're male or female, in which case you'd better be male because a male represents ordinary human beings, unfortunately as things stand at the moment, whereas a woman is always a woman![7]

This is not to say that the complacencies of her male narrators are not ironically subverted; the central character of *A Severed Head* (1961) receives enough unpleasant surprises about the women he has taken utterly for granted to last him a lifetime, and he is not the only Murdoch hero to have this experience. Yet the impression remains that Murdoch has considerable difficulty in handling female characters with the sympathy and insight she gives to her men. One problem inherent in the form of the novel, as her generation inherited it, is that it is designed to express emotional nuances among a small group of leisured people. The cast of a nineteenth-century novel characteristically exist in the boundless leisure of inherited income and no job; similarly, the characters in *A Fairly Honourable Defeat* (1970), despite laboriously created credentials as academics, curators and senior civil servants, seem to have infinite leisure in which to pursue the philosophical and emotional intricacies of the plot. This tendency to hark back to the Victorian philosophical novel as perfected by George Eliot perhaps finds its fullest expression in *The Philosopher's Pupil* (1983), which is a full and leisurely evocation of the social and spiritual life of a provincial town.

The novels of Margaret Drabble (*b*.1939) occupy much the same territory: the articulate, highly educated characters, the settings in London and university towns, the conversations about philosophy and responsibility. *The Millstone* (1965) describes the struggles of an intelligent heroine towards independence; *The Ice Age* (1977) attempts an ambitious anatomy of Britain: rotting cities and characters who feel that they are powerless in the face of social decline, 'a weed on the tide of history'. *The Middle Ground* (1980) is also concerned with urban middle-class life, but is technically rather different, a loose structure reflecting the influence of contingency and chance on the characters within it.

Anita Brookner (*b*.1938) writes with sensitivity about much the same kind of characters. *Providence* (1982) concerns itself with the intellectual struggles of a lecturer at a provincial university, the narrative divided between a transcript of her thoughts and an unsympathetic third person narration. In several novels Brookner is much concerned with the worries of the lecturing classes, particularly the clash between a wish for classical order and the need for romantic freedom.

Mary Lavin (*b*.1912) is a distinguished modern Irish writer working from a Catholic perspective. Most of her *oeuvre* consists of short stories, but she has also written two novels. *Mary O'Grady* (1950) tells the story of a countrywoman who comes to Dublin with her husband in the early years of the century, and experiences a life of unremitting drudgery punctuated by tragedy. Her husband dies young, one son goes to America, then returns mentally ill, two daughters are killed in an accident, and the youngest son fulfils the traditional dream of the Catholic mother by being accepted for the priesthood, only to be rejected at a late stage of his training. Mary, an uneducated, naïve and sentimental woman, is able to transcend these successive appalling shocks with the help of her faith, and thus to make a complete success of living a life which would have reduced most women to despair. It is a study of a type of personality – practical, unintrospective and intuitive – rarely explored in fiction. Lavin's many short stories focus specifically on women's experience, and on continuity within women's lives, for example, 'A Cup of Tea', in which a college-educated woman rejects her mother and her unhappy married life, but, since she is accustomed to rely on her intellect, fails to see the significance of a momentary insight when she recognises the likeness of herself and her fiancé in old photographs of her parents as a young couple.

Edna O'Brien (b.1930) is a very different type of Irish writer. Whereas Mary Lavin grounds her work on her position within rural Ireland, Edna O'Brien moved to London in her thirties and writes from a more detached perspective. Her novels are overtly concerned with women's issues: female repression and female sexuality. This is particularly seen in *Casualties of Peace* (1967) which traces its heroine's struggles from an opening dream of death to her final murder. Her early trilogy *The Country Girls* (1959–64) charts the maturation of two contrasted Irish girls as they move from romantic innocence to disillusionment with marriage and men.

Antonia White (1889–1980) can in some ways be compared with these Irish writers, since her overriding concern as a writer is with Catholicism. Her early *Frost in May* (1933) is a semi-autobiographical account of a convent schoolgirl who is rejected by her father and expelled from her adored school after writing an ingenuous novel which is perceived by others as obscene. White's subsequent trilogy (*The Lost Traveller,* 1950; *The Sugar House,* 1952; *Beyond the Glass,* 1954) changes the name of the central character, but is clearly a continuation of the same story. All Clara's unhappy experiences are mediated through the central place of Catholicism in her life, both as a complex of religious belief, and as an organising structure.

Maureen Duffy (b.1933) shares some thematic interests with the Rhodesian writer Doris Lessing (since she had left Africa long before Rhodesia became Zimbabwe, the term seems appropriate), but perhaps her principal concern is with continuity and discontinuous experience. *Capital* (1975), one of her three London novels, is discontinuous in time: the main plot-line unfolds in the London of the 1970s, centred on Meepers, a lonely, homeless man whose war injuries have left him psychically sensitive to the very distant past, and a university lecturer in eighteenth-century history who befriends him. This narrative is intercut with vignettes of other lives lived in the same geographical area: a Neanderthal man, pre-Celtic tribesmen, a Roman, Saxons and Normans, the Black Death personified as a flea, and a medieval whore. The voices combine to give a sense of city life as one which is necessarily shaped by the patterns of the past even when one is not conscious of it. *Londoners* (1983) is thematically similar, but different in structure: Al, the central character, is absorbed in translating the work of the fourteenth-century French poet, non-conformist and criminal François Villon, and is living in London's bed-sitter land, surrounded by poor and rootless people, foreigners, whores, old people trying to survive on tiny pensions, and other members of the urban underclass. He (or she: this is never clarified) acts as a spokesman for Maureen Duffy's own perception of the value of a sense of the past when s/he says:

> It's perverse to be at heart a medievalist in the computer age, to have an imagination with a five-hundred-year time warp, to see the Paris of Joan of Arc and the London of Marie Lloyd as one eternal city so that the snows of yesteryear slop over the top of my track shoes and soak the legs of my jeans ink blue when I step over the threshold.            (ch. 1)

Maureen Duffy is acutely aware of the past, and of the pressure on personalities trying to survive and maintain a sense of individual dignity in the hostile environment of a great city. Her vision is essentially humane: *Londoners,* even more explicitly than her earlier works, explores and acts out the thesis that human beings, even in the profoundly lonely and disconnected world of bed-sitter land, are connected with one another. The death of a young Irish drug addict, briefly met, is experienced by Al as something directly relevant to his/her own sense of self. The novel is a powerful plea for accepting the human worth of others, however alien in their habits and beliefs. It ends with a demonstration of one logical outcome of refusing to acknowledge any sense of common humanity with strangers: the blowing up of the pub in which Al is drinking as an act of random political terrorism.

One writer who is apparently without a moral axe of any variety to grind is Beryl Bainbridge (*b.*1934), who came to prominence in the 1960s with a series of short, blackly comic novels. Her characters are observed and anatomised from a vantage point of extreme detachment. She tends to portray very ordinary people exposed to extreme situations. For example, in *The Bottle Factory Outing* (1974), the liveliest character in the book – fat, bossy Freda – organises a works outing during which she is accidentally killed. Her workmates, unwilling to face a police enquiry, collaborate in getting her corpse back to the bottle factory without attracting public attention and inter it in an empty sherry barrel. The comedy lies in the precisely delineated reactions of her characters to events: since the reader is told what they think as well as what they say, their complete failure to understand one another's points of view is thus made available for the reader's entertainment.

Brigid Brophy (*b.*1929) also rose to fame in the 1960s. *The Snow Ball* (1964), set at a New Year masked ball, is thematically and structurally connected with Mozart's *Don Giovanni,* and was published in the same year as her *Mozart the Dramatist.* Another highly intellectual novel, *Palace without Chairs* (1978), is a baroque fantasy centred on the flight to London of the teenage lesbian archduchess Heather following a Fascist revolution in the imaginary country of Evarchia, and a subsequent Evarchian history of abdications and assassinations. The use of a royal family links the novel with the tradition of fairy tale, and underlines the author's desire to present her characters as symbolic rather than imitative of life. The novel is an expression of Brophy's critical theories about the pleasure and value of highly self-conscious fiction, and, just as *The Snow Ball* is a fictional version of her critical work on Mozart, *Palace without Chairs* reflects her study of the immaculately artificial Ronald Firbank, *Prancing Novelist* (1973).

It would give entirely the wrong impression to say that Molly Keane, born in 1904 but still writing in the 1980s, stands at the end of the tradition of the 'Big House' Irish novels of the much earlier Somerville and Ross and her near-contemporary Elizabeth Bowen. Her books are certainly full of the decline of great gentry families: unpaid debts, horses sold, home farms falling to ruin and the crumbling of the big house itself. That is merely the context; her treatment of this material is closer to that of Beryl Bainbridge. She is, however, a celebratory writer: wild, anarchic and intensely compassionate. The grim and fantastical *Good Behaviour* (1981) demonstrates how its monstrous heroine, seen at the beginning of the book in her rampant middle age, grew slowly and through a series of very real disasters into the inhuman and yet sentimental creature of her decline. The grand family grows further and further out of touch with the realities of modern Irish life. The cultural clashes which form the high comedy of Somerville and Ross are here matter for the blackest of black comedies.

Molly Keane was herself born into the world which she anatomises in her novels. It is worth noting that, although she wrote novels and plays in the 1920s and 30s, these were all published as the work of 'M.J. Farrell': social pressure would have prevented anyone in her world of hunting and racing from claiming authorship. A convention decreed not only that nobody should be seen to have literary interests but also, as she records, that it was bad form simply to carry a pen. In the novels of her maturity, published under her own name, this and all other conventions are left firmly behind.

*Time after Time* (1983) is a strangely positive and joyous work. The cast of literally and spiritually deformed siblings inhabiting a typically doomed big house would seem to promise nothing but tragedy; however, a genuinely comic spirit impels the novel forward, so that (via a Trappist monk and a ham sandwich, a war-crimes investigator and an episode of spirited shoplifting) in the end the wicked are left in the purgatory of each other's company while the sympathetic characters receive a satisfactory chance to live happily within the framework of contemporary Ireland.

In one sense or another, most of the women writers of the late twentieth century write from a detached standpoint. All writers attempt to express what they perceive as significant; but the conscious engagement of the reader in a complex moral drama is rare. A.S. Byatt (*b*.1936) is a notable exception: one of the few women writers of the twentieth century consciously working on a large scale and with a Victorian sense of detail. *The Virgin in the Garden* (1979) and its sequel, *Still Life* (1985), are consciously and deliberately historical, evoking the 1950s and Queen

Elizabeth II's coronation; long, densely textured, ambitious novels, with the sense of the exemplary and significant nature of ordinary experience for which George Eliot is the natural model. The whole nature of writing, the perception of what one is trying to achieve by exerting the authority of authorship, has been growing increasingly problematic and difficult since the end of the nineteenth century. Authority has long had difficulty with women, since the dominant ideology of patriarchy has always accused authoritative women of lack of femininity. In reaction, many twentieth-century women writers have not only chosen to abandon an authoritative stance, but have declared such a stance ideologically unsound. Therefore, one can see the unashamed seriousness, fullness and depth of A.S. Byatt's novels as doubly courageous, in that they are moving against the mainstream of contemporary critical theory and novelistic practice. They draw specifically on a nineteenth-century female tradition of writing, and succeed, like the work of the best Victorian novelists, in creating a context of moral seriousness and significance for the trivial and day-to-day events of provincial life. Her most recent novel is a profoundly ambitious undertaking: *Possession* (1990) traces the paths of two young academics of the late 1980s, Roland and Maud, as they decipher the progress of an affair between two (imaginary) Victorian poets, Randolph Henry Ash and Christabel LaMotte. The novel has extraordinary depth and reality: Byatt performs acts of literary ventriloquism which go far beyond pastiche and produces poems of real quality for the imaginary poets, as well as journals and letters convincing in every detail. The Victorian re-creations are impressive, but the novel places itself even more firmly in the tradition of George Eliot in that it deals with philosophical and moral issues in a serious way: the characters do not talk about philosophy; instead, philosophical concerns are an inextricable part of the fabric of the book. Not the least courageous aspect of it is the analysis of what has happened to literature and learning in the contemporary world: literature is seen as a commodity, a deadly means by which competitive academics scrabble for advancement. The lopsidedness of extreme feminist criticism is exposed, the meretricious games of extreme literary theoreticians are analysed and found seriously wanting, as are the profoundly negative tendencies of Leavisite critical theory. The novel explores the difference between human intentions, at once self-serving and consciously idealistic, and practical effects, often so different from the conscious intentions of the actors. Maud and Roland are saved by their lurking belief in the value of art as part of human life. Intensely aware of feminist issues, Byatt has the courage in this book to make a weighty plea for human values, beyond trends in art and divisive gender stereotyping.

If *Possession* is a worthy product of the school of George Eliot, the works of a slightly earlier novelist, Barbara Pym (1913–80), are a faint reflection of the manner of Jane Austen. She lacks Austen's fierceness, but her fiction is essentially concerned with tracing the interrelations of small groups of middle- or upper-middle-class English characters as they move through small and beautifully observed worlds to happiness or self-knowledge. There is much concern with the influence of religious, particularly Anglo-Catholic, belief. Her best-known novels, *A Glass of Blessings* (1958) and *Excellent Women* (1952), are particularly fine examples of this delicate, unspectacular art: there are no violent events, few strong emotions reach the surface of the novels, but there are no flaws in observation, and the intimation of a quiet providence at work in the lives of the characters is convincing and disturbing – a Victorian world and sensibility oddly at home in a modern context.

In the last decade, a number of novelists have emerged who write from a radical feminist perspective. Their writing is wholly different in kind and intention from that of A.S. Byatt and Barbara Pym, inheritors of the nineteenth-century realistic novel. Instead, the complex, interwoven structures of writers such as Maureen Duffy, and the detached perspective of writers such as Beryl Bainbridge, are important influences on this non-naturalistic, symbolist tradition, shaped by non-mainstream genres such as fantasy, Gothic and science fiction.

The novels and short stories of Angela Carter (1940–92) are bleakly funny, set in a variety of worlds which bear a tangential, distorted relationship to what we perceive as reality. Her palette of images and events is surreal, violent and paradoxical, and she is concerned above all with the interplay of reality and appearances. The hero of her novel *The Passion of New Eve* (1977), which is set in an apocalyptic America of the near future, is captured by a group of surgically minded radical feminists and reshaped from a handsome man into a beautiful woman. Eve, as he has become, then undergoes a brutal initiation into what it means to be female in the modern world:

> intensive study of feminine manners, as well as my everyday work about the homestead, kept me in a state of permanent exhaustion. I was tense and preoccupied; although I was a woman, I was now also passing for a woman, but, then, many women born spend their whole lives in just such an imitation. (ch. 8)

What Angela Carter is exploring, through Eve and many other characters in her novels, is the way that men and women (but especially women, the main focus of her concentration) are shaped and warped by the expectations of their culture. Her very young heroines, Melanie in *The Magic Toyshop* (1967), Marianne in *Heroes and Villains* (1969), are shown to be inventing their adult selves out of whatever materials are to hand. The conscious artificiality and the cerebral quality of her work are not a symptom of inadequacy but an essential tool for a writer so fundamentally concerned with self-creation and the playing of parts. The text forms an intellectually satisfying complement to the content. Her plots, typically, include dramatic twists and turns, which surprise the protagonists but are not allowed to surprise the reader. Four pages into *The Infernal Desire Machines of Doctor Hoffman* (1972), we already know that the hero Desiderio will meet and love Albertina Hoffman, and that he will ultimately murder her. The narrator (this, like *The Passion of New Eve*, is a first-person narrative) may recall his earlier self feeling astonishment, but the reader is not permitted to share it.

Another notable fabulist is Emma Tennant (*b*.1938), who shares Angela Carter's surrealism, and her sense of humour. *The Bad Sister* (1978) is a remarkable creative translation of James Hogg's nineteenth-century study of madness and alienation, *Confessions of a Justified Sinner* (1819). In what passes for the real world of this novel, Jane, the schizophrenic subject, is the illegitimate daughter of a wealthy man, who also has a legitimate daughter of almost the same age. Jane is a kind of malignant shadow of this other girl, and ultimately murders both her and their common father. Emma Tennant's *Wild Nights* (1979), with a title taken from Emily Dickinson, is a fantastical, symbolic narrative of tension and conflict between North and South, landowner and tenant, and, most centrally, men and women. The bizarre battles played out by the various forces of conventionality and unconventionality are seen through the uncritical eyes of a child, a narrative device which leaves the reader unable to locate a set of 'normal' reactions against which the characters' behaviour can be tested. The life of a landed family in the Scottish Borders is transmuted into the wildest and most exhilarating fantasy.

Emma Tennant's 'translations' of Hogg and Robert Louis Stevenson (*The Bad Sister* and *Two Women of London* (1989)) also illustrate a tendency in women's writing found as early as the seventeenth century, which is the deliberate revision, or paralleling, of existing male-centred narratives through female versions. Two early examples of this are Charlotte Lennox's *The Female Quixote* (1752), and 'Philo-Phillipa''s revision of the myth of Apollo and Daphne at the beginning of her poem to Katherine Philips (before 1667). A modern example is Esmé Dodderidge's entertaining and sardonic *The New Gulliver, or, The Adventures of Lemuel Gulliver Jr in Capovolta* (1979), which takes the basic plot-structure of Swift's *Gulliver's Travels* and uses it to feminist ends by creating a society in which women harass, abuse and exploit men. In the case of *Two Women of London*, Tennant has shifted the focus of the story from the issue of good and evil in the same character, explored by Stevenson, to the ease with which a woman encumbered by children can lose her personal and social identity. As a deserted mother of two, Mrs Hyde is trapped in a state of poverty and desperation; the single career-girl Miss Jekyll can borrow with impunity to finance an elegant middle-class lifestyle:

if Mrs Hyde was the poor poor – that is, too poor to exist without State support...then Eliza was the 'rich poor', the individual encouraged to take out a hundred per cent mortgage: which 'I' could, of course, with a job at the Shade and the hint from Sir James that I'd go on to run his design business in the South West...                    ('Editor's Postscript')

The story is thus a parable of women's lives, and an examination of the constraints which affect them.

Fay Weldon (*b*.1933) has written a number of novels dealing principally with motherhood and friendship and rivalry between women. Perhaps the most extreme of these is *The Life and Loves of a She-Devil* (1984), which addresses questions of women's status, among other things. The central character, Ruth (a big woman), decides to revenge herself on her unfaithful husband Bobbo and his mistress Mary, a petite, attractive and successful novelist. She succeeds in burdening her rival with her own problems (notably her unattractive children), and undergoes extensive and drastic surgery to turn herself into a physical replica of the other woman, taking over, in time, her role, life, house and professional career. This disturbing fable suggests how far women will go in response to male demands – apart from wrecking the lives of the adulterous pair, the She-Devil has in effect annihilated herself. It also, like Tennant's *Two Women of London,* suggests how much women's lives are interpreted in terms of potentially mobile signifiers – fatness or thinness, motherhood or single independence.

Jeanette Winterson (*b*.1959) has already written a series of very well-received novels, from *Oranges are Not the Only Fruit* (1985) to *Sexing the Cherry* (1990). She writes from a specifically lesbian perspective, in a highly experimental style which exploits and underscores the fictionality of her fiction; her novels are witty, fantastic and disturbing, making serious points about the nature of writing, memory, time and the construction of personality in a very playful manner. Her work suggests that lesbian fiction has come a very long way since *The Well of Loneliness,* as does that of the Scottish writer Ellen Galford, whose 1986 novel, *The Fires of Bride,* locates her story on a remote Hebridean island among a virtually all-female cast of characters to whom men are more or less irrelevant, neither feared nor desired.

# Drama

### Lady Gregory and the Abbey Theatre

The rise of women dramatists in the *fin de siècle* and the early twentieth century was very much a part of a changing culture in the theatre, in which plays which presented an idea or a problem, rather than merely an entertaining spectacle, became increasingly popular.

One remarkable example of the new theatrical culture was the Abbey Theatre in Dublin, which opened in 1904, and was very much a dramatist's theatre. Many of its most successful plays were written by Lady Augusta

Gregory (1852–1932); it was her box-office hits which made it possible for the Abbey to go on staging experimental plays by W.B. Yeats, J.M. Synge and Sean O'Casey, some of which puzzled or angered their early audiences (Synge's *The Playboy of the Western World* caused riots when it was first put on in 1907). The Abbey owed its origin to the generosity of another woman, a Manchester tea heiress called Annie Horniman (1860–1937), who gave £20,000 to build it.[8] She continuted to pay the actors' and managers' salaries for six years; and later founded the Gaiety in her own city of Manchester.[9] It might be assumed that the titled Lady Gregory would have been wealthy enough to act as 'backer'. In fact, she had relatively little money she could call her own: as a widow, she held her estate at Coole in trust for her oldest son, and was certainly not legally able to touch any of his capital to subsidise the theatre she loved.

The most successful of her many plays was *The Rising of the Moon* (1907).[10] She wrote both comedies and tragedies, all of them in a very distinctive Anglo-Irish dialect, the English of people whose speech-patterns are formed by Gaelic. Her plays are swift-moving, many with small casts, and very varied in subject-matter. Few deal with romantic love: even *Grania* (1912), a three-act play with only three characters, based on the legend of Grania, who is married (against her will) to the much older Finn, elopes with Diarmuid, but goes back to Finn after Diarmuid's death, deals most crucially with the fact that the principal emotional bond in the play is between Diarmuid and Finn, and that although Grania has successfully wrecked their relationship, neither of them has ever really transferred his love to her. This sombre play was never performed. The kind of tragedy which filled seats at the Abbey is represented by her one-act play *The Gaol Gate* (1909). The structure of this play focuses on the political situation in Ireland, and the enormous distance in sympathy between the Protestant Ascendancy and the Irish people. The principal characters are two women at the gaol gate, wife and mother of Denis. Denis had been arrested for murder, with two of his friends. The entire village knows that one of the others, Terry, fired the shot, but the authorities have direct evidence only against Denis. It has been rumoured that Denis has informed on his friends and been freed; a letter has come for the women, which (being illiterate) they cannot read, and are reluctant to show anyone else, so they have come to Galway to find out what is happening. In spite of the fact that Denis is generally known not to be the killer, the mother's attitude is that if he has turned informer, it is a shame worse than death. The wife, by contrast, would forgive him anything if he would come back to her. Their different attitudes are used to explore the emotional complexities of the situation. In the end, they find out that he has been convicted and hanged (the letter was to tell them of this decision), and the other two have been set free. The wife is heart-broken; the mother rises above her grief in pride and thankfulness that her son died like a hero, and did not inform to save himself. The play dramatises, very starkly and effectively, the moral imperatives of life in an occupied country, and is also unusual in that the entire drama is sustained by the two women, providing splendid opportunities for the actresses.

Although *The Rising of the Moon* is a comedy, it makes the same political point about Irish solidarity in the face of English oppression, most notably when the poor ballad-singer says of the reward offered for an escaped Republican: 'is it a poor man like me, that has to be going the roads and singing in fairs, to have the name on him that he took a reward?' It also emphasises the cultural cohesiveness of Ireland: the policeman who is the main character is gradually won round by the ballad-singer's evocation of the songs they both know.

### Suffragette drama

The relationship between successful runs of plays by women and the presence of women behind the scenes in management, production or finance is not fortuitous, since it is the management which dictates which plays actually appear before the public. This can be seen in English theatres as well as in Dublin: the American-born actress, playwright and novelist Elizabeth Robins (1862–1952), together with fellow-actress Marian Lea, took the Vaudeville theatre as managers in 1892, and put on *Karin,* a play by a Norwegian woman, Alfhild Agrell. Elizabeth Robins had been heavily involved in publicising and championing the plays of Ibsen (she learned Norwegian so as to read him in the original); it is interesting therefore that when she had a theatre of her own, it was a Norwegian woman's play she chose to put on. By 1912, there were four actress-managers of London theatres, and Lilian Bayliss (1874–1937), the woman who created the Old Vic, had managed to get a theatre licence for what was then the Victoria Music Hall in Waterloo Road.[11] This control of theatres by women managers was instrumental in allowing women writers to put their plays before the public.

Elizabeth Robins co-wrote *Alan's Wife* with Florence Bell (1851–1930), performed in 1893. It appeared anonymously and caused a furore: the heroine, Jean, a working-class girl, is widowed at the end of the first act, and murders her handicapped baby because she doubts her ability to support him alone.[12] A later play by Elizabeth Robins, *Votes for Women,* was staged by the distinguished director Harley Granville-Barker in 1907, and was successful both as a play and as a political statement. The context of such dramas is the increasing popularity of 'problem plays' from the 1890s onwards: plays which aired a social issue and provoked discussion, in ways which are analogous to television documentaries in our own time.

Elizabeth Robins was far from being the only suffragette to write a play. The very successful one-act comedy *How the Vote was Won* was written by Cicely Hamilton (1872–1952) and Christopher St John (a woman; *d*.1960), and produced by Edith Craig (1869–1908; daughter of the great late

Victorian actress Ellen Terry) in 1909. It ran and ran in London, and then toured the country with great success; it was even favourably received by the critics of the *Times*, the *Daily Graphic* and the *Pall Mall Gazette*, papers which were certainly no friends of suffragettes in general. Its success is linked by the critic of the *Pall Mall Gazette* with the recent change in theatrical fashion:

> the fact that it is so acutely controversial is not at all against it – is, in fact, a virtue rather than a defect, for the Theatre of Ideas is upon us. All that really matters is that it is clever and it is witty.[13]

The plot of the play is based on the idea of a women's strike. A principal anti-suffrage argument was that women were looked after by men and were not independent adults, therefore did not deserve the franchise. The suffragettes, therefore, persuade all women to stop work, and present themselves either to their nearest male relative or to the workhouse, thus requiring men actually to support them, individually or through the rates. The play takes place in the little house of Horace Cole, who is faced with the ghastly possibility of having to support his sister, his niece, a distant relation, his first cousin and his aunt, who arrive at intervals throughout the play. The scales drop from his eyes – 'if this rotten Government think we're going to maintain millions of women in idleness just because they don't like the idea of my Aunt Lizzie making a scratch on a bit of paper and shoving it in a ballot-box once every five years, this government have reckoned without the men!' (the assembled female relatives all cheer, and Horace and his friends march on Westminster). The fun of the play lies mostly in the wide cross-section of types displayed, and the absence of sermonising: instead of trying to argue Horace out of his position, the women put him in a position where he reverses his own views without noticing that he has done so. Evelyn Glover's *A Chat with Mrs Chicky* (1912) and *Miss Appleyard's Awakening* (1913) are less entertaining because they are less successful in integrating their message with the requirements of drama: the characters just stand and argue. A noteworthy feature of both these plays is that working-class women are shown as more politically aware, better informed and more intelligent than the middle-class ladies who employ them.[14]

Not all Edwardian women's plays centred on women's suffrage. *Rutherford and Son* (1912), which ran for a whole season at the Vaudeville, London, was a very successful play (in dialect) by Githa Sowerby (1876–1970).[15] Its main character, John Rutherford, is the master of a successful pottery, and a domestic tyrant, whose children live in permanent terror of him. By the end of the play, he has managed to drive all of them away, and faces the fear that his achievement, without a son to pass it on to, is meaningless. His downtrodden daughter-in-law is revealed as a woman of ruthless maternal passion, as she bargains with him over her son, the only grandchild – to whose interests she has already sacrificed her own husband.

In the 1920s, the public appetite for 'problem plays' continued. Even Marie Stopes (1880–1958), champion of effective contraception, managed to persuade the Royal Court to stage her play *Our Ostriches* (the title refers to the Birth Rate Commissioners) in 1923, even though she was a wildly self-indulgent and undisciplined writer. It was less a play than a dramatised tract (like all her fiction), and was not a hit with the public: but it is interesting that a twenties theatrical management thought it a good risk. Slightly earlier in the same year, she made a different attempt at getting her message across to the widest possible audience by writing the script for a film, *Maisie's Marriage*; this was not shown in London until 1925, but was quite successful in the provinces.[16]

### Drama between the wars

The inter-war period saw public taste move away from 'problem plays' and towards more sophisticated forms of entertainment in which the message, if there was one, was presented in less blatant forms. M.J. Farrell (Molly Keane) was successful with a number of light-hearted society comedies, the first of which was *Spring Meeting* (1938). A different kind of playwright, Elizabeth Mackintosh (1896–1952), who wrote plays under the name Gordon Daviot and detective stories as Josephine Tey, wrote a historical play which was a critical and popular success, *Richard of Bordeaux* (1933), though an attempt to repeat the success with *Queen of Scots* in the following year was a disappointment. She also wrote *A Shilling for Candles* (1936), both as a play and a book.

### Post-war and contemporary drama

The post-war period saw a number of highly competent, popular and unambitious plays by women. Dodie Smith (1896–1990) was one such writer. *Dear Octopus* (1938) is her best-loved play: the Octopus of the title is a matriarch presiding over the reunion of her family. The play ran until the theatres were closed by the outbreak of war in September 1939, and was successfully revived in the 1960s. *I Capture the Castle* (1954) was another effective and well-received play. Enid Bagnold (1889–1981) is best remembered for *National Velvet* (1946), adapted for the stage from her own book (later it became a well-known Hollywood film) and *The Chalk Garden* (1956). The play *The Mousetrap* by the detective novelist Agatha Christie (1890–1976) has made theatrical history by running continuously in the West End for forty years (since 1952); it must thus rank as one of the most successful plays ever produced. Thus, a number of professional women playwrights were, as in the Victorian period, successfully competing with men in creating a type of drama which was, on the whole, well-crafted and non-controversial.

There is a major turning-point in the history of modern English drama in the year 1968: the repeal of government censorship. The repressive nature of this censorship has been outlined in an earlier chapter; it did, of course, cause endless trouble for Edwardian playwrights, such as Elizabeth Robins,who went anywhere near socially contentious issues. But it became even more of a problem in the 1950s and 60s, as post-war writers struggled to represent a changing society in an appropriate language. The Lord Chamberlain's office cut expletives, whether scatological, sexual or blasphemous (however appropriate to the character); and reference to homosexuality, divorce, members of the Royal Family, or eminent modern persons; anything which might be even remotely understood as an attack on Christian institutions, the Crown, or the established order of society; or anything which might not be considered in good taste: this policy resulted in the banning of productions of Sophocles's *Oedipus Tyrannus,* and the *Oberammergau Passion Play,* among many other dramas.[17] The feminist drama of the last two decades became possible only when the campaign to abolish this censorship was finally successful in 1968.

Two women's plays of this transitional period were significant contributions to the new serious theatre of the 1960s. Shelagh Delaney (*b.*1939) wrote *A Taste of Honey* when she was only eighteen, and it became an immediate popular and critical success. Like her contemporaries, John Osborne and Harold Pinter, Delaney explored characters and situations which the very middle-class theatre of the preceding decades had preferred to overlook. The play centres on a working-class mother and her adolescent daughter in Salford, Lancashire; their respective boyfriends; and the tensions between them. Jo, the daughter, wants to get away from her mother, Helen, who, in turn, says, 'Why don't you learn from my mistakes?' However, pressures which they experience, but cannot articulate, cause Jo to follow in her mother's footsteps. She becomes pregnant by Jimmy, a young black man doing his National Service, and faces single parenthood. The play opens up themes of fear, anger and tension in motherhood which in 1958 represented ground-breaking exploration of taboo subjects. In Act II, Jo, now pregnant, is living with Geoff, a gay man who is much more whole-heartedly 'motherly' than Jo herself. This relationship comes to an end when Helen, who has been thrown out by her new lover, returns to the flat. Jo, who is very ambivalent towards her own baby, is both able and willing to 'mother' her own mother: 'For the first time in my life I feel really important. I feel as though I could take care of the whole world.' The complexities and power-politics of caretaking are explored from a variety of angles.

The other ground-breaking woman playwright of the 1960s was Ann Jellicoe (*b.*1927), who, unlike Delaney, is primarily concerned with male emotional patterns. *The Sport of My Mad Mother,* first performed in 1958, is a play about violence and tribal identity. The action is steered and controlled by Greta, a mother-goddess figure, pregnant throughout the second and third acts, who exercises an effective emotional authority over both men and other women. *The Knack* (1961) is also a play about power and hostility rather than about love. Three men share a house: Tolen, who is outstandingly successful sexually; Colin, who envies him; and Tom, who seems to be indifferent. Tolen claims that attracting women is a 'knack', directly dependent on exerting an appropriately masculine authority: 'First you must realise that women are not individuals, but types. No, not even types, just women. They want to surrender but they don't want the responsibility of surrendering' (Act I). When a girl, Nancy, appears in the street outside and asks them for directions to the YWCA, they take her as a specimen to prove Tolen's point. Jellicoe's points are to do with power, relationships of submission and dominance. The victimisation of Nancy is a painful demonstration of this, but so is the way that Tolen and Colin (who actually owns the house) are completely agreed in perceiving Colin as a failure, and Tolen a success. It is a play about roles, rather than about gender.

The importance of women in theatrical management to the staging of women's drama, particularly of more experimental kinds, is still considerable. Joan Littlewood's Theatre Workshop Company, based at the Theatre Royal in the East End of London in the late 1950s and early 60s staged new plays written for the company, including Delaney's *A Taste of Honey*. Littlewood also bore the overall responsibility for Theatre Workshop's best-known production, *Oh, What a Lovely War* (1963), collectively composed by company members. Similarly, Joan Plowright's position as a producer in the National Theatre Company in the 1960s enabled her to press for positive discrimination in the commissioning of new plays by women – Maureen Duffy's *Rites* (1969) was a result of this initiative.[18] The play is connected in theme with Euripides's *Bacchae*, which has as the spring of its tragic action women's resentment at a male attempt to pry into their mysteries. It is set in a women's public toilet, a space where women can talk and act freely without men. The action reaches its climax when a short-haired figure in a suit and coat emerges from one of the cubicles and tries to escape; the women turn on this person and beat it to death, only realising too late that it is actually a woman. The play thus begins by showing the positive aspects of gender-based solidarity, and ends with murderous lashing out against the outsider.

Since the early 1970s, feminist theatre companies such as Monstrous Regiment, with which Caryl Churchill created *Vinegar Tom,* Mrs Worthington's Daughters, and the Woman's Theatre Group, have collectively created a forum for new work questioning women's social and political roles.[19]

Pam Gems (*b*.1925) has written a number of plays which focus on the lives of women. *Piaf* (1978) is a play about the working-class French singer Edith Piaf, whose only sustained relationship is with her woman friend Toine. The structure is episodic, moving back and forth over Piaf's life, rounding out the picture of a remarkable woman who never spared herself, her lovers or her friends in her effort to put all of herself into her singing. It offers a bravura starring role for the main actress. *Dusa, Fish, Stas and Vi* (1976) is a very different type of play, in which interest is divided among the four women of the title. The plot centres on the attempts of the four women to retrieve Dusa's children, kidnapped by her ex-husband. The women lead very different lives: Dusa is not working, and would be a full-time mother if she could only get her children back; Fish is a professional radical, a speaker for a left-wing group; Stas is a physiotherapist who wants to do a PhD in marine biology and is saving money towards this by working at night as a 'hostess', a high-class prostitute; Vi is young, working-class and anorexic. Each woman is struggling to live her own life as best she can, but is also prepared to help and support her friends. The counterpointing of the four stories gives them a collective significance as a statement about women's lives which none of the four stories could sustain on its own.

Claire Luckham's (*b.*1944) *Trafford Tanzi* (1978) is a very successful play which uses a sustained metaphor of wrestling for the difficulties a girl faces in growing up: the cliché 'wrestling with problems' is brought vividly to life as Luckham uses the full-bloodedly dramatic repertoire of movement in all-in wrestling to represent Tanzi's strife with her parents and husband. This structuring, besides making the play extremely funny and giving the audience a fast-moving and visually exciting show, enables her both to end the play on an upbeat note of Tanzi's victory, and to imply the virtual certainty of a re-match: Tanzi, whether we see her as a professional wrestler or as Everywoman, will never be able to rest on her laurels.

*Steaming* (1981), by Nell Dunn, author of the sixties novels *Up the Junction* and *Poor Cow,* is another play which pushed back the frontiers of the theatrically permissible. It has a cast of six women, all of them well over thirty, and takes place in a dilapidated public Turkish bathhouse. It is thus a private, women-only space which is not somebody's home, and a haven for the women, both working-class and middle-class, who visit it. At the end of Act I, the women learn that the baths are to be closed in six weeks, and band together as a community to try (unsuccessfully) to save them. The play is therefore unusual in focusing on women's enjoyment of each other's company, and in representing women's bodies as a source of pleasure to themselves, particularly in the case of the mentally retarded Dawn, who is encouraged to take all her clothes off and enjoy a moment of freedom from her mother's repressive rule. The play disregards the tacit theatrical convention that only beautiful bodies should be exposed on stage, in order to give pleasure to the onlookers, and insists on older women's right to be seen as playful, sensual and fully human.

The plays of Caryl Churchill (*b.*1938) have been consistently inventive and audacious, both technically and thematically. *Top Girls* (1982) is a play with a characteristically complex texture. The first act takes place in a restaurant, where a 1980s woman, Marlene, who has just been made managing director of an employment agency, has invited five inspirational heroines to dinner: Isabella Bird, the Victorian explorer; Lady Nijo, a thirteenth-century Japanese imperial courtesan, later a nun; Pope Joan; Dull Gret, a peasant from a Breughel painting; and Patient Griselda. Marlene and the women talk about their lives. All of them have been faced with difficult choices. One of these is children: Isabella had none, Nijo and Griselda, both of whom had been obedient daughters and wives, had their children taken away. Joan was stoned to death when the birth of her baby revealed her sex to the Roman people. Act II opens in Marlene's employment agency, where Marlene is interviewing yet another female under-achiever with ruthless competence. Then the scene shifts to Angie, sixteen years old, who seems more immature than her friend, who is twelve. Angie, Marlene's niece, is confused and childish, perhaps subnormal. In the last scene, Angie turns up at the employment agency, hopelessly attaching herself to the glamorous Marlene, whom she has seen twice in seven years. Act III is a flashback to the previous year, to Marlene's visit to her sister, which had been engineered by Angie. The sister, Joyce, is herself a working-class under-achiever: she works as a cleaner, and her husband has left her. As the sisters talk, we discover that Angie is Marlene's child whom Marlene had when she was seventeen; the older sister adopted her. Moreover, caring for Angie as a very demanding baby caused Joyce to miscarry the only child she ever conceived herself. Marlene is a Thatcherite go-getter, upwardly mobile, attacking her sister for not doing anything with her life: 'Anyone can do anything if they've got what it takes...if they're stupid or lazy or frightened, I'm not going to help them get a job, why should I?' But Joyce brings this back to the personal level: 'What about Angie?...She's stupid, lazy and frightened, so what about her?' Marlene has no answer to this, and Joyce forces her to a recognition that her success has been dependent on Joyce's willingness to free her: she and Angie are members of the underclass without which Marlene's upward mobility would be impossible. The story of Marlene, trying to live by confident assumptions about success and achievement, and the account of how these are put in context by her permanent entanglement with a subnormal child, is set in historical context by the five heroines of Act I, who, in their separate ways, make it plain that civilisation has always been designed for men rather than women. Dull Gret's enraged resistance, leading her women neighbours on a manic charge through Hell – 'you just keep running on and fighting' – seems the only reasonable response. It is not what Marlene wanted to hear, either in this act or from her sister Joyce in Act III, but the realities of women's lives are resistant to morally simple solutions. The last word in the play is from Angie, the helplessly destructive child who will always have to be looked after: 'Frightened'.

Churchill's 1987 hit, *Serious Money,* is a powerful satire on greed in the 'Thatcher years': the political context is made explicit. The surreal energy of the profit for profit's sake life of money traders, fuelled on adrenalin, champagne and cocaine, maintains a comic momentum which becomes shocking as one begins to realise the huge impact of this savage battle for immediate financial gain ('a cross between roulette and space invaders') on the lives of the whole population of the world. There are no heroes in this play. The pretensions of the traditional upper-class male brokers to social and moral responsibility are savagely denied:

> FROSBY: My lovely city's sadly changed.
> Sic transit gloria! Glory passes!
> Any wonder I'm deranged,
> Surrounded by the criminal classes...
> GRIMES: We're only doing just the same
> All you bastards always done.
> New faces in your old square mile,
> Making money with a smile,
> Just as clever, just as vile. (Act II)

This, however, is not a simple-minded exercise in knocking the establishment. Traditionally excluded classes have flooded into the city – women, yobs, black and Third World people – but they are not given any kind of moral alibi as victims of oppression; instead, Churchill presents greed as a straightforwardly human trait, based as it is on the common instinct for personal survival. The only difference is that representatives of the traditional underclasses are more clear-sighted and less sentimental. The relationship of profit to production and jobs is stated only by a Peruvian tycoon, Jacinta Condor, who has decided to sell her assets in South America (except her indispensable access to cocaine production) in order to go to the West and make money out of money – 'why should my money stay in Peru and suffer?'. She has just put several thousand people out of work, and contributed substantially to the collapse of her country's economy; the only difference between her and the other City people is that she is directly aware of doing so.

*Serious Money* is technically interesting in a number of ways. Caryl Churchill disciplines the obscene slang of the money-market by the unobtrusive but consistent use of verse, which distances and contains the speakers, helping to maintain the precise balance which will allow the audience to go on laughing and still absorb the political message. Another device (which she also uses in *Top Girls,* among other plays) is creating a very dense aural texture by having one (or more than one) speaker begin before the previous speaker has finished, which requires very careful timing by the actors, but speeds up the drama by keeping the audience's attention switching from one focus to another, in effect mimicking the frenetic pace of City life.

# Poetry

## The onset of Modernism

To discuss English women poets of the twentieth century in a single section is perhaps to impose a somewhat arbitrary categorisation on very different writers. Edith Sitwell (1887–1964), despite current critical eclipse, was one of the first English women poets of the modern period to make a name for herself. She engaged in a unique experiment with language, putting herself through a training in the technical manipulation of sound unparalleled in its rigour. She approached the art of poetry as a painter approaches painting, which is to say, by learning the abstract values of tone and colour, and how to juxtapose them, rather than starting from the need to communicate meaning in its raw form. In an age of abstract painting, in which colour and form were separated from the need to imitate nature, she became an abstract poet. Her early series of poems, *Façade* (1922), demonstrates the distinctiveness of her poetic practice, and also its elegance and wit. 'Waltz', which evokes an early Victorian atmosphere, opens:

Daisy and Lily,
Lazy and silly,
Walk by the shore of the wan grassy sea, –
Talking once more 'neath a swan-bosomed tree.
Rose castles,
Tourelles,
Those bustles
Where swells
Each foam-bell of ermine,
They roam and determine
What fashions have been and what fashions will be, –
What tartan leaves born,
What crinolines worn.

It is unfortunate that the media made her into an icon of Byzantine extravagance and aristocratic irrelevance: she is perhaps the most important of the women poets of the twentieth century whose reputation has been eclipsed. The spiritual poems of 1939–45 alone are worthy of study as a re-invention of a lost tradition of women's spirituality. Her late poems, particularly 'The Yellow Girl' and 'La Bella Bona Roba', are extraordinary, and require re-evaluation.

There are several important women poets of the Modernist movement in the 1920s who were either English or, like H.D., American by nationality but European by preference, and spent most of their time in England. H.D., who was psychoanalysed by Freud himself, and fascinated by his new insights into human character and perceptions, solved her difficulty in locating a female voice by going back, like Freud with his creative use of the

Oedipus myth, to the ancient Greeks. The only major Greek woman poet whose works are preserved is Sappho (seventh/sixth century BC), but the corpus of Greek myths provides an extraordinary range of vital and dynamic female characters. For H.D., the events of her own life and emotions were compellingly refracted through these archetypal patterns of story. Her use of classical myths was wide-ranging and eclectic, but the figures of Helen, the supremely desirable woman, Hermes, the ambiguous god of magic, thievery and trickery, and Osiris, the Egyptian god who married his twin sister, died and was resurrected, are frequently recurring images in her writing. One of her aims was to convey the double consciousness of mind and body, a mythologising of the womb as a centre of identity and primitive wisdom which parallels her contemporary and friend D.H. Lawrence's phallic preoccupations. Her Imagist writing, as well as deploying symbolic objects as tokens of human emotion, is strengthened by an interplay of mythic reference. A reader who is not familiar with classical literature will often find that in order to understand her allusions, it is necessary to make continuous reference to a dictionary of classical mythology. It is true of most literature that the more you share the author's own background of knowledge, the richer and more interesting you will find their work; but H.D., like T.S. Eliot and Ezra Pound, presents the reader with a text which is a mosaic of quotations and allusions in which the background of the writer's own literary heritage is so close to the surface that the work in hand is formidably difficult on its own.

Two Englishwomen were also prominent members of the very international Modernist movement: Mary Butts (1890–1937) and Mina Loy (1882–1966). Mary Butts was personally notorious for her self-destructive life-style, which included an involvement with black magic and heavy consumption of alcohol and opium, but managed to publish six novels, three collections of stories and an autobiography. Mina Loy was principally a poet, and published *Lunar Baedeker* in 1958.[20]

## Stevie Smith and her contemporaries

Stevie Smith, a somewhat younger poet than Mary Butts and Mina Loy, has already been discussed in the context of her prose writing. Her voice, both as prose writer and poet, was so completely individual that many writers and readers have found it difficult to come to terms with her, though her fellow poets have from time to time praised her highly, and pointed out that her lyrics, reminiscent of both nursery rhymes and Anglican hymns in structure, but subtle in their use of assonance, are considerably less simple than they appear. These poems are almost deliberately spinsterish and pedantic in their diction, but their content, both emotional and philosophical, is often complex. Here is a characteristic example:

I always remember your beautiful flowers
And the beautiful kimono you wore

When you sat on the couch
With that tigerish crouch
And told me you loved me no more.
What I cannot remember is how I felt when you were unkind
All I know is, if you were unkind now I should not mind.
Ah me, the power to feel exaggerated, angry and sad
The years have taken from me,
    Softly I go now, pad pad.

As far as her personal life was concerned, despite a wide circle of friends
and lovers, she chose to live happily with her aunt for most of her adult life,
and to celebrate, with all the wit and energy at her command, the value of
very ordinary women's friendships and non-sexual relationships. She takes
an apparently perverse delight in celebrating the sheer surburban
ordinariness of the life she chose to lead. Both her poetry and her prose,
though their rhythms are delicate and controlled, celebrate 'the talking
voice that runs on'. Her prose is equally deceptive, slapdash, dashaway, a
clever pretence at being random and unstructured chatter, but in fact
showing her perception of the poetic possibilities of slang and apparently
unremarkable speech. Her preferred stance is one of ironic detachment and
analysis; she writes as an outsider, like a cat on the window-sill watching
with sharp-focused interest the passions and follies of the family inside.

Other women poets of this century are an eclectic group. The
relationship of women poets to one another is not in any sense a constant.
H.D. was conscious of a need in her writing for female role models as, in the
previous century, was Elizabeth Barrett Browning, when she said 'where
are the poetesses?...I look everywhere for grandmothers.'[21] Similarly
Elaine Feinstein has dedicated much of her creative endeavour to the
recreation in English of the Russian poetry of Marina Tsvetayeva, whom
she describes as 'my teacher of courage'.

### Post-war and contemporary poetry

On the other hand, Elizabeth Jennings (b. 1926), according to her analysis
of herself in *The Bloodaxe Book of Contemporary Women Poets*, is
conscious of the influence of W.H. Auden, Edwin Muir and Robert Graves
in her work. She mentions no woman poet, and the idea of having a place in
a specifically female tradition of writing is evidently one of little or no
importance to her. Elizabeth Bishop (1911–79, collected poems 1983) was
more than merely indifferent: she objected in principle to her poetry
appearing in a women's anthology, stating, 'undoubtedly gender does play
an important part in the making of any art, but art is art and to separate
writings...into two sexes is to emphasise values in them that are *not* art.'[22]
Yet in spite of this stance, Bishop's poem 'Casabianca' is a direct reworking
of an earlier woman's work (Felicia Hemans's poem) in a way which must by
now be familiar to readers of this book:

> Love's the boy who stood on the burning deck
> trying to recite 'The boy stood on
> the burning deck.'

Sylvia Plath (1932–63) has received consistently favourable, if sometimes unhelpful, critical attention. As an American who worked in England, she is only partially relevant to this study, but she is too important a figure to ignore. The main influences on her mature poetry are probably Robert Lowell, who opened up the possibility of dealing very directly with personal pain with his *Life Studies* (1959), and Ted Hughes, to whom Plath was married. She was also aware (uneasily) of her contemporary, Adrienne Rich (*b*. 1929), as Virginia Woolf was of Katherine Mansfield, and deeply impressed by Stevie Smith, to whom she wrote a fan letter in 1962, the year of her own highest achievement. She declared herself 'a desperate Smith-addict', and described her delight in poets 'possessed by ... the rhythms of their own breathing'.[23] Like many comments by working poets on other poets, this last tells us as much about Sylvia Plath as it does about Stevie Smith, although it is true that Smith's extension beyond a conversational speaking voice, her use of basic, common metres, like the four-line, end-stopped format of many English hymns, may have helped to free Plath from her early formalism and dependence on a consciously poetic diction. Her greatest poems, notably the blackly humorous 'Daddy', in *Ariel* (1965), with its flat, childish rhyme, pulling against both syntax and rhythm, seem to owe something to Smith's patient mastery of the off-key as a deliberate poetic technique.

Sylvia Plath's senior, Kathleen Raine (*b*. 1908), has been writing steadily since her first publications in the 1930s and is still active. Her major books are *Collected Poems 1935–1980* (published in 1981), *The Lost Country* (1971) and *The Oracle in the Heart* (1980). She has also published three volumes of autobiography: *Farewell Happy Fields* (1973), *The Land Unknown* (1975) and *The Lion's Mouth* (1977).

Although her initial subject of study was science, Kathleen Raine has come to specialise in those poets of the British tradition who might be called 'secular mystics': she is particularly expert in the study of Blake and Yeats as well as in the neo-Platonic tradition in English literature to which these poets belong. All these influences permeate her own work. She is interested in spiritual things, in otherworldly things, and an intense personal mysticism, expressed in sparse, deceptively simple words, is at the core of her poetry. She is preoccupied with moments of vision and expansion of consciousness, as in the poem 'Heirloom':

> 'When I was a lass,' she said,
> 'Sitting among the heather,
> Suddenly I saw
> That the moor was alive!

I have told no-one before'...
She saw the living skein
Of which the world is woven,
And having seen, knew all...

Often her poems recall those of the Jesuit poet Gerard Manley Hopkins in their intense awareness of the spiritual dimension which holds worldly things in being. All nature is a constant revelation, a showing forth of unexpected power. Within this heightened sensibility, Kathleen Raine is at ease, as plain in her speech as a woman visionary of the Middle Ages:

We do not see them come.
Their great wings furled, their boundless forms infolded
Smaller than poppy-seed or grain of corn
To enter the dimensions of our world...

Elizabeth Jennings might also be described as a spiritual poet: she draws on the influences of a tradition very different to that of Kathleen Raine, namely the tradition of Roman Catholic spiritual poetry in English, and has already been mentioned as a writer whose sense of poetic identity is not consciously dependent on gender. She is thus to an extent an outsider, a woman in a tradition which has been, since the Middle Ages predominantly male, and a sacred poet in an age of urgent and secular women's writing. Her *Collected Poems* were published in 1967, since when there have been four volumes, the most recent being *Celebrations and Elegies* (1982). She has also published *Every Changing Shape* (1961), a study of mystical poetry. There are resemblances between her poetry and that of Kathleen Raine: the spiritual dimension is ever present and both poets owe an obvious debt to Hopkins; but Elizabeth Jennings allows herself richer textures of versification and a more sensuous choice of words:

I caught a night-bird on a shaft of wind.
I thought and found it sleeping in my mind.

I took a leaf and held it in my palm.
It sent no shiver through me but pure calm.

Her keen awareness of the otherworldly is seen in 'In a Garden', a poem full, as are many, of reminders, memories, unlikely and yet convincing connections:

...I need not have stood long
Mocked by the smell of a mown lawn, and yet
I did. Sickness for Eden was so strong.

Anne Ridler (*b*. 1912) has published six collections at intervals between 1939 and 1988. Her work has points of similarity with that of Elizabeth Jennings, though her choice of subjects addresses specifically female experience more directly, for instance, 'For a Child Expected' (1943) and 'Mirror Image' (1972), themes which can be paralleled in eighteenth-century women's poetry.[24] Other poems, such as 'A Taste for Truth' (1972), wrestling with the problem of pain, or 'Free Fall' (1988), are more theological in focus.

Elaine Feinstein (b. 1930) is less preoccupied with the spiritual, intensely involved with life, relationships and the present. *Some Unease and Angels: Selected Poems* was published in 1977. She has also published translations from the Russian poet Marina Tsvetayeva and six intense, almost confessional novels, in which contemporary Jewish identity and experience are a principal theme. She has written that she was much influenced by the poetry which she has translated, that through it she found the freedom of individual expression: the ability to write exactly what she wants without regard for convention. She writes about many subjects, but she is particularly drawn to the experiences of women and the roles which women play in different societies:

> ...say I am a witch:
> black is the
> mirror you give me
> drawn inward at siege
> sightless, mumbling:
> criminal, to bear three
> children...

Through nearly all her poetry, even the celebrations of love, runs an undercurrent of tension, a strong bleakness:

> No tenure, in garden trees, I
>     hang like a leaf, and stare
> at cartilaginous shapes
>     my shadow their visitor.
> And words cannot brazen it out.
>     Nothing can hold for ever.

She also, as one would expect from a writer closely involved with Russian poets, shows a strong sense of history and politics in her writing.

Anne Stevenson (b. 1933) was educated in America, but has spent most of her life in Britain. She is very aware of her existence as a poet in a country and era not friendly to poetry. She has written in an essay:

> In these days of superfluous affluence, rewarded wickedness and sophisticated violence, my answer is to live simply, reducing my needs to the level of the beautiful and the necessary.

Her poetry is both private and accessible: she writes with passionate concern about very ordinary things, but gives these experiences a reality which the reader can share. She is aware of the fragility of the intelligent individual in a conformist society, aware how easily children, relationships and hopes can be damaged:

Snail! Scary knot of desires!
Hungry snarl! Small son.
Why do I have to love you?
How have you won?

Despite this caution, there is also an element of the positive: there is a point to her equation of the *beautiful* with the *necessary*:

Sleepers over oceans in the mill of the world's breathing.
The grace to say they live in another firmament.
A way to say the miracle will not occur,
And watch the miracle.

Among the poets of the younger generation, there are a number of highly individual voices. *The Honeycomb* (1989), by Pauline Stainer (*b*. 1941), is a collection of remarkable variety, united by a strongly metaphysical cast of mind, finely judged control of sound, and an original and wide-ranging willingness to use scientific or medical imagery to form precise, inescapable conceits. The range of the collection is such that it encompasses historical meditations set forth with the detachment of a true historian, as in 'Casting the Bronze Horse':

Downriver at dawn
on the sliding pallor of the flood,
the bronze for the great horse
is shipped away to Ferrara
and reduced into cannon

while also including the haunted evocation of an East Anglia as compelling as those historical inventions of Sylvia Townsend Warner's which it recalls:

'They are bearing a silver fish
Out of the thinning mist'
*Pull down the blind, mother*
*Whilst the skaters go past*

'Or is it a milk-white hound
caught in the sluice?'
*Turn the lamp high, mother;*
*Heart's blood is a fugitive dye.*

Carol Rumens (*b*. 1944) is, like Elaine Feinstein, a writer who allows a sense of Jewishness to lead her into exploring the connection between Western Europe and countries of the former Soviet empire. The recent collection *Direct Dialling* (1985) includes 'Outside Oswiecim', a poem based on a visit to the Nazi death-camp at Auschwitz, and evoking the thousands of people who died there. However, it ends *outside*, as the title suggests, not denying, but transcending the overwhelming message of death:

> So we died for the last unforgeable scrap
> – Ourselves. Got free for being something harder
> Even than zoo-meat. Fought like the Crusader
> To nail our resurrection to the map.

'Revolutionary Women' and 'Direct Dialling' are other poems in this collection which engage with the experience of people whose lives include choices so agonising that they are hard for us to imagine.

Wendy Mulford (*b*. 1941) has written on a wide variety of themes in a highly distinctive, imagistic style. Her poems avoid narrative connection between one line and the next; meaning resides both in the words and the spaces between them, but resists any attempt to be read as prose. The three-line poem 'Exceptional Needs' (from the collection *Late Spring Next Year* (1987), as are the other poems mentioned here) is typical of her method in that it contains words whose grammatical status is unclear and whose meaning thus remains ambiguous. The six words of the poem nevertheless seem to suggest a coherent idea: that actions seen as important in their own time lose significance once they are overtaken by later events. Not all her poems are so abstract; 'Elegy: For Male Lovers (Bradford, 1980)', on the mass-murderer who killed thirteen women in Yorkshire, is a far more conventionally structured meditation on male violence and the nature of women's involvement with it. Similarly, 'Setting Sail for the Falkland Isles: Fools' Paradise' is a direct juxtaposition of a political event widely perceived as a meaningless and inappropriate gesture, and the breakdown of a personal relationship.

Denise Riley (*b*. 1948) has published two collections (*No Fee* and *Some Poems, 1968–1978*) with Wendy Mulford, but speaks with a very different voice, sometimes comically ironic, as in her 'Making a Liberty Belle':

> my exercise book of twenty
> years ago says neatly, I guess
> copied out of an Annual
> 'to make a Liberty Belle
> White Ballet
> Skirt with a
> Layer of Blue Net...'         (*Dry Air*, 1985)

The poem works by implying the gross disjunction between this cutely feminine costume (which does not even aspire to the dignity either of the Liberty Bell itself, or even the Statue of Liberty's classical robes) and what 'liberty' as a concept might actually mean in a girl's life. The detail of the old exercise book is also significant, in that it suggests the way in which girls are socialised into accepting pitifully inadequate symbols rather than searching for their own truths.

Carol Ann Duffy (*b.* 1955) is a young writer who commands a variety of styles. 'Translating the English, 1989' (*The Other Country*, 1990) is a satirical catalogue of the least attractive features of life in England, recited with innocent pride by a speaker proud to be British, whose speech-rhythms suggest that he (the tone suggests a male) is in fact an immigrant:

> Welcome to my country! We have here Edwina Currie
> and The Sun newspaper. Much excitement
> Also the weather has been most improving
> even in February. Daffodils. (Wordsworth. Up North.)
> If you like
> Shakespeare or even Opera we have too the Black Market.
> For two hundred quids we are talking Les Miserables,
> nods being as good as winks. Don't eat the eggs.
> Wheel-clamp. Dogs. Vagrants. A tour of our wonderful
> capital city is not to be missed...

The movement between comedy and seriousness in this poem is characteristic of her work. Similarly, 'The Act of Imagination (*under the Act, the following things may be prosecuted for appalling the Imagination*)' is much less of a joke than it first seems:

> Ten More Years.
> A dog playing Beethoven's 'Moonlight Sonata'.
> President Quayle.
>
> The pyjamas of Tax Inspectors.
> The Beef Tapeworm (*Taenia Saginata*).
> British Rail.
>
> Picking someone else's nose.
> The Repatriation Charter.
> Gaol.
> The men. The Crucifix. The nails...

Other poems are about the right to speak: 'We Remember Your Childhood Well' is addressed to a person in anguish, overriding his or her perception as without significance: 'Your questions were answered fully. No. That didn't occur... What you recall are impressions, we have the facts.' 'Liar' is about a woman increasingly involved in her fantasy-life, who is eventually committed:

> You know the rest. The man in the long white wig
> who found her sadly confused. The top psychiatrist

who studied her in gaol, and then went back home and did
What he does every night to the Princess of Wales.

The poem begins with the woman dressing as a man: the description of the
judge as someone dressed up, and the implication that the fantasy-life of the
psychiatrist is as irresponsible and out of control as that of his patient,
suggest that the difference between Susan's fantasies and those of the men
who commit her are that theirs are endorsed by society, and hers are not.
Carol Ann Duffy is also capable of sharply focused autobiographical poetry,
for example, 'In Mrs Tischer's Class', lyrical love poetry such as 'Who
Loves You', and dramatic monologue: 'Too Bad', a first-person poem about
a gunman, by implication in Northern Ireland, is particularly successful in
its reticence.

Liz Lochead (*b.* 1947), poet, dramatist and maker of cabarets, has all the
vigour, sense and gallows humour of her native Glasgow without being
simply or reductively 'a regional poet'. Her career has developed through
performance poetry into cabaret, musical and full-length drama. Her skill
as a parodist (equal to that of her English contemporary Wendy Cope (*b.*
1945)) is far-ranging and deadly: a country-and-western song of extreme
banality, for example, turns into a depiction of the powerlessness of the
individual faced with the prospect of nuclear catastrophe. Her monologues
are on some levels entertainments of a high quality, but, read in quantity, a
city emerges from the scattered voices: the sixth-former in love with her
English teacher and identifying with Emily Brontë to the point of dementia,
the lonely, suddenly affluent wife with her husband away on the oil-rigs, the
ghastly Minister's wife trying with real fear to reduce all art to the level
of the cosy.

The plays, musicals and monologues exist alongside a body of non-
performance poetry of considerable achievement: *Dreaming Frankenstein*
(1985) ranges widely among fairy tales, autobiography, evocations of place.
Among the most impressive poems are the group concerned almost
passionately with a review of the work of Mary Shelley, poems which show
an individual commitment to the idea of a women's tradition in writing:

No maidservant ever
in her narrow attic, combing
out her hair in the midnight mirror
on Hallowe'en (having eaten
that egg with its yolk hollowed out
then filled with salt)
– oh never one had such success as this
she had not courted...

Eyes on those high peaks
in the reasonable sun of the morning,

she dressed in dampened muslin
and sat down to quill and ink
and icy paper.

It is fitting that this survey of women's writing since the beginning of English society should end with a poem which so firmly and gracefully assumes the presence and value of a female cultural tradition, represented here by the female folklore of Halloween divination rituals, and the figure of that highly educated woman, Mary Shelley.

NOTES
1 'George Eliot', *The Common Reader*, First Series (1925).
2 At least, if we exclude Mary de la Rivière Manley's *New Atlantis* (1709), which tells anecdotes about a group of wealthy lesbians. It should perhaps be added that 'the Lesbian' has long been a stock figure for male writers, particularly pornographers. Cleland's *Fanny Hill* (1748–9) includes an early example of this.
3 See, for example, J. Rule, *Lesbian Images*, Peter Davies, London, 1976, pp.50–61, for a discussion of this.
4 A further curious aspect of the unease which lesbianism as an acceptable fictional topic has provoked even among lesbians is the phenomenon of women writers, most notably the South African Mary Renault and the French Marguerite Yourcenar, who do not write about lesbianism, but devote novel after novel to a sensitive and sympathetic analysis of male homosexuality, while themselves remaining sexually evasive.
5 V. Woolf, *Women and Writing*, ed. M. Barratt, Women's Press, London, 1979, p.31.
6 D. Richardson, 'Women in the Arts', *Vanity Fair*, May 1925.
7 D. Johnson, *Iris Murdoch*, Harvester, Brighton, 1987, p.xii.
8 R. Pogson, *Miss Horniman and the Gaiety Theatre*, Barrie & Rockliff, London, 1952.
9 Coxhead, *Lady Gregory: A Literary Portrait*, pp.76–8.
10 Lady Gregory, *Collected Plays*, ed. A. Saddlemyer, Colin Smythe, Gerrards Cross, 4 vols, 1970.
11 Holledge, *Innocent Flowers: Women in the Edwardian Theatre*, p.42.
12 *New Woman Plays*, ed. L. Fitzsimmons and V. Gardner, Methuen, London, 1991, prints *Alan's Wife* together with three other plays by women dramatists of the 1890s.
13 The play is printed in *How the Vote was Won and Other Suffragette Plays*, ed. D. Spender and C. Hayman, Methuen, London, 1985, pp.23–33, which also prints critical comments, pp.19–20.
14 *How the Vote was Won*, pp.104–24.
15 *New Woman Plays*, pp.135–89.
16 R. Hall, *Marie Stopes: A Biography*, André Deutsch, London, 1977, pp.243–7.
17 K. Tynan, 'The Royal Smut-Hound', in M. Wandor, *Look Back in Gender: Sexuality and the Family in Post-war British Drama*, pp.73–85.
18 *Plays by Women, Volume Two*, ed. M. Wandor, Methuen, London, 1983, 'afterword' by Maureen Duffy, p.26.
19 H. Keyssar, *Feminist Theatre*, Macmillan, London, 1984.
20 G. Hanscombe and V.L. Smyers, *Writing for Their Lives: The Modernist Woman, 1910–1940*, Women's Press, London, 1987, pp.106–28.
21 *The Letters of Elizabeth Barrett Browning*, ed. F.C. Kenyon, Macmillan, New York and London, 1897, pp.231–2.
22 *The Faber Book of Twentieth-century Women's Poetry*, ed. F. Adcock, Faber and Faber, London, 1987, p.97.

23 *London Magazine*, February 1962, p.46.
24 For example, Anna Laetitia Barbauld's 'To a Little Invisible Being', and Elizabeth Teft's 'On Viewing Herself in a Glass', in *Eighteenth-century Women Poets*, pp.307 and 125.

**Genre fiction: detection, romance, children's books**

The earlier sections of this study have pointed out the economic factors which imposed significant constraints on the nature and volume of women's writing in the seventeenth, eighteenth and nineteenth centuries. The economics of literature are relevant to the twentieth century also. Although it is now easier for women to earn money than it has ever been before, writing formula fiction, which can be done at home while children are at school, still has much to commend it. The ratio of male to female writers in different genres of popular fiction still varies enormously. 'Horror' is dominated by male writers, and so are 'science fiction and fantasy', though there are some highly successful women (notably Patricia Highsmith (*b.* 1921) and Ruth Rendell (*b.* 1930)) working in the former category, and the latter is increasingly being infiltrated by female writers and, indeed, female readers. This recent development was emphasised when the Women's Press launched a successful science fiction series in 1985: although C.L. Moore wrote science fiction in the 1950s (including the remarkable story 'Shambleau'), she concealed her gender behind initials. Romance, conversely, is the classic case of a literature essentially by and for women.

A salient aspect of women's contribution to popular fiction is the development of the English detective story, a genre which, unlike the other genres referred to, is bought and read by both sexes with equal enthusiasm, and which has unquestionably been dominated, in terms of sales and influence alike, by women writers, notably Agatha Christie (1890–1976), the most popular of all; Dorothy Sayers (1893–1957), Margery Allingham (1904–66) and Ngaio Marsh (1899–1982), who were better craftsmen with more sense of style; and, more recently, P.D. James (*b.* 1920). The English detective story is characterised by a peculiar combination of cosiness and mayhem: classically, a group of nice, ordinary, middle-to-upper-class people are all forced to assess each other's capability of the one major crime which can plausibly be committed by almost anyone if the circumstances are right. The nature of the detective story is to lay bare the cracks, tensions and discontinuities in the humdrum surface texture of ordinary family life, and it is perhaps for this reason that women, whose social role involves the preservation of apparent harmony in difficult circumstances, should be so good at analysing its underside.

Historical fiction and romance are of course peculiarly a woman's genre. There is a distinction to be drawn between fictions which are sold by the publisher's imprint, that is, where the purchaser is persuaded to buy 'a new Mills & Boon', unmindful of the name on the title-page, and confident that the content will be the mixture as before, and novels by such well-known authors as Georgette Heyer (1902–74) or Catherine Cookson (*b.* 1906), which are sold and bought, like other fiction, on the strength of the author's name and reputation. The sheer scale of romantic fiction as a commercial enterprise is astonishing: Harlequin, only one of the many companies involved, has a 28 per cent share of all paperbacks sold in Canada, and 10–12 per cent of the total USA paperback market. More romances, therefore, are bought and sold than any other single fictional category. It is therefore appropriate that the doyenne of this genre, Barbara Cartland (*b.* 1901), has a place in the *Guinness Book of Records* as the most prolific living author. The formula for this type of book is that a vulnerable, virginal girl meets an older, wealthier, more sophisticated, attractive man; she gets into some kind of predicament from which he rescues her; and they recognise their mutual love. Another type of formula fiction which commands a very wide readership is the 'family saga', in which the fortunes of a group of people are charted over three generations or so. Normally, a powerful, strong-minded woman is the central figure of the narrative.

Not all works sharing broadly similar themes are identical in value. *Jane Eyre*, *Cinderella* and *The Taming of the Shrew* may be the templates from which the industrious pulp-novelists of Harlequin or Mills & Boon cut out their characters, but the creation of a vast mass of lowest-common-denominator fiction, poverty-stricken in conception, execution, characterisation and style, does not retrospectively invalidate the achievement of a Charlotte Brontë or a Shakespeare. It is also, given the arbitrariness of literary categorisation in our time, dangerous to assume that all books which are lumped together under the category of 'romance' are necessarily equally bad. Daphne Du Maurier (1907–90) achieved with *Rebecca* (1938) a story which, while profoundly clichéd in its approach to character, is brilliantly plotted as narrative. Historical fiction is an even more ambiguous area. George Eliot's novels are set some distance back in time; and *Romola* (1863) is set in fifteenth-century Florence. In the twentieth century, Rose Macaulay, Naomi Mitchison and Sylvia Townsend Warner are only three of the many serious novelists to have set at least one major novel in a distant culture. Certain other women, notably Dorothy Dunnett and the South African Mary Renault (1905–83), are known exclusively as 'historical novelists', but that is not to say that their work is necessarily lacking in complexity and subtlety.

Another area of women's writing which should be treated here is the writing of children's books. This was seen as a peculiarly women's province as early as the eighteenth century. Probably the earliest English children's writer of any note is Sarah Fielding, whose *The Governess, or The Little Female Academy* (1749) describes a range of character types among adolescent girls in a fashionable boarding-school. A generation later, the equally moral works of Mme de Genlis (1746–1830) set the tone for much subsequent writing when her principal works were translated into English, between 1784 and 1792. Her most effective imitator in England was Maria

Edgeworth, who had twenty-one younger siblings, and thus had good reason to be concerned with the education of children. Edgeworth's *Moral Tales* (1801) are considerably livelier than those of her French predecessor. Her Harry and Lucy stories were concerned with inculcating practical science and useful knowledge rather than simply with appropriate behaviour, which had the enlivening effect of shifting attention from the children to the world around them. Mary Wollstonecraft, a little earlier (1788), also published a book designed to form young minds on correct principles – *Original Stories from Real Life*[1] – and improving literature for children formed an important part of the stock kept by her husband William Godwin at his bookshop in London. A particularly notable milestone in the slow process of expanding the intellectual and moral range of children's fiction was *Tales from Shakespeare* (1807) by two other members of the same intellectual circle, brother and sister writers Charles and Mary Lamb (1775–1834 and 1764–1847 respectively). These tales were designed to introduce children to the nation's greatest playwright in a simplified and shortened format.

The nineteenth century saw the publication of a flood of moral tales for children, many of them written by women. A notorious example is the *History of the Fairchild Family* (1818–47) by Mary Sherwood (1775–1851), a grim work in which any lapse from virtue is horribly punished. Perhaps the only representative of this period of children's literature still available to modern children is *Black Beauty* (1877), the tear-jerking 'autobiography of a horse' by Anna Sewell (1820–78), which is an effective plea for the humanitarian treatment of animals. An equally serious and didactic writer, who concerned herself with the development of an evangelical conscience rather than with cruelty to animals, was Charlotte Mary Yonge (1823–1901), author of a total of 160 books, all relentlessly uplifting, and less attractive to a twentieth-century readership.

The nineteenth century also produced a number of women writing for children who were less obsessed with moral instruction. Probably the earliest of these was Catherine Sinclair (1800–64), whose *Holiday House*, which appeared in 1839, '[endeavours] to paint that species of noisy, frolicsome, mischievous children, now almost extinct'. Louisa Molesworth (1839–1921) was a writer who mixed fantasy with realism, placing far from perfect children in magical environments. In *The Cuckoo Clock* (1877), Griselda, who is staying with two old aunts, makes friends with the cuckoo from the cuckoo-clock who leads her into the world of magic, and confronts a variety of truths about herself. Geraldine, in *The Carved Lions* (1898), runs away from an unsatisfactory childhood to seek shelter in the shop with the carved lions. Mrs Molesworth's best work, as these two books indicate, is about lonely, imaginative children, and still has an appeal for their twentieth-century successors, since it is always absolutely in sympathy with the child, rather than didactically concerned to revise the child's views in accordance with adult morality. Lucy Lane Clifford (1853–1929) wrote the very successful *Anyhow Stories* (1882) which include bizarre and frightening tales of madness and alienation, notably 'Wooden Tony' and 'The New Mother'.[2]

At the end of the nineteenth century, E. (Edith) Nesbit (1858–1924) wrote much more entertaining and less self-consciously improving books, with a strong emphasis on real life as it was experienced by middle-class London children in her day, adroitly combining fantasy and mundane domestic realism. Her children are often comically contrasted with the angels of supernatural goodness in the fiction they read themselves, and their occasional attempts to model themselves on fictional heroes, in the approved manner, always meet with disaster.

Several women made a successful career out of writing books aimed specifically at schoolgirls, notably Angela Brazil (1869–1947). Her books deal with groups of clean-cut middle-class English schoolgirls in the hermetically enclosed world of an all-girls' boarding school. They offer an unselfconscious portrayal of an all-female world which is entirely physically and emotionally self-sufficient, though Angela Brazil's tendency to name heroines Lesbia (for example, Lesbia Farrars in *Loyal to the School* (1920)) was, it is virtually certain, not consciously intended as a coded message that these relationships should be seen as homosexual. Somewhat later, Richmal Crompton (1890–1969) created in William Brown (*Just William*, first published in 1922) a juvenile English reflection of Huckleberry Finn: a tough, gauche, well-meaning little boy, continually upsetting his family's precarious sense of social position. Her books, with their ironies and mock-epic tone, were initially intended for adults, but proved in the event to be immensely successful with child readers of both sexes.

Beatrix Potter's (1866–1943) lapidary little books for very young children are deservedly classic. Again, she struck a note of realism which was a new departure in writing for children: the natural behaviour of animals was something she observed very closely, and she saw no reason to gloss unduly over the fact that foxes eat ducks if they get the chance, and that although generations of children have taken the plight of Peter Rabbit deeply to heart, Peter's father was baked in a pie by the gardener's wife, and he himself risked the same fate when he went to steal lettuce. Her illustrations contribute greatly to the distinction of her books, and have a worthy place in the tradition of the nineteenth-century British watercolour.

The first of P.L. Travers's (*b*. 1906) Mary Poppins books appeared in 1935, with their peculiarly anarchic authority-figure: a nanny who is childlike in her vanity, but possessed of extensive magical powers. Mary Norton's (*b*. 1903) Borrowers, a dying race of six-inch-high people, were another highly original creation (the five books appeared between 1952 and 1982). The books are vivid and interesting about the logistical problems these tiny people face and overcome, and the texture of the writing is nostalgic, beautifully detailed and precise. The theme of the Borrowers is loneliness, friendship and independence: all the humans who make contact with Borrowers are extremely isolated, and Arietty, the Borrower who is at the centre of the narrative, suffers agonies of loneliness and frustration.

Distinguished writers for children more recently include Lucy Boston (1892–1989), whose series of books about Green Knowe introduce the problems of time and death to young children in a most sensitive and imaginative way. Philippa Pearce (*b.* 1920) is also concerned with introducing a sense of the nature of time in *Tom's Midnight Garden* (1958), in which Tom escapes from his unattractive and isolated life into the past, and comes to terms with his present situation. Penelope Lively (*b.* 1933), who has also written adult fiction (her *Moon Tiger* won the Booker Prize in 1987), charts similar territory in books such as *The Ghost of Thomas Kempe* (1973) and *The Revenge of Samuel Stokes* (1981), which represent the continued presence of historical figures in the twentieth-century world. Susan Cooper (*b.* 1935) is concerned with problems of good and evil in her series *The Dark is Rising*, which charts the conflict between the Light and the Dark, and makes effective use of Welsh myth.

Yet the biggest seller of all, and perhaps one of the most successful writers, in terms of the sheer volume of her output in England this century, was Enid Blyton (1897–1968). Her astonishing success almost defies comment, except to note that the extreme predictability of style, content and structure has made her work as soothing and undemanding for the average child as a Mills & Boon romance is for the mass-market woman reader.

NOTES
1 The second edition (1791), illustrated by William Blake, has been reprinted by Woodstone Books, Spelsbury, 1990.
2 A. Lurie, *Don't Tell the Grown-ups: Subversive Children's Literature*, Bloomsbury, London, 1990, pp.85–91.

**Translation, letters, diaries and essays**

Non-fiction writing by women has a long history going back to Julian of
Norwich in the fourteenth century. The Christian duty of speaking out, of
proclaiming a perhaps unpalatable truth, or sharing a revelation, motivated
many women to write in the fifteenth, sixteenth and seventeenth centuries
who would otherwise have certainly maintained silence. The Christian
religion has often been an instrument of repression, but the stress which it
puts on the guidance of the individual's conscience has made it a perennially
ambivalent ally of partriarchal government. A woman such as Margery
Kempe in the fourteenth century was empowered by her sense of her
relationship with God to reject all the social expectations which constrained
the life of a wife, businesswoman and mother. The Protestant Reformation,
in its formative stages in the England of the sixteenth century, brought
women out as speakers pleading for the cause of one theological position or
another, for example Catherine Parr (1513–48), the sixth wife of Henry
VIII, who published two widely read books: *Prayers, or Meditations*
(1545) and *Lamentacion or Complaynt of a Sinner* (1547).

Women, similarly, found a political voice in the context of the massive
upheaval of the English Civil War, though this was also profoundly involved
with theology: the Royalist position was High Church (Charles I was
married to a Catholic), and the Roundheads' zeal was fuelled by radical
Protestantism as well as by economic and social considerations.[1] Thus, from
the sixteenth century onwards, a surprisingly large number of women
printed at least one prophetic work. Notable women prophets and
visionaries include Lady Eleanor Douglas (1590–1652), author of *The New
Jerusalem at Hand* (1649) and other works, Jane Lead (1623–1704) who
experienced a long series of visions decrying the pursuit of scientific reason
(as distinct from insight, or true wisdom) and looking forward to the
Second Coming, and Joanna Southcott (1750–1814), a prophetess who
founded a successful religious sect. Women's writing in the form of essays,
propaganda and prophecy, while having only a tangential relationship to
literature, is linked with it, in that the publication of such works indicates a
degree of public tolerance for women expressing themselves on issues of
particular concern to them.

Another semi-literary art in which a number of women have
conspicuously excelled is that of translation. There are occasional examples
of translations by women from the sixteenth to the eighteenth century:
Mary Sidney's sixteenth-century translation of *The Triumph of Death* from
Petrarch's Italian, and *Antonie* (1592) from Robert Garnier's French play
*Marc-Antoine*, for example, or Elizabeth Carter's much-praised translation
of the Greek philosopher Epictetus in 1758. Helen Maria Williams

(*c*.1761–1827), poet, novelist and enthusiast for the French Revolution, was imprisoned by Robespierre during the Reign of Terror (1793) and used the time to translate J.H.Bernadin de St-Pierre's seminal novel, *Paul et Virginie* (1787). Her English translation, published in 1796, was highly successful. The extension of women's educational opportunities in the nineteenth century naturally increased the numbers of successful female translators. George Eliot herself first made her name as the translator of David Friedrich Strauss's *Life of Jesus* (1846) and Ludwig Feuerbach's *Essence of Christianity* (1854) – her first attempt at fiction did not appear until 1857. The history of Anglo-Irish literature is a particular case where translation played a significant role in the development of an Irish national consciousness, and Lady Gregory's translations of Irish epics were seminal in her own time. In the twentieth century, the Anglo-Irish scholar Helen Waddell (1889–1965) introduced an almost forgotten literary tradition to the English-speaking world with her *Medieval Latin Lyrics* (1929). Her one novel, *Peter Abelard* (1933), arose from her academic interest in medieval poetry and philosophy, and is extraordinarily successful in evoking the harsh and vivid world of twelfth-century Paris. More recently, Dorothy Sayers, in addition to her unusually penetrating and sophisticated detective fiction, published what has become virtually the standard English version of Dante's *Divine Comedy* between 1949 and 1962. Helen Lowe-Porter's translations of the German novels of Thomas Mann, created in close association with the original writer, are widely recognised as works of literature in their own right. The novelist Sylvia Townsend Warner, late in her life, became the English translator of Proust's *Contre Sainte-Beuve* (1958); Willa Muir (1890–1970) translated the works of Franz Kafka (among other German authors); and Antonia White has translated many of the works of Colette.

Many women have been distinguished letter-writers and diarists. Lady Anne Clifford (1590–1676) is one of the earliest Englishwomen to leave a diary; other contemporary diarists included Mary Rich (1625–78) and Alice Thornton (1627–1707).[2] The *Journal* of Dorothy Wordsworth has been deservedly famous since its first publication in 1897, as has Frances Burney's *Diary*, which was valued for its vivid spontaneity long before the rehabilitation of her reputation as a serious novelist. In the twentieth century, Katherine Mansfield's *Journal*, published in 1924, is known as well as her fiction, if not better, and Virginia Woolf's *Diary* has also been widely read since its publication.

Women's letters in England have a history which goes back to the seventh century, and include the surviving letters from the circle of St Boniface in the eighth century and the Paston family in the fifteenth and sixteenth. In both these instances, women's letters are preserved as part of a collection of letters relating to a particular circle, not collected as the work of a particular woman. From these beginnings, the literary letter in England took off as a popular genre in the eighteenth century.

Hester Thrale (1741–1821), a close friend of Dr Johnson, published *Anecdotes of the Late Samuel Johnson* in 1786, and her correspondence with him (even though it had originated as private letters) in 1788. An extreme example of this exposure of private correspondence to the public gaze was William Godwin's publication of his wife Mary Wollstonecraft's early letters to her lover, Gilbert Imlay, in his *Memoirs of the Author of a Vindication of the Rights of Woman* (1798), which contemporaries, though interested, considered a gesture in poor taste. The publishability of genuine letters in the eighteenth century and later may be associated with the rise of the epistolary novel, a convention which tends to blur the distinction between fact and fiction. However, the interest of the reading public in literary letters outlived the popularity of the epistolary novel and continued to grow throughout the nineteenth century. For example, the letters of Dorothy Osborne (1627–95), originally written as private letters to her husband Sir William Temple, were published for their literary interest in the later nineteenth century, as were the *Journals and Correspondence* of Mary Berry (1763–1852), the friend and literary executor of Horace Walpole. Many of the letters of Lady Mary Wortley Montagu, notably her *Turkish Letters* (published 1763), are effectively short and entertaining essays on the various topics which presented themselves to her attention.

A further area where certain women's names are outstanding is the literary essay. As a genre, it merges imperceptibly with the more-or-less public letter, journalism and the journal tradition. Many women writers, past and present, have been journalists: even in the eighteenth century, Mary de la Rivière Manley succeded Jonathan Swift as editor of the *Examiner* (in 1711), while Eliza Haywood presided over *The Female Spectator* (1744–6), an amusing and often scandalous monthly magazine. An unsuccessful periodical of the later eighteenth century, *The Lady's Museum* (1760–1), was edited by the novelist Charlotte Lennox. Mary Wollstonecraft became the editorial assistant on *The Analytical Review* in 1787, and Maria Edgeworth proposed to Anna Laetitia Barbauld that they should collaborate in inaugurating a politically liberal women's journal to be called *The Feminead*. This did not come off, but it is an interesting indication of how involved women of the late eighteenth century had become with contemporary politics. In the next century, Harriet Martineau, Charlotte M. Yonge and George Eliot were among the Victorian women who were journalists as well as novelists. Barbara Leigh Smith (1827–90), first cousin to Florence Nightingale, and a friend of George Eliot, created *The English Woman's Journal* (which was not a magazine devoted to fashion, light fiction and recipes, but a serious forum for discussion) in 1858.[3] In the 1920s, Margaret, Lady Rhondda (1883–1958) inaugurated *Time and Tide* (which refers to the proverb ending 'wait for no man') as a suffragette magazine; it was commercially successful, and brought radical women's views, including those of Rebecca West, Antonia White, Virginia Woolf, E.M. Delafield (1890–1943) and Naomi Mitchison, to a wide audience. Many twentieth-century women have combined fiction with journalism, and many novelists have published at least one book of essays, or have worked for part of their writing lives as journalists. A notable example is Rebecca West, whose coverage of the great war crimes trial at Nuremberg after the Second World War is both journalistic in its immediacy and philosophical in its sense of the implications and significance of law and lawlessness in an international context. Another non-fiction book which played a particularly significant part in her development as a writer of both fact and fiction was her biography of the fourth-century African thinker, St Augustine of Hippo (1933). This work caused her to explore the mentality of Augustine, one of the subtlest and most self-analytical thinkers of all time, and a principal architect of Western European approaches both to God and to society. It also brought her face to face with the decline and fall of the Roman Empire, in which she saw instructive parallels with the historical developments of her own time. Her two-volume masterwork, published in 1941, is *Black Lamb and Grey Falcon*, an account of a journey through Yugoslavia in 1937 which focuses her considered intellectual and emotional response to a Europe heading rapidly towards war:

> I resolved to put on paper what a typical Englishwoman felt and thought in the late nineteen thirties when, already convinced of the inevitability of the second Anglo-German war, she had been able to follow the dark waters of that event back to its source. That committed me to what was in effect some years of a retreat spent among fundamentals. I was obliged to write a long and complicated history, and to swell that with an account of myself and the people who went with me on my travels, since it was my aim to show the past side by side with the present it created.
>
> (Epilogue)

The result is a long, profoundly serious work which compares and contrasts historical knowledge with personal experience, the individual and the theoretical. It is novelistic in its evocation of individual personalities, but the historical and political analyses which are an equally important part of its structure tend to place it with academic writing. Ultimately, like St Augustine's *City of God*, it is a uniquely structured and highly individual exploration of the present in the light of the past.

Among more recent writers, Angela Carter may be singled out for her essays on contemporary manners and *mores*, most of which first appeared in the journal *New Society*, collected under the title *Nothing Sacred* (1982). Brigid Brophy and Germaine Greer (*b*.1939) are other twentieth-century novelists who have published collections of essays: Brophy's *Don't Never*

*Forget* (1966) and *Baroque 'n' Roll* (1986), and Greer's *The Madwoman's Underclothes* (1989).

There have been numerous women essayists in Britain since the nineteenth century. An outstanding early example is Harriet Martineau, whose *Illustrations of Political Economy* (1823–4) showed a genius for interpreting complex factual information to the ordinary reader. Mary Russell Mitford wrote a collection of essays and sketches of rural life, published as *Our Village* (1824–32), evoking the life of a small and secure community. Her other claim to interest is that she was an old friend and supporter of the much younger Elizabeth Barrett during the period of isolation and confinement which preceded her dramatic elopement with Robert Browning. The Catholic poet Alice Meynell is another interesting essayist whose numerous volumes are of a consistent quality and perceptiveness. They include *The Rhythm of Life* (1893) and *The Second Person Singular* (1921). However, the most significant and influential woman essayist of the early twentieth century is Virginia Woolf. Her series of essays collected under the title of *The Common Reader* (1925 and 1932) are essentially studies of earlier writers, some of them at that time little known to the reading public. Her academic style and mildly antiquarian subject matter owe much to the prevailing tone of the Edwardian literary essayists who included her father Sir Leslie Stephen and George Saintsbury (Professor of English literature at Edinburgh University from 1895 to 1915), though she is an unusually graceful, concise and amusing exponent of the genre.

Academic historians are outside the bounds of this survey, since their works are not read by the general public, but one woman who is worth noting is Catherine Macaulay (1731–91), the first Englishwoman to write a serious work of history. Her *History of England* (1763–83) was based on original research in the British Museum's collections of parliamentary and legal documents, and was a serious, deeply considered work, perceived in her own time as the Whig answer to the Tory interpretation of seventeenth-century history offered by Hume. Macaulay's *History* was methodologically ahead of its time in giving meticulous footnote reference to the original sources. She was a woman of staunch republican principles, and turned to practical politics in the 1770s, writing in support of the right of the American colonies to rebel against Britain. The later history of Macaulay and her work is instructive: at the age of forty-seven, Macaulay took as her second husband William Graham, aged twenty-one. Friends and critics alike reacted with incredulous contempt (at least in England); Americans, notably Elizabeth Cady Stanton and Susan B. Anthony, continued to be interested in her ideas, but the perception of her personal life as immoral led to the eclipse of her work as also in some nebulous fashion tainted.

In the field of popular history, there have been a number of notably successful women writers. One of the earliest is Charlotte M. Yonge, whose 'Cameos from English History' appeared in *The Monthly Packet* (a widely read evangelical journal, of which she was also the editor) from 1815 to 1898. C.V. (Veronica) Wedgwood (*b*.1910) and Antonia Fraser (*b*.1932) have both written ably on early modern history: Dame Veronica is best known for her comprehensive and elegantly written histories of the Stuart period, particularly *The King's Peace* (1955) and *The King's War* (1958), whereas Lady Antonia Fraser has essentially written more popular biographies of such figures as Mary, Queen of Scots and Oliver Cromwell. Cecil Woodham-Smith's (1896–1977) account of the Crimean War (*The Reason Why*, 1953) and the Irish famine of the 1840s (*The Great Hunger*, 1962) are deservedly classic in their combination of extensive research with clear exposition and a great gift for evocation.

NOTES
1 Hobby, *Virtue of Necessity*, pp.26–84.
2 *Virtue of Necessity*, pp.76–9.
3 *Barbara Leigh Smith Bodichon and the Langham Place Group*, ed. C.A. Lacey, Routledge and Kegan Paul, London, 1987.

# Bibliography

## 1  A general guide to finding primary texts

Most of the novels and poems referred to are currently available in print, or have been reprinted within the last ten years. The Penguin Classics, Oxford World's Classics and Pandora Mothers of the Novel series among them have printed a good selection of women's fiction going back as far as the seventeenth century. For the nineteenth and twentieth centuries, Penguin and Virago between them have brought many novels back into print. The Women's Press concentrates mainly on new writing by women, but brings out occasional reprints, notably Elizabeth Barrett Browning's long poem *Aurora Leigh*.

Women's poetry is often harder to find. By far the most inclusive source for early modern women's poetry is *Kissing the Rod: An Anthology of Seventeenth-century Women's Verse*, ed. G. Greer, S. Hastings, J. Medoff and M. Sansone, Virago, London, 1988. Samples of verse from a wide variety of eighteenth-century women are collected together in *Eighteenth-century Women Poets*, ed. R. Lonsdale, Oxford University Press, Oxford, 1990, which also includes biographical notes on the writers. Faber have published collections of some modern poets, such as Sylvia Plath, Kathleen Raine and Anne Stevenson. Useful anthologies of nineteenth- and twentieth-century poems include *Bread and Roses: Women's Poetry of the Nineteenth and Twentieth Centuries*, ed. D. Scott, Virago, 1982; *Scars Upon My Heart: Women's Poetry and Verse of the First World War*, ed. C.W. Reilly, Virago, London, 1981; *The Faber Book of Twentieth-century Women's Poetry*, ed. F. Adcock, Faber, London, 1987; and *The Bloodaxe Book of Contemporary Women Poets*, ed. J. Couzyn, Bloodaxe, Newcastle upon Tyne, 1985.

Representative collections of seventeenth-century plays can be found in *The Female Wits: Women Playwrights of the Restoration*, ed. Fidelis Morgan, Virago, London, 1981, and *Love and Thunder: Plays by Women in the Age of Queen Anne*, ed. Kendall, Methuen, London, 1988. Five plays by Aphra Behn have been published together (edited by Maureen Duffy) by Methuen, London, 1988. Of the eighteenth-century plays mentioned, only Frances Burney, *A Busy Day*, Rutgers University Press, New Brunswick, NJ, 1984, and Joanna Baillie, *A Series of Plays*, reprinted from the first volume of her *Plays on the Passions* (1798) by Woodstock Books, Spelsbury, 1990, are available in a modern edition. None of the Victorian women's plays mentioned is in print, except for those which appear in the nineteenth-century collected editions of British plays such as B.N. Webster's *The Acting National Drama* (1837–50). A sample collection of Edwardian plays is in *New Woman Plays*, ed. L. Fitzsimmons and V. Gardner, Methuen, London, 1991. Eight volumes of modern plays by women have appeared in the Methuen Drama Series, most of them are edited by Micheline Wandor, and two volumes of lesbian plays, edited by Jill Davies. Another interesting, recent collection is *Monstrous Regiment: Four Plays and a Collective Celebration*, ed. G. Hanna, Nick Hern Books, London, 1991.

## 2 Reference works

BELL, M., PARFITT, S., SHEPHERD, S.: *A Biographical Dictionary of English Women Writers, 1580–1720*, Harvester Wheatsheaf, Hemel Hempstead, 1990.

BLAIR, V., CLEMENTS, P., GRUNDY, I: *The Feminist Companion to Literature in English: Women Writers from the Middle Ages to the Present*, Batsford, London, 1990.

DRABBLE, M.: *The Oxford Companion to English Literature*, 5th edn, Oxford University Press, Oxford, 1985.

HARTNOLL, P.: *The Oxford Companion to the Theatre*, 4th edn, Oxford University Press, Oxford, 1983.

TODD, J.: *A Dictionary of British and American Women Writers, 1600–1800*, Methuen, London, 1984.

TODD, J.: *A Dictionary of British Women Writers*, Routledge, London, 1989.

UGLOW, J.S. and HINTON, F.: *The Macmillan Dictionary of Women's Biography*, Macmillan, London, 1982.

## 3 General criticism

AUERBACH, N.: *Women and the Demon: The Life of a Victorian Myth*, Harvard University Press, Cambridge, Mass., 1982.

BROWNSTEIN, R.: *Becoming a Heroine: Reading About Women in Novels*, Penguin, Harmondsworth, 1984.

COTTON, N.: *Women Playwrights in England c. 1363–1750*, Bucknell University Press, Lewisburg, 1980.

DAVID, D.: *Intellectual Women and the Victorian Patriarchy*, Macmillan, London, 1987.

DRONKE, P.: *Medieval Women Writers*, Cambridge University Press, Cambridge, 1984.

DUSINBERRE, J.: *Alice to the Lighthouse: Children's Books and Radical Experiments in Art*, Macmillan, London, 1987.

ELLMANN, M.: *Thinking About Women*, Virago, London, 1979.

FIGES, E.: *Sex and Subterfuge: Women Writers to 1850*, Macmillan, London, 1982.

GILBERT, S.M. and GUBAR, S.: *The Madwoman in the Attic: The Woman Writer and the Ninteenth-century Literary Imagination*, Yale University Press, New Haven and London, 1984.

GREER, G.: *The Female Eunuch*, Paladin, London, 1971.

HANSCOMBE, G. and SMYERS, V.L.: *Writing for Their Lives: The Modernist Women, 1910–1940*, Women's Press, London, 1987.

HOBBY, E.: *Virtue of Necessity: English Women's Writing 1649–88*, Virago, London, 1988.

HOLLEDGE, J.: *Innocent Flowers: Women in the Edwardian Theatre*, Virago, London, 1981.

KEYSSAR, H.: *Feminist Theatre: An Introduction to Plays of Contemporary British and American Women*, Macmillan, London, 1984.

LEIGHTON, A.: *Victorian Women Poets: Writing Against the Heart*, Harvester Wheatsheaf, Hemel Hempstead, 1992.

MAHL, M. and KROON, H.: *The Female Spectator: English Women Writers before 1800*, Indiana University Press, Bloomington and Indianapolis, 1977.

MOERS, E.: *Literary Women: The Great Writers*, Women's Press, London, 1978.

MOI, T.: *Sexual/Textual Politics: Feminist Literary Theory*, Methuen, London and New York, 1985.

MORGAN, F.: *The Female Wits: Women Playwrights of the Restoration*, Virago, London, 1981.

PALMER, P.: *Contemporary Women's Fiction: Narrative Practice and Feminist Theory*, Harvester Wheatsheaf, Hemel Hempstead, 1989.

PEARSON, J.: *The Prostituted Muse: Images of Women and Women Dramatists 1642–1737*, Harvester Wheatsheaf, Hemel Hempstead, 1988.

RUSS, J.: *How to Suppress Women's Writing*, Women's Press, London, 1984.

SHOWALTER, E.: *A Literature of Their Own: British Women Novelists from Brontë to Lessing*, Virago, London, 1978.

SHOWALTER, E. (ed.): *The New Feminist Criticism: Essays on Women, Literature and Theory*, Virago, London, 1986.

SPENCER, J.: *The Rise of the Woman Novelist: From Aphra Behn to Jane Austen*, Basil Blackwell, Oxford, 1986.

SPENDER, D.: *Mothers of the Novel: 100 Good Women Writers before Jane Austen*, Pandora, London and New York, 1986.

TODD, J.: *Sensibility: An Introduction*, Methuen, London and New York, 1986.

TODD, J.: *Feminist Literary History*, Polity, Cambridge, 1988.

TODD, J.: *The Sign of Angellica: Women, Writing and Fiction, 1660–1800*, Virago, London, 1989.

## 4 Biographical and critical works on specific writers (by writer)

*Austen, Jane*: BUTLER, M.: *Jane Austen and the War of Ideas*, Clarendon Press, Oxford, 1975.

*Austen, Jane*: SOUTHAM, B.C. (ed.): *Jane Austen: The Critical Heritage*, Routledge & Kegan Paul, London, 1968.

*Behn, Aphra*: GOREAU, A.: *Reconstructing Aphra: A Social Biography of Aphra Behn*, Dial Press, New York, 1980.

*Bowen, Elizabeth*: LASSNER, P.: *Elizabeth Bowen*, Macmillan, London, 1989.

*Braddon, Mary E.*: WOLFF, R.L., *The Sensational Victorian: The Life and Fiction of M.E. Braddon*, Garland, New York and London, 1979.

*Brontë, Anne, Charlotte, Emily*: ALLOTT, M. (ed.): *The Brontës: The Critical Heritage*, Routledge & Kegan Paul, London, 1974.

*Brontë, Anne*: LONGLAND, E.: *Anne Brontë, the Other One*, Macmillan, London, 1989.

*Brontë, Charlotte*: GASKELL, E.: *The Life of Charlotte Brontë* (1857), repr. Arthur Dobson, Bradford, 1968.

*Brontë, Charlotte*: NESTOR, P.: *Charlotte Brontë*, Macmillan, London, 1987.

*Brontë, Emily*: GÉRIN, W.: *Emily Brontë*, Clarendon Press, Oxford, 1971.

*Browning, Elizabeth Barrett*: LEIGHTON, A.: *Elizabeth Barrett Browning*, Harvester, Brighton, 1986.

*Browning, Elizabeth Barrett*: STONE, M.: *Elizabeth Barrett Browning*, Macmillan, London, forthcoming.

*Burney, Frances*: DOODY, M.A.: *Frances Burney: The Life in the Works*, Cambridge University Press, Cambridge, 1988.

*Burney, Frances*: SIMONS, J.: *Fanny Burney*, Macmillan, London, 1987.

*Centlivre, Susannah*: BOWYER, J.W.: *The Celebrated Mrs Centlivre*, Duke University Press, Durham, NC, 1952.

*Compton-Burnett, Ivy*: GENTILE, K.: *Ivy Compton Burnett*, Macmillan, London, forthcoming.

*Drabble, Margaret*: CREIGHTON, J.V.: *Margaret Drabble*, Methuen, London, 1985.

*Edgeworth, Maria*: BUTLER, M.: *Maria Edgeworth: A Literary Biography*, Clarendon, Oxford, 1972.

*Eliot, George*: BEER, G.: *George Eliot*, Harvester, Brighton, 1986.

*Eliot, George*: CARROLL, D.(ed.): *George Eliot: The Critical Heritage*, Routledge & Kegan Paul, London, 1971.

*Gaskell, Elizabeth*: EASSON, A. *Elizabeth Gaskell*, Routledge, London, 1979.

*Gaskell, Elizabeth*: EASSON, A. (ed.): *Elizabeth Gaskell: The Critical Heritage*, Routledge, 1990.

*Gaskell, Elizabeth*: SPENCER, J.: *Mrs Gaskell*, Macmillan, London, forthcoming.

*Gregory, Augusta, Lady*: COXHEAD, E.: *Lady Gregory: A Literary Portrait*, Macmillan, London, 1961.

*Hall, Radclyffe*: BAKER, M.: *Our Three Selves: The Life of Radclyffe Hall*, Hamish Hamilton, London, 1985.

*H.D.*: DUPLESSIS, R.B.: *H.D.: The Career of That Struggle*, Harvester, Brighton, 1986.

*Inchbald, Elizabeth*: LITTLEWOOD, S.R.: *Elizabeth Inchbald and Her Circle*, Daniel O'Connor, London, 1921.

*Jewsbury, Geraldine*: HOWE, S.: *Geraldine Jewsbury*, Aberdeen University Press, Aberdeen, 1935.

*Linton, Eliza Lynn*: ANDERSON, N.F.: *Woman against Woman in Victorian England: A Life of Eliza Lynn Linton*, Indiana University Press, Bloomington and Indianapolis, 1987.

*Macaulay, Rose*: BABINGTON SMITH, C.: *Rose Macaulay*, Collins, London, 1972.

*Manley, Mary de la Rivière*: MORGAN, F. (ed.): *A Woman of No Character: An Autobiography of Mrs Manley*, Faber, London, 1986.

*Mansfield, Katherine*: BERKUMA, S.: *Katherine Mansfield: A Critical Study*, Oxford University Press, Oxford, 1952.

*Mansfield, Katherine*: DE BELL, D.: *Katherine Mansfield*, Macmillan, London, forthcoming.

*Martineau, Harriet*: PICHANICK, V.K.: *Harriet Martineau: The Woman and Her Work*, University of Michigan Press, Ann Arbor, 1988.

*Montagu, Lady Mary Wortley*: HALSBAND, R.: *The Life of Lady Mary Wortley Montagu*, Oxford University Press, Oxford, 1956.

*More, Hannah*: JONES, M.G.: *Hannah More*, Cambridge University Press, Cambridge, 1952.

*Morgan, Lady (Sydney Owenson)*: CAMPBELL, M.: *Lady Morgan: The Life and Times of Sydney Owenson*, Pandora, London and New York, 1988.

*Murdoch, Iris*: JOHNSON, D.: *Iris Murdoch*, Harvester, Brighton, 1987.

*Newcastle, Duchess of (Margaret Cavendish)*: JONES, K.: *A Glorious Fame: The Life of Margaret Cavendish, Duchess of Newcastle*, Bloomsbury, London, 1988.

*Radcliffe, Ann*: MCINTYRE, C.F.: *Ann Radcliffe in Relation to Her Time*, Yale University Press, New Haven, CO, 1920.

*Rhys, Jean*: HOWELLS, C.A.: *Jean Rhys*, Harvester Wheatsheaf, Hemel Hempstead, 1991.

*Richardson, Dorothy*: RADFORD, J.: *Dorothy Richardson*, Harvester Wheatsheaf, Hemel Hempstead, 1991.

*Richardson, Samuel*: EAGLETON, T.: *The Rape of Clarissa*, Basil Blackwell, Oxford, 1982.

*Rossetti, Christina*: BATTISCOMBE, G.: *Christina Rossetti: A Divided Life*, Constable, London, 1981.

*Rossetti, Christina*: MARSHALL, L.: *Christina Rossetti*, Macmillan, London, forthcoming.

*Shelley, Mary*: MELLOR, A.K.: *Mary Shelley: Her Life, Her Fiction, Her Monsters*, Routledge, London, 1988.

*Shelley, Mary*: SPARK, M.: *Mary Shelley*, Constable, London, 1988.

*Sitwell, Edith*: SALTER, E.: *Edith Sitwell*, Oresko Books, London, 1979.

*Smith, Stevie*: CIVELLO, C.: *Stevie Smith*, Macmillan, London, forthcoming.

*Smith, Stevie*: SPALDING, F.: *Stevie Smith: A Critical Biography*, Faber, London, 1988.

*Spark, Muriel*: SPROXTON, J.: *Muriel Spark*, Macmillan, London, forthcoming.

*Ward, Mrs Humphry*: SMITH, E.M.G.: *Mrs Humphry Ward*, Twayne, Boston, 1980.

*Wollstonecraft, Mary*: ST CLAIR, W.: *The Godwins and the Shelleys, the Biography of a Family*, Faber, London, 1989.

*Woolf, Virginia*: MARCUS, J. (ed.): *New Feminist Essays on Virginia Woolf*, Macmillan, London, 1981.

*Wordsworth, Dorothy*: GITTINGS, R. and MANTON, J.: *Dorothy Wordsworth*, Oxford University Press, Oxford, 1985.

*Yonge, Charlotte M.*: BATTISCOMBE, G.: *Charlotte Yonge: The Story of an Uneventful Life*, Constable, London, 1943.

# Index

Page numbers in **bold** indicate a main entry for a writer.

# The author of this handbook

JANE STEVENSON read Anglo-Saxon, Norse and Celtic and English at Newnham College, Cambridge. Having completed a PhD on early Irish Latin literature, also at Newnham, she was appointed to a Research Fellowship at Pembroke College, Cambridge. During that time, she worked on medieval liturgy, the development of literacy in early Ireland, the school of Canterbury in the seventh century, and began research for this book. In 1988, she became a lecturer in Late Antique and Early Medieval History at the University of Sheffield. She now divides her research interests between the British Isles in the early Middle Ages, and early nineteenth-century literature. She has recently completed (with Peter Davidson) an edition of Walter Scott's *Old Mortality*, and is now working on an edition and translation of the Latin hymns of the early Irish Church. Other recent work includes a study of the background to Maria Edgeworth's Irish novels, and a study of eighth-century English women's letters. She is married, and lives in Warwickshire.

THE LIBRARY
SAINT FRANCIS XAVIER
SIXTH FORM COLLEGE
MALWOOD ROAD, SW12 8EN